A THEORY OF PAY

A THEORY OF PAY

ADRIAN WOOD

CAMBRIDGE UNIVERSITY PRESS

CAMBRIDGE
LONDON · NEW YORK · MELBOURNE

Published by the Syndics of the Cambridge University Press
The Pitt Building, Trumpington Street, Cambridge CB2 1RP
Bentley House, 200 Euston Road, London NW1 2DB
32 East 57th Street, New York, NY 10022, USA
296 Beaconsfield Parade, Middle Park, Melbourne 3206, Australia

First published 1978

Printed in Great Britain
at the University Press, Cambridge

Library of Congress Cataloguing in Publication Data
Wood, Adrian.
A theory of pay.
Bibliography: p.
Includes index.
1. Wages. I. Title.
HD4906.W66   331.2'1'01   78-1038
ISBN 0 521 22073 4

TO JOYCE

CONTENTS

CONTENTS

PREFACE

In writing this book I have been helped by a large number of people. I am especially indebted to Dr J. Pemberton. Over the last four years I have learned a great deal from reading and discussing his work. In addition, he read the whole of the penultimate draft of this book and made many valuable suggestions for improvements. Substantial parts of the penultimate draft were read also by Dr C. R. S. Dougherty, Professor R. F. Kahn, Mr A. Lawson, Professor W. B. Reddaway, Mr J. A. Trevithick and Mr F. Wilkinson, whose perceptive and penetrating comments were of the greatest assistance to me in revising the manuscript. At an earlier stage I received good advice from Professor A. B. Atkinson, Professor D. G. Champernowne, Dr J. H. Goldthorpe and Professor N. Kaldor. I have also benefited greatly from the comments and reactions, positive and negative, of the Cambridge students to whom I have lectured on some of the ideas in this book at various stages of their development. Finally, I would like to express my gratitude to Professor E. H. Phelps Brown, who very kindly lent me an advance copy of his recent important book, *The inequality of pay*, thus enabling me to profit from reading it in the final throes of writing my own book.

ADRIAN WOOD

King's College
Cambridge
October 1977

1

THEORIES OF PAY

The object of this book is to propound a theory of the determination of rates of pay in modern capitalist economies. The book and the theory are concerned primarily with the relative pay of different jobs and individuals, and with the average level of pay in money terms, both of which are directly determined in the labour market, but not (or only peripherally) with the average level of pay in real terms, which, though to some degree affected by events in the labour market, is fundamentally determined by what Keynes called 'the other forces of the economic system'.*

It is hardly necessary to emphasise the practical significance of the subject matter of this book. Pay (by which I shall mean not only wages and salaries but also the incomes of those employers and self-employed people who work with little or no capital of their own) makes up about three quarters of the national income. Thus the inequality of pay is the main determinant of the inequality of personal income, except at its extremes, and indeed also of the inequality of personal wealth (Blinder, 1974; Wolfson, 1977). Similarly, the behaviour of the average level of pay in money terms is normally the main influence on the behaviour of the general price level. To understand what governs these things is therefore of great importance in formulating policies to redistribute income or to control inflation.

There is of course an established body of economic thought on the determination of rates of pay, which may be found in any contemporary textbook. But orthodox theory, though by no means so otiose as is sometimes suggested, is to my mind deficient in certain major respects. In particular, it fails to take account of the influence of ideas of fairness, especially in the minds of employees, or to come to terms with the behaviour of groups (including unions), as distinct from

---

* Keynes (1936), p. 14. For a more precise statement of this proposition, see pp. 231–2 below.

individuals, or to appreciate the significance of certain other institutional features of modern labour markets.

A string of more or less unorthodox writers have grappled with these issues, but not very successfully. Most have failed to develop their ideas in a rigorous way. Some, while building theoretically satisfactory models, have dealt only with limited and specific areas, and have provided no coherent alternative view of the working of the labour market as a whole. And others, it seems to me, have been mistaken in their view of how the labour market works, especially in their wholesale abandonment of orthodox principles.

My purpose in this book is to take and develop a particular vein of unorthodox thought and to integrate it with some extremely orthodox ideas in such a way as to produce a new and general theory of the determination of pay. I shall also attempt to test this theory, and to draw out some of its implications for policy.

I do not wish to exaggerate the novelty of my theory. It is constructed to a considerable extent from ingredients which are not new, and I recognise that to many people it may be more acceptable or comprehensible when regarded as a special case or an extension of some other theory. It is thus natural to devote the remainder of this chapter to a brief review of existing theories of pay. The review will not be complete, especially in a bibliographical sense. The object is rather to survey and comment on the main *ideas*, some of which will receive more extensive treatment in subsequent chapters.

1.2 COMPETITION

The force on which economists have traditionally laid greatest stress in discussing the determination of pay is a particular sort of competition. More precisely, the basic assumption of competitive theories of pay is that employers and employees behave in something like the following way. If at any time an employer wishes to hire more labour than is willing to work for him at the wage he is currently paying, he will offer a higher wage to attract employees from other employers. Conversely, if at the prevailing wage more employees wish to work for a particular employer than he is willing to hire, they will compete with one another for jobs by offering their services for a lower wage.

Competition, then, is essentially a disequilibrium process by which excess demand and excess supply cause changes in wages. In exploring its outcome, competitive theorists also assume (a) that neither employers nor employees combine together to influence conditions of demand or supply and (b) that competition is perfect in the sense that in each labour submarket (the market for a particular type of labour in a particular locality) there tends to prevail a uniform wage which no individual employer or employee can influence. The numbers of employees supplied and demanded in any given submarket are thus functions of (among other things) this wage, which makes it comparatively straightforward to explain what determines its equilibrium or market-clearing level.

Given the conditions of demand and supply in all the submarkets in the economy, which are interdependent in several respects, it is customary to assume that a unique equilibrium set of wage rates exists. It is also usually presumed (although this has been challenged by those who have analysed disequilibrium and information failures in multi-market economies) that the process of competition causes the actual set of wage rates to tend towards, and indeed to approximate, the equilibrium set.

To impart substance to this sort of theory, it is necessary to say more about the determinants of demand and supply. In this respect it is convenient to distinguish between influences on relative wage rates and influences on the general money wage level.

(i) *Relativities*

Throughout this book, a number of fundamental and familiar determinants of the demand for and the supply of labour will be taken for granted. On the demand side, these include the pattern of (individual and collective) preferences for all kinds of consumption goods, the technology of production, the availability of non-labour inputs to production, and the structure of competition in (and other institutional attributes of) product markets. On the supply side, they include the demographic characteristics of the population, the availability of unemployment benefits and other types of non-wage income, and preferences, conventions and laws relating to work and leisure. Given these basic considerations, competition would cause pay relativities to be governed primarily by four more specific influences on supply and demand.

(1) The intrinsic non-pecuniary advantages and disadvantages of

3

jobs. Different jobs are to different degrees interesting, arduous, dirty and dangerous; they offer different degrees of security and regularity of employment; they command differing amounts of social prestige; and to undertake them employees must expend, with varying chances of success, varying amounts of money, time and effort on education and training (a consideration stressed in recent years by the human capital school – Mincer, 1970; Blaug, 1976). Competition for jobs which are attractive in these respects would tend to cause them to be paid less than jobs which are unattractive, by an amount such as to make the marginal employee indifferent between them.

(2) Differences in the industriousness and in the innate or fortuitously acquired abilities of individual people.* For obvious reasons, employers tend to prefer more efficient employees. As a result, competition should cause the pay of more able and industrious individuals to exceed the pay of less able and industrious individuals by an amount such as to cause the marginal employer to be indifferent between them. (A number of writers, though, have recently stressed the inadequacy of the information available to employers in this regard, and have thus provided fresh insights into the role of educational qualifications and the nature of discrimination against women and racial minorities – Blaug, 1976, pp. 845–50; Cain, 1976, pp. 1232–3.)

(3) The imperfect mobility of labour (and capital) between different areas and different jobs. This is the result of such things as ignorance and uncertainty, reluctance to rupture ties of friendship and family, the expense of moving and retraining, and the fact that the experience gained by working in a particular job often leads to the development of a comparative advantage in that job. In a competitive world, these factors would permit the existence of differences in pay between submarkets which could not be explained by differences in non-pecuniary advantages or innate abilities, especially as a consequence of unanticipated changes in the pattern of demand.

(4) Economic and social barriers to equality of opportunity (including those recently emphasised in connection with secondary labour markets and the culture of poverty – Cain, 1976, pp. 1222–3). For

* This influence on pay relativities has been emphasised to the exclusion of all others by a school of economists who have argued that the shape of the size distribution of pay is determined by the shape of the size distribution of human ability; see the survey in Lydall (1968, ch. 2), the comments in Wood (1972, ch. 2, pp. 22–3), and the related but more sophisticated work of Tinbergen (1956), Mayer (1960, app.), Reder (1968) and Phelps Brown (1977).

example, unequal access to education and training might be caused by capital market imperfections or by the orientation of the educational system towards activities and values absent from the family backgrounds of the children of less educated parents. In an otherwise competitive world, these social constraints could cause the net (pecuniary and non-pecuniary) advantages of jobs requiring education and training to exceed the net advantages of other jobs by a margin which could not be ascribed to the influence of scarce innate abilities.

(ii) *Wage inflation*

In competitive theory, movements of the general money wage level are caused by imbalances between the aggregate monetary demand for and the aggregate supply of labour, although in most models it is the behaviour of aggregate demand that gets most of the attention. It is beyond the scope of this book to explore the determinants of aggregate demand, or to review the dispute between Keynesians and monetarists concerning the influence of governmental fiscal and monetary policy, or to consider the practical problems of demand management. I shall thus simply assume in what follows that the government can and does, in one way or another, and with a reasonable degree of accuracy, regulate the aggregate monetary demand for labour. It is, however, worth looking at certain other aspects of the competitive theory of wage inflation.

First, one must mention the important role that expectations have played in recent models (which are surveyed by Laidler, 1975, and Trevithick, 1975). More precisely, a number of economists have argued, some with reference to purely competitive models, that variations in the pace of inflation are governed both by variations in the aggregate demand–supply balance and by variations in expectations of future inflation, which in turn are generated by more or less sophisticated extrapolation of past inflation (*adaptive* expectations), or by a deeper understanding of the working of the economy (*rational* expectations), or in some other way. These economists have thus suggested that the general money wage level may change without aggregate excess demand or supply; and they have shown that under certain assumptions imbalances between aggregate demand and supply determine not the rate of change of the general money wage level but whether this rate of change is accelerating or decelerating.

In this connection, it is worth considering the definition of aggregate excess demand and supply, with special reference to the problem that in practice, at any given time, there is likely to be excess demand in some labour submarkets and excess supply in others. In this sort of situation, one cannot say whether there is aggregate excess demand or aggregate excess supply or neither without explicitly or implicitly adopting some 'averaging' procedure. There are many possible such averaging procedures, all of which are imperfect in some respect, and there are thus many possible definitions of aggregate excess demand or supply.

One definition that has recently received a good deal of attention, especially in connection with models involving expectations, is that which is implicit in the concept of the *natural* rate of unemployment (Tobin, 1972; Trevithick, 1976). It is that there is aggregate excess demand whenever the net effect of the various excess demands and supplies in individual submarkets is to impart an upward tendency to the general money wage level (the various individual shortages and surpluses thus being weighted in accordance with their effects on wage rates). The lowest level of unemployment at which there is no such upward tendency is the natural rate.

It has been pointed out by Trevithick that wage inflation need not respond symmetrically to unemployment *above* the natural rate, and by Tobin that the natural rate of unemployment need not be the same thing as *full employment* (i.e. an arbitrarily small but positive amount of involuntary unemployment). But there must be a strong presumption, even making allowance for variations in the reaction speeds of individual submarkets and for imperfections in the flow of information, that if the world were truly competitive, then (a) the effects of excess aggregate demand and excess aggregate supply would be roughly symmetrical and (b) full employment and the natural rate of unemployment would in general be much the same thing.

1.3 MONOPOLY

Two assumptions of competitive theory are that employers and employees do not combine to influence demand or supply conditions and that markets are perfect. To abandon these assumptions does not necessarily imply that the considerations discussed in the preceding section have no effect on pay. To begin with, if the degree of monopoly in labour submarkets were uniformly low, a perfectly competitive model would provide an acceptable, albeit approximate, description of a monopolistic world. Moreover, even if the degree of monopoly in particular submarkets is high, the basic competitive process of bidding wages up and down in response to shortages and surpluses of labour may play a part in the attainment of equilibrium. And the underlying determinants of supply and demand in competitive markets – such as consumer preferences, technology, and social restrictions on the availability of education – will usually also exert an important influence in monopolistic markets.

To abandon the assumptions of competitive theory, however, does complicate matters, for example because several wage rates may prevail in equilibrium in each submarket, and because one must take account of the supply and demand conditions which confront individual buyers and sellers within particular submarkets. More fundamentally, monopoly creates certain gaps in the orthodox theory of pay, and raises certain questions about behaviour, some of which orthodox theorists have been unable to answer in a satisfactory way. To illustrate this, I shall review the orthodox account of three different types of monopolistic situation at a partial equilibrium level, and the orthodox analysis of their general equilibrium and macroeconomic implications, before turning in the next section to examine some unorthodox theories.

It is worth explaining the rationale of the line which I shall draw between orthodox and unorthodox theories. The distinguishing feature of orthodox theories of pay, competitive and monopolistic, is that they ignore the influence of ideas of fairness or propriety. Such ideas I shall call *pay norms*. Orthodox theories thus assume that the world is effectively *anomic* (i.e. non-normative). By contrast, most of what I shall call the unorthodox theories of pay ascribe considerable practical significance to pay norms.

(i) *Monopsony*

Let us look first at the case in which an employer has some control over the wage in the particular sense that his supply of labour is limited but varies to a greater or lesser extent in response to changes in his wage rate (and let us provisionally assume that employees must simply take or leave whatever wage is offered). The orthodox partial equilibrium analysis of the effects of monopsony is straightforward and familiar. It rests on the general principle that a rational employer will hire labour of any given type up to the point at which the marginal gross gain (measured in terms of money) from hiring an extra person is equal to the marginal cost.

It is usually assumed that a monopsonistic employer pays the same wage to all employees of a given type and thus that the marginal cost to a monopsonist of an additional employee exceeds his wage. For to increase his supply of labour by one man a monopsonist must raise the wage, and he must pay this higher wage to all his employees. In a perfectly competitive labour market, by contrast, the marginal cost to an individual employer of an additional employee is simply his wage. A monopsonist will therefore tend to hire a smaller number of employees and pay them a lower wage than he would if the submarket were perfectly competitive, to a degree inversely related to the elasticity of his labour supply function.

Things would be somewhat different if a monopsonist were not obliged to pay the same wage to all employees of a given type. A discriminating monopsonist would pay each employee only his supply price, being the minimum wage necessary to inhibit him from taking employment elsewhere, and thus the marginal cost of an additional employee would only be his wage. In consequence, a discriminating monopsonist would tend to hire the same number of men and pay the marginal employee the same as if the submarket were perfectly competitive. But every other employee would receive less than the competitive wage by an amount inversely related to the attractiveness of his alternative employment prospects.

(ii) *Individual monopoly*

Let us now turn to monopoly on the supply side of the labour market, considering first those cases in which individual employees have some control over the wage at which they can sell their labour but in which they do not act collectively.

The most striking, though not the most common, sort of individual monopoly occurs in the case of unique abilities, such as those of entertainment and sports stars. Each individual of this kind is a very imperfect substitute for other individuals, and in consequence (since there is normally intense competition among potential employers) faces an imperfectly elastic demand curve. For example, an opera star must choose between making a small number of appearances, each of which will command a very high fee, and a larger number of appearances, each of which will command a rather smaller fee. The orthodox approach to this type of situation is simply to assume that the employee has a well-defined set of preferences as between money and leisure and thus chooses the point on his demand curve which maximises his individual utility.

A much more common sort of individual monopoly is caused by the costs to employers of hiring and firing employees, including the expense of employer-specific training. Such transactions costs make 'outside' employees imperfect substitutes for existing employees, since a rational employer, rather than lose an existing employee, would pay him more than a new recruit similar in all other respects. Moreover, since changing employers usually imposes transactions costs also on the employee, a rational employee, rather than leave his existing employer, would accept a wage less than the best he could obtain elsewhere. There thus tends to be a difference between the maximum wage that an employer would be willing to pay and the minimum wage that an employee would be willing to accept. Where within this range the actual wage will lie is something which orthodox theory does not explain, although it is customary to state that it depends on the relative bargaining power of the two parties.

(iii) *Collective monopoly*

The most conspicuous type of labour market monopoly in modern capitalist economies is that which arises when employees combine together into trade unions, professional associations, and similar groupings, formal and informal (all of which I shall refer to indiscriminately as 'unions'). Yet the treatment of this sort of collective monopoly is the weakest aspect of the orthodox theory of pay. Despite a considerable amount of work, there is no coherent and accepted body of theoretical generalisations about the character and consequences of union action even at the partial equilibrium level. The orthodox analysis of collective monopoly is thus difficult to survey. For convenience I shall divide it into three (not strictly independent) parts, considering first union methods, second union power, and third union goals.

9

(1) *Union methods*. Economists usually portray unions as exerting an influence on wages by imposing restrictions on entry into certain jobs, including the establishment of minimum qualifications and periods of training, limitations on the capacity of the institutions providing such training, and rules about who may do what (and how much) work. Such artificial restriction of supply, it is argued, causes employers to compete more intensely with one another for labour and to bid the wage up to the level desired by the union.

This is a good description of the modus operandi of some unions. But most do not operate in this indirect fashion. Instead, they try to insist directly that a particular wage be paid to all the employees in a particular job, often allowing the employer to decide how many employees to hire at this wage. Few orthodox economists have recognised this; even fewer have attempted to explain why some unions choose the direct and others the indirect method of influencing wages, or the consequences of this choice.

(2) *Union power*. Whichever method of operation a union adopts, it must be able to enforce its decisions. In the one instance it must be able to prevent employers from hiring non-union (or non-qualified) labour. In the other it must be able to prevent employers from deviating from its prescribed wage. Thus common to both methods is the question of power.

One aspect of union power, which has been thoroughly analysed by orthodox economists, is the nature of the tradeoff in specific submarkets between the wage and the level of employment. In a submarket with many small employers, this tradeoff is simply the demand curve, whose elasticity determines what wage will result from any given restriction of supply or, equivalently, what level of employment will result from the enforcement of any given wage.

But the wage–employment tradeoff is only an outer limit on the power of a union in a specific submarket. A second, equally important, aspect of union power is the extent to which the union *can* control the wage. Even if the wage–employment tradeoff were very inelastic, the union might be so weak that any attempt on its part to raise the wage would result in all union members losing their jobs and being replaced by non-union (or ex-union) labour. On the other hand, there may be submarkets in which the wage–employment tradeoff is relatively elastic but in which the union is powerful enough to dictate whatever wage it desires.

Economists have been less successful in analysing this second aspect of union power. It is evident that the degree to which a union can control the wage in a specific submarket is a function of the amount of leverage it can exert on its members, on non-union employees and on employers, and of the amount of leverage which employers, individually and collectively, can exert on the union and its members. But economic theorists have made little progress in their attempts to construct models which treat the causes and effects of this sort of power in a way which is both general and illuminating.

This is apparent, for example, in the orthodox analysis of bilateral monopoly (Reynolds, 1974, pp. 467–9). Given the competitive labour supply function, the model of non-discriminating monopsonistic behaviour discussed earlier implies that the employer, if he were free to do so, would choose to set the wage at a particular level. And it is conventional to assume that the union, if it were free to do so, would choose to set the wage at some other, higher, level. Within these limits, as in the case of individual monopoly, it is customary to state that the wage is determined by relative bargaining power. But despite a number of valuable suggestions, there is no accepted measure of bargaining power or theory of bargaining processes, and thus it cannot be said that the orthodox model explains what governs the level of the wage in situations of this kind.

However, it would in my view be wrong to attach much significance to the failure of orthodox economists to deal satisfactorily with this second aspect of union power at a theoretical level. For this failure is common to orthodox and unorthodox theorists alike. Moreover, it seems to me that bargaining power is something whose causes and effects are usually comparatively easy to identify in practice. Thus the absence of a general theoretical framework does not necessarily imply that it is impossible (or even difficult) to explain or predict the outcomes of bargaining processes in particular instances.

(3) *Union goals*. The most fundamental weakness of the orthodox treatment of collective monopoly in my opinion is that it provides no convincing general account of union goals. This weakness is exposed in a particularly direct way by the proclivity of orthodox economists to

stress that unions must normally accept that in specific jobs higher wages will in the long run be associated with lower employment than would otherwise have been the case.* This implies that unions, insofar as they have the power to control wages, must choose between higher wages and higher employment. But what principles guide the representative union's choice of a position on the wage–employment tradeoff is a question to which orthodox economic theory gives no satisfactory answer.†

Many economists have avoided the question of union goals altogether. Marshall, for example, never raised it, and both Smith and Mill were distinctly vague about the objectives of guilds and corporations. More recently, some of those who (following Fellner, 1949) have represented union preferences concerning wages and employment by indifference curves have failed to specify the shape or determinants of these curves, while Johnson (1970) assumed that a union would seek a 'fixed proportional differential excess' of the wage over the competitive level, without explaining what might govern the size of this excess.

Other economists (including Reynolds, 1974, pp. 418–20) have tended to maintain that no valid generalisations about union goals are possible. But there must be *some* best generalisation (or set of generalisations), however imperfect. Moreover, arguments of this kind tend to confuse goals and constraints. In particular, they come close on occasion to concluding that unions have no goals simply on the grounds that unions are often unable to achieve their goals.

Another traditional school of thought argues that unions in specific jobs will choose not to raise wages above the competitive level, in order to avoid causing unemployment among their members. This argument is not very compelling even if one accepts its implied premises, which are (a) that the alternative to employment in the job in question is unemployment and (b) that the membership of a union consists of all those who would be employed in the job in question if the wage were at its competitive level. For a majority of members might vote for

* Except (over a certain range) when a monopsonistic submarket is unionised, or when a union can influence demand by, say, lobbying for tariffs on imported substitutes.
† To pose the question in this form takes for granted (a) that there is a one-to-one correspondence between unions and jobs, (b) that labour within specific jobs is homogeneous, (c) that in specific jobs there exist well-defined wage–employment tradeoffs for union labour, and (d) that each union behaves as a non-discriminating monopolist, insisting on the same wage for all its members, rather than extracting different wages from different employers according to their ability to pay.

higher wages for themselves at the expense of the employment of a minority.

But the premises themselves are dubious. (a) In most cases the alternative to employment in a specific job is not unemployment but employment in some other, albeit less attractive, job. (b) More important, in the long run the membership of a union in a specific job is normally limited to those who are either currently employed in that job or who have been recently employed and expect to be employed again. Thus the usual result of the enforcement of a high wage by a union in a specific job is not high 'unemployment' among its members but a small membership.

Dunlop (1944) has put forward several related hypotheses. The most prominent is that the representative union will choose that point on the wage–employment tradeoff which maximises the total wage bill of its members. But as Atherton (1973) has noted, there is little empirical support for this hypothesis, and it is hard to justify it on a priori grounds (whether or not one follows Dunlop in assuming that union membership is an increasing function of the wage, rather than, as was argued above, a function of employment). Much the same is true of the hypothesis of Braff (1969, p. 225) and others that the goal of the representative union is to maximise the excess of the wage bill over the wage bill that would be paid at the same level of employment if the wage were equal to the average supply price of labour.*

Cartter (1959) has suggested a rather different sort of hypothesis, which is that in any particular situation a union will treat the existing wage as a lower bound and the existing level of employment as an upper bound. Thus if the wage–employment tradeoff becomes more favourable, the union will try to raise the wage while maintaining employment at its initial level, but if the wage–employment tradeoff becomes less favourable, the union will try to maintain the wage at its initial level while allowing the level of employment to decline. This view also is supported by little empirical evidence; and the hypothesis itself is unsatisfactory in that it does not explain why the union chooses a particular position on the 'initial' wage–employment tradeoff.

* This is sometimes referred to as the 'business union' hypothesis, since it supposes that the union will choose that point on the demand curve (the wage–employment tradeoff) at which 'marginal revenue' (the marginal change in the wage bill with respect to employment) is equal to 'marginal cost' (the supply price of the marginal employee).

Another hypothesis, which commands a good deal of popular support, is that the goal of the typical union is to maximise the wage rate of its members. But this hypothesis has never appealed to economists, whose awareness of the concept of the wage–employment tradeoff has led them to criticise it on the grounds that no union would pursue a strategy which maximised unemployment among its members.* This criticism loses some of its force if, as was argued earlier, the alternative to employment in a specific job is not usually unemployment, and if union membership is a simple function of employment.

But the idea of a union consisting (or seeking to consist) of one very highly paid member is also extremely bizarre. More generally, there is not much evidence to suggest that unions usually want *unlimited* increases in wages. Instead, they seem in general to have fairly specific wage targets, which they will fight (not always successfully) to attain with all the means at their disposal, but beyond which they will not try to drive the wage even though they may have the power to do so (Daniel, 1976, p. 105). What governs these union wage targets, however, is something which orthodox economists have failed to explain.

(iv) *Relativities and wage inflation*

This review of the orthodox analysis of the various sorts of labour market monopoly has so far been confined to the partial equilibrium level. But to investigate the effects of monopoly on pay relativities and the general money wage level, our primary objects of interest, it is essential to introduce general equilibrium and macroeconomic considerations. In this respect, orthodox theory is rather underdeveloped, in part at least because of its failure to resolve some of the partial equilibrium issues mentioned above, especially those concerned with unions. A certain amount of work has beeen done on monopoly in general equilibrium models (for example, Arrow, 1971), including some applications of game theory, but not much has emerged in the way of specific propositions applicable to the labour market.

An exception to this is a particular type of two-sector model, developed by Kaldor (1968), Johnson (1970), Friedman (1973) and Reynolds (1974, pp. 547–8).† The model has been applied and interpreted in

---

* Thus Mansfield (1970) suggests that the typical union might seek to maximise the wage rate subject to the constraint that some (unspecified) minimum number of its members be employed.

† See also Wood (1975), p. 143, and the discussion and references on p. 1242 of Cain (1976).

various ways, but in the present context it is appropriate to assume that the economy consists simply of a unionised sector and a non-unionised competitive sector. The central proposition of the model is that if the wage is forced up in the unionised sector, employment there will decline, which will increase the supply of labour to, and thus drive down the wage in, the competitive sector. (The demand for labour in the competitive sector will therefore increase, absorbing some or all of the workers released by the unionised sector.) In this way, the action of the unions will have a double effect on relative wages.

This model is relevant also to the effects of unions on the general money wage level, as may be seen by considering a somewhat extreme case. Suppose that the wage in the competitive sector falls far enough to cause the entire surplus of labour from the unionised sector to be absorbed (which requires, among other things, the aggregate supply of labour to be completely inelastic), and that the aggregate level of employment therefore does not change. Suppose further that unless the government takes some purposive action, the aggregate monetary demand for labour will not alter. As a result, the action of the unions will affect only relative wages and will have *no effect* on the general money wage level (which is by definition the aggregate monetary demand for labour divided by the aggregate level of employment).

This particular proposition relies on assumptions which many orthodox economists would regard as unacceptably strong. Some would stress that it is an equilibrium proposition, and that lags and immobility would cause union action to have a temporary effect on the general money wage level and the aggregate level of employment, or indeed that the dynamic process of disequilibrium adjustment is of such a kind that the requisite equilibrium state might never be attained. Others would challenge the assumption that a change in relative wages would not affect the aggregate monetary demand for labour, on the grounds that it might alter, for example, the aggregate propensity to save, or the aggregate amount of investment undertaken at any given rate of interest, or the relationship between the aggregate demand for goods and the aggregate demand for labour.

In addition, many orthodox economists would take issue with the assumption that there exists a competitive sector large enough, and with sufficient downward flexibility of its (relative) wage, to absorb the entire surplus of labour from the unionised sector. This might not be the case in practice for several reasons. One, of course, might be that all sectors were unionised. Another might be a minimum wage law applicable to the competitive sector. A third might be the attractions of leisure, which would make people unwilling to work in the competitive sector for less than a certain wage. In all these cases, even if the aggregate monetary demand for labour were unaltered, the action of unions could reduce the aggregate level of employment and raise the general money wage level.

For reasons of this sort (one supposes), many orthodox economists have maintained that unions can and do influence not only pay relativities but also the general money wage level. Some have suggested that unions prevent the general money wage level from falling; others that they actually push it up; and yet others that they raise the natural rate of unemployment, causing the general money wage level to be pulled up by excess demand in specific submarkets before full employment is attained. But exactly how, and why, and to what extent unions do these things is not adequately or coherently explained by orthodox economic theory.

1.4 UNORTHODOX VIEWS

A great number and variety of unorthodox opinions concerning the determination of pay relativities and the general money wage level have been advanced at one time or another (sometimes by otherwise entirely orthodox economists). But I shall concentrate on those which maintain that pay is influenced by ideas of fairness or propriety.

This notion is in my opinion essential to a proper understanding of the behaviour of pay in modern capitalist economies. It also enables one to fill in some of the gaps in the orthodox theory of the determination of pay under conditions of monopoly. Not least, the concept of fairness provides the basis for a coherent and plausible explanation of union wage goals. Indeed, it seems to me to explain why unions *exist*.

(i) *Relativities*

The belief that ideas of fairness or propriety influence pay relativities has a surprisingly long history. Smith (1904, p. 107) was echoing earlier writers* when he stated that 'the wages of labour vary accordingly to the great or small trust which must be reposed in the workmen' and, more specifically, that 'we trust our health to the

---

* See the references to Cantillon and Hume in Cannan's notes on p. 107 of Smith (1904). See also Fogarty (1961, app.) on the scholastic theory of the just wage.

physician; our fortune and sometimes our life and reputation to the lawyer and attorney. Such confidence could not safely be reposed in people of a very mean or low condition. Their reward must be such, therefore, as may give them that rank in the society which so important a trust requires.'

This influence on relative pay is quite different from the others that Smith noted in the same chapter, which arise from competitive pressure to equalise net advantages. The net advantages of being, say, a physician cannot (according to Smith) tend to equality with the net advantages of other jobs because the relative pay of physicians must be high enough to enable them to maintain a particular social standing.

Mill noted this anomaly in Smith's account of the determinants of relative pay.* Indeed, he included in his book on distribution a whole chapter arguing that Smith and other English economists had actually exaggerated the influence of competition and had unduly neglected the conflicting influence of custom (1886, pp. 147–51). In his later chapter on pay relativities he gave examples (p. 244) of the kinds of labour whose pay is fixed by convention. These include women, and professional and other people in responsible jobs (of whom Mill said 'it is usual to pay greatly beyond the market price of their labour all persons in whom the employer wishes to place peculiar trust').

Mill's views in this regard were repudiated by Marshall (1949, p. 465), whose restatement of Smith, omitting all mention of trust, and supplemented by a strong emphasis on individual differences in ability and efficiency, became the basis of most twentieth-century economic thought on the subject of pay relativities. But a number of economists have challenged Marshall's narrowly anomic approach.

Wootton (1955), and later Routh (1965, ch. iv), rejected the orthodox competitive explanation and argued that pay relativities are primarily determined by conventional ideas of fairness.† This point of view,

---

* Although he confused matters by placing two quite different interpretations on it. To begin with, he portrayed the influence of trust on pay as an example of the effect of a naturally scarce talent – trustworthiness (Mill, 1886, p. 236). But as Smith puts it forward, the influence of trust on pay has nothing to do with the innate characteristics of the people occupying responsible jobs, but is, as Mill subsequently recognised, the consequence of a social convention concerning the pay of jobs which involve responsibility. The trustworthiness of the individual incumbents of such jobs is the result, not the cause, of their high pay.

† A similar view is expressed in UN (1967), ch. 1, p. 8. And even so orthodox an economist as Hicks has accorded some influence to ideas concerning fair relativities: Hicks (1963), chs. ii and iv and pp. 316–21 of the Commentary; Hicks (1955), pp. 396–404.

some of whose implications were investigated by Reddaway (1959), has subsequently acquired quite a strong hold in British official circles, especially among people involved in administering incomes policies (Clegg, 1971, ch. IV; Jones, 1973, pp. 19–22; Pay Board, 1973, 1974; Brittan, 1977, p. 178). Moreover, quite a number of other economists, in Britain and elsewhere, have acknowledged the influence of comparisons and beliefs about fair relativities on union wage targets and on the outcome of wage negotiations; indeed, this feature of collective bargaining has been formalised into such concepts as 'wage contours', 'orbits of coercive comparison', and 'pattern bargaining' (Reynolds, 1974, pp. 418–20, 551–2; Ross, 1948; Dunlop, 1957, p. 17; Seltzer, 1951; Atherton, 1973).

More directly related to Smith's and Mill's views concerning the influence of trust on pay is Simon's (1957) theory of the determination of relativities within bureaucratic organisations (which was further developed by Marris, 1964).* The influence of ideas of fairness on pay relativities within specific organisations has been emphasised also by Doeringer (1971) and other students of internal labour markets. That wages in particular firms and sectors are governed by convention rather than market forces has likewise been suggested by some theorists of dual or segmented labour markets (Cain, 1976), most notably Thurow (1976).

These various contributions, though extremely valuable, are very underdeveloped. The writers mentioned have not in general addressed themselves sufficiently closely to the mechanisms by which ideas of fairness might influence actual relativities. In particular, they have not satisfactorily investigated (especially in a general equilibrium context) what happens when there are conflicting ideas of fairness, or when ideas of fairness conflict with orthodox economic pressures. Largely as a consequence of this, and despite the apparent willingness of some of those mentioned to jettison orthodox theory in its entirety, the scope and relevance of the hypothesis that ideas of fairness govern relativities has been nothing like adequately explored, either theoretically or (with the major exception of Phelps Brown, 1977) empirically.

* Lydall (1959) has advanced a theory which is formally similar, but whose content is wholly orthodox (Lydall, 1968, p. 127).

(ii) *Wage inflation*

Quite a number of economists have put forward wage-push theories of inflation which explicitly or implicitly involve the notion that the behaviour of the general money wage level is influenced by ideas of fairness. It is appropriate to distinguish between those who have emphasised fairness in *real* terms and those who have emphasised fairness in *relative* terms.

(1) *Wage–price spiral theories.* The typical theory of the former sort maintains that unions have particular ideas about what would constitute a fair real wage, and thus that wage demands and settlements are dependent on the (past or expected future) behaviour of the general price level. More precisely, inflation is argued to occur because union real wage targets are in excess of what the economy can deliver; variations in the pace of inflation over time are thus caused primarily by variations in the relationship between real wage targets and the actual real wage (see, for example, the writers cited by Laidler, 1975, p. 764; see also Hicks, 1975, and Pemberton, 1975). In some versions of the theory, it is the *disposable* real wage that is crucial (Wilkinson, 1972; Coutts, 1976). In others, the desire to squeeze the share of profits (which is one among several determinants of the average real wage) is seen as particularly important.

Two shortcomings of most wage–price spiral theories may be noted in passing. One is that they tend to portray unions (and indeed employees in general) as a monolithic block and to overlook the fact that wage bargaining is normally a decentralised and uncoordinated process – thus, among other things, laying themselves open to the charge that they assume that unions (by not taking account of the effect of money wage increases on prices) act irrationally or myopically. The other shortcoming, which is more fundamental, is that these theories provide no satisfactory general account of the determination of real wage targets, and are thus in a basic sense incomplete.

(2) *Wage–wage spiral theories.* That ideas of fairness concerning pay relativities might affect the general money wage level was first suggested by Keynes, who argued (1936, pp. 14, 264) that money wages were rather inflexible in a downward direction because each individual

group of workers was afraid of losing out in relative terms. This insight has been noted and generalised by Trevithick (1976, 1976a).

Much the same principle plays an important part in 'wage leadership' theories of inflation, according to which customary ideas of fair relativities cause the wage increases in one sector to be imitated in other sectors (see, for example, Kaldor, 1976, pp. 708–9; Daniel 1976a; Trevithick, 1975, pp. 103–4). This mechanism is consistent with a variety of explanations of the rate of wage increase in the leading sector – which in this sort of model determines the rate of wage inflation. It could be governed by increases in prices and beliefs about fairness in real terms; or it might have nothing to do with considerations of fairness, being governed instead, say, by excess demand in the sector in question.

Several economists, including Kahn (1958, para. 48; OECD, 1961, pp. 54, 446–7), Tobin (1972) and Pemberton (1975), have taken this approach one stage further, and have put forward 'wage–wage spiral' theories. In models of this kind the general money wage level is driven up endogenously by a leap-frogging process of interaction between the wage settlements of different groups anxious about (and sometimes with inconsistent aspirations concerning) their relative rates of pay.

Those who have emphasised the importance of ideas about fair relativities, and wage–wage spiral theorists in particular, seem to me to have put their finger on one of the most important features of wage inflation in modern capitalist economies. Nonetheless, their models are far from fully developed. They are for the most part short on microeconomic behavioural underpinning; and the characteristics of the processes they describe have not been properly explored either at the general equilibrium or at the macroeconomic level. Among other things, no adequate investigation has been made of the various ways in which orthodox economic forces might conflict or interact with pressures to establish fair relativities.

1.5 OUTLINE OF THE BOOK

In chapter 2 I consider the nature and sources of pay norms (i.e. ideas about fair pay), and the way in which they may change over time. In chapter 3 I examine the methods by which employees might go about coercing employers into complying with their pay norms. I also examine the pressures on employers (and employees) not to comply with pay norms, and the several sorts of conflicts to which these may give rise.

In chapters 4 and 5, drawing on the discussion in earlier chapters, I develop a theoretical model (first at the partial equilibrium level and then for the economy as a whole) of the way in which pay relativities and the general money wage level are determined. I explore in some detail the consequences of conflicts between different pay norms and between pay norms and orthodox economic pressures.

In chapter 6 I examine the evidence with regard to the determinants of (a) various types of relativities and (b) the behaviour of the general money wage level. I endeavour to test the theory developed in chapters 4 and 5, and to present a balanced account of what actually governs pay in modern capitalist economies.

Finally, in chapter 7 I draw out some of the implications of my theory for government policy, focussing on the issue of inflation. I analyse the deficiencies of various sorts of policies, and I suggest a more promising approach.

2

PAY NORMS

2.1 FAIRNESS AND RELATIVITIES

An essential ingredient of any theory that ideas of fairness influence pay is evidently the ideas themselves. This chapter is accordingly devoted to a discussion of pay norms. It is not, it should be emphasised, about how or when or whether pay norms might influence actual rates of pay, which will be explored in subsequent chapters.

(i) *Real and relative norms*

At any particular time, beliefs about what constitutes a fair rate of pay in a particular instance are usually couched in absolute money terms. But beliefs of this kind are superficial and frequently revised. The underlying, more important, pay norms are what govern these revisions. As mentioned earlier, there are two main possible types of pay norm; *real* norms (implying that beliefs about fair pay in money terms are revised in response to changes in prices), and *relative* norms (implying that beliefs about fair pay in money terms for particular people or jobs are revised in response to changes in other rates of pay).

A major premise of this book (which is consistent with most of the available evidence, discussed on pages 213–15) is that ideas of fair pay in relative terms are more fundamental than, and eventually always dominate, ideas of fair pay in real terms. I shall not altogether ignore ideas of fairness in real terms. But from this point onwards I shall confine the use of the term pay norm to beliefs about fair relativities.

I shall also assume (although the substance of most of what follows does not depend on this assumption) that pay norms are proportional. In the short run, beliefs about fair or proper pay relationships may be couched in absolute rather than percentage terms (Daniel, 1976a, pp. 25–7). And absolute differences in pay are sometimes deliberately kept constant in the face of increases in absolute levels of pay as a means of reducing proportional relativities. But ultimately, I think, beliefs about proper absolute differences in pay are subordinate to beliefs about proper proportional differences.

One should also, in a world of non-proportional taxation, consider whether pay norms are couched in gross or net of tax terms – and indeed how fringe benefits should be treated. I shall suppose that fringe benefits, appropriately valued in monetary terms (and taking due account of their liability to taxation or otherwise), are simply an integral part of pay. As regards taxation, although little of the subsequent argument turns on this point, I shall suggest below on a priori grounds that many, but not all, sorts of beliefs about fair relativities are couched in net of tax terms.

(ii) *Comparisons*

What is regarded as a fair rate of pay (in money terms) for a specific job or employee depends both upon norms concerning relativities and upon the rates of pay prevailing in some comparative *reference set* of employees or jobs. Most of this chapter will be about norms as such. But it is convenient to begin with some preliminary remarks about comparisons.

In principle, the pay of any given employee or job could be compared with that of every other employee or job (and indeed with every other individual income of any kind) in the economy. But in practice the scope of the comparisons made in specific instances is usually quite limited (Runciman, 1966; Daniel, 1975, pp. 20–3, 1976, pp. 20–2). The sizes and shapes of reference sets are determined by the interaction of two sorts of considerations.

(1) Normative sentiments about which pay relativities are important. Any given group of employees, for example, will feel particularly strongly about their position relative to some groups, and less strongly (or not at all) about their position relative to others.

(2) The availability of information. Some rates of pay are easily discovered; to find out about others is difficult or expensive, and in some cases impossible. Even when information is freely available, its application is limited by the restricted data-assimilating capacity of the human brain.

Reference sets thus tend to contain those employees and jobs whose relative pay is the subject of strong feeling or easily ascertainable, and to exclude those whose relative pay is a matter of indifference or difficult to discover. Specifically, people connected with a particular job tend to know and care more about pay in the same establishment, industry, occupation, union and region than in other establishments, industries, occupations, unions and regions.

Even so, it is frequently impossible for comparisons to be precise. Some statistics cover only basic wage rates and omit other components of pay such as overtime earnings, shiftwork premia and payment by results. In many cases data on fringe benefits, hours of work and working conditions are unobtainable. And the dates to which figures refer and the intervals at which they are available are not always the same. Thus even when the underlying data are reliable (and a considerable amount of informal misinformation about rates of pay is always in circulation) the most accurate possible pay comparisons are sometimes rather rough.

(iii) *Agreement and disagreeement*

At any rate on the face of it, there would seem to be little reason why different people should share the same pay norms. Indeed, a large number of industrial disputes explicitly or implicitly involve disagreements about what would constitute fair relativities. And the number of these disputes surely understates the amount of dissension, since the absence of overt disagreement may signify not agreement but ignorance or weakness (Mann, 1970).

An alternative source of information about normative disagreements is surveys of opinion, although these are scarce. They reveal not only considerable heterogeneity of opinion concerning pay relativities, but also some correlation between the opinions of respondents and their actual pay. For example, a recent survey in Britain (Fosh, 1974) asked people if they thought there was too great a difference between pay in top jobs and pay in bottom jobs. Managerial and professional respondents were evenly divided on this issue. But 83 per cent of the semiskilled and unskilled respondents felt that existing differentials were too large (although the *strength* of their feelings was not investigated – Daniel, 1976, p. 25). A similar picture emerges in Runciman (1966, table 22) and, for the United States, in Sussman (1976).

There are, then, many instances in which different people entertain conflicting pay norms, a fact which will receive a great deal of attention in subsequent chapters. But there is also a substantial, indeed a remarkable, amount of agreement about what various kinds of pay relativities ought to be. Moreover, many people adhere to pay norms which are counter to their self-interest.

The degree of consensus tends to be more pronounced, the narrower the occupational or social group concerned. For example, a large majority of the employees in any particular job usually have roughly the same idea about what is a proper rate of pay for their job, relative to other jobs, and it is not difficult to find cases in which employees in different jobs, especially within a given establishment or occupation, share common beliefs about fair pay relativities between those jobs. There is also a significant measure of agreement between broader social groups. For instance, 80 per cent of the respondents in Fosh (1974) were agreed that people with special skills should get a lot more pay than those with no special skills – and even 77 per cent of the semiskilled and unskilled respondents adhered to this view. Likewise, many employees in relatively highly paid jobs do not wish to widen the gap between their own pay and pay in less well paid jobs.

The causes of this superficially rather surprising degree of consensus are to be found in the way in which pay norms evolve. Ideas of fairness are not established in a vacuum, spontaneously in the mind of each individual. They are implanted by exposure to the beliefs and behaviour of other individuals. Thus a group of individuals will tend to hold similar views either if they derive their views from a common external source or if the views of each member of the group are influenced by the views of other members. Both possibilities are relevant in the present context.

(1) Custom has great moral force. Thus precedent and tradition are frequently invoked in the course of discussions and negotiations over pay, and the past history of actual relativities is a major influence on current pay norms. Moreover, because the past is unique, custom tends to be a source of normative consensus, especially when historical precedent is consistent, and especially within groups whose composition varies slowly over time and whose members therefore share a common body of specific experience.

(2) When disagreements over pay relativities occur, pressures of various kinds are exerted by those who hold one view against those who hold other views. Much of this pressure is coercive, being designed

to thwart the will of the other party. But some of it is persuasive, being designed to induce the other party to change its mind. Persuasion involves the use of reasoned argument, force of personality, approval and disapproval, and the extension and withdrawal of friendship, all of which normally require face-to-face contact. Thus mutual persuasion is of negligible importance as a source of normative consensus where there is little social intercourse, and it is at its most effective within fairly small groups, such as workers in the same job or establishment.

2.2 SECONDARY NORMS

For some purposes it is sufficient to know that particular people entertain specific beliefs (which I shall call *primary norms*) about what pay relativities within or between particular jobs ought to be. But for other purposes it is important to ask about the *sources* of primary norms. One would like to know, for example, what it is that causes certain people to think that some specific pair of jobs should be paid the same, and what differentiates them from some other job which the same people think should be paid more. If one knew this, one would have begun to uncover deeper and more general beliefs (which I shall call *secondary norms*)* about the sorts of considerations which are relevant in assessing the fairness of pay.

To the extent that one understands the nature of secondary norms, one is in a better position to explain why particular primary norms are what they are. One can also explain certain sorts of changes over time in primary norms. And one obtains a better understanding of conflicts between different primary norms, many of which are caused by conflicts between different secondary norms. For these reasons, the present section is devoted to a review of secondary norms.

It would be impossible to produce an exhaustive list of the many and various moral principles which at one time or another have been invoked to justify or condemn the size of particular pay relativities – even if one excludes, as I shall do, (a) propositions based on considerations of economic efficiency, (b) propositions concerning the fairness of the mechanism which governs relativities, rather than its results, and (c) propositions regarding the accessibility of particular jobs to particular individuals or groups. But most secondary norms appear to fall into four broad categories, which may be labelled need,

* Cf. Hart's (1961) distinction between primary and secondary rules.

sacrifice, social position and responsibility. The secondary norms of any given individual can thus usually be represented as some specific mixture of these categories.

(i) *Need*

The view that people ought to be paid in proportion to their needs is commonly, though not always, associated with the belief that the consumption needs of different people are fundamentally similar. Thus it is the usual rationalisation of the familiar idea that everyone should be paid the same (although the principle of equal pay also has other, deeper, roots). This idea is powerful and pervasive; even when people are not paid the same, it is generally felt necessary to defend the inequality in question on moral or economic grounds.

One important manifestation of egalitarianism is the rate for the job principle – the belief that all the employees in any given job should be paid the same, regardless of individual differences in ability or efficiency or bargaining power. This belief has always been one of the most fundamental tenets of trade unionism, and most manual, clerical and professional unions have attempted to put it into practice in one form or another. An extension of this principle is that similar jobs in different establishments, or with different employers, should also be paid alike.

The idea that everyone should be paid the same also exerts an important influence on opinions about pay relativities between dissimilar jobs. In some cases it is the basis of demands literally for equal pay in different industries or occupations. In another, larger class of cases it affects beliefs about the proper magnitude of differences in pay between jobs. For example, even if one thinks that more arduous or responsible jobs ought to be more highly paid, it remains to decide how much more highly paid, and in this regard the strength of one's egalitarian sentiments will be important.

Thus far it has been taken for granted that payment in accordance with need is a secondary norm whose implications are always egalitarian. This is not so, need being also, for example, the basis of the view that pay should vary according to the number of an employee's dependents. In addition, one must reckon with the principle of relative deprivation (Runciman, 1966).

The essence of this principle is that need should be subjectively rather than objectively defined. In particular, it is argued that the happiness or unhappiness of individual people depends not on the extent to which their needs as measured by some external yardstick are satisfied, but on the extent to which their expectations are or are not fulfilled. If this is so, it is important to know how expectations are formed. Of the various possibilities in this regard, it would appear that precedent is particularly influential. Thus payment in accordance with subjective need is one possible rationalisation of the belief that existing pay relativities ought to be preserved. It is also the basis of the idea that it is unfair to reduce anyone's pay in absolute real terms.

(ii) *Sacrifice*

Another very common and compelling idea is that pay ought to be proportional to the effort, cost and inconvenience – or, in a word, to the sacrifice – involved in acquiring it. This also is an egalitarian principle, in a more general sense than the principle of payment in accordance with need, with which it is liable to conflict, since it advocates in effect the equalisation not of pay but of utility, taking account of both the pecuniary and the non-pecuniary advantages (and disadvantages) of work.

There are many different sorts of sacrifice, and thus there are correspondingly many different specific applications of this secondary norm, some of which tend to conflict with others, especially since different people often attach different weights to particular sorts of sacrifice. There is, for example, the belief that those whose work is intrinsically pleasant and rewarding should be paid less than those whose work is unpleasant and unsatisfying. There is also the belief that those who have spent or forgone money in the course of education and training deserve higher pay than those who have not. And there is the belief that higher pay should accrue to those who work longer hours, or harder, or at less convenient times or in less convenient places.

The principle of payment according to sacrifice, incidentally, seems to me to underlie most moral (as distinct from economic) statements to the effect that pay should be related to productivity. What is usually meant by 'more productive' in this context, that is, is harder working or more highly trained. It is less common to encounter the belief that one should on moral grounds reward greater productivity independent of effort or other sacrifice, such as might arise from the use of a more efficient machine or from superior inherited abilities.

(iii) *Social position*

Many people also believe that pay ought to depend on social position, in two principal senses, namely sex and what I shall call estate. A third sense, which is important in some societies but which I shall not discuss, is race.

(1) *Sex*. The idea that women should on moral grounds be paid less than men is very familiar. In some cases it is based on the proposition that the typical woman's consumption is financed by her husband's income, and in this respect might be said to be simply a rational variant of the idea that pay should be proportional to need. But more commonly, I believe, it reflects the traditional view that men are and ought to be socially dominant and that this basic inequality should be symbolised by inequality of pay, both within and between jobs.

(2) *Estate*. By 'estate' I mean that dimension of social stratification (which Smith called 'rank in society' and Weber* called 'status') along which are to be found such groups as gentlemen, the lower middle class, respectable people and common workers. These are not classes in the Marxian sense. They are distinguished not in terms of ownership of the means of production, but in terms of differences of accent, manners, dress and social outlook, which people acquire primarily from their parents. These distinctions have their origins in pre-industrial systems of stratification, and for this reason are both of greater salience in Europe than in the United States (whose present society had little pre-industrial history), and of declining importance in contemporary societies generally. Even so, considerable significance continues to adhere to, for example, the distinctions between manual and non-manual work and between apprenticeship and professional training – both of which reflect mainly the social status attached to formal education.

In any event, there exists in some circles the idea that occupations whose typical incumbents are of relatively high estate should be relatively highly paid (Wootton, 1962, pp. 40, 128–9; Houghton, 1974, p.

* See 'Class, status, party' in Gerth (1948). See also Runciman (1966), pp. 36–40.

36). This view is now most frequently voiced by professional groups – doctors, lawyers, teachers, and so on – and in a sense is yet another variant of the idea that pay should be proportional to need. For it rests on the proposition that the maintenance of a particular social position requires a particular relative level of consumption (although the connection is not precise, because social position depends to some extent on the composition rather than the level of consumption).

(iv) *Responsibility*

Finally, let us consider the longstanding and widely held view that the relative pay of different jobs ought to reflect the relative degrees of responsibility involved. Responsibility is not altogether easy to define, but in general terms it depends on two things. (1) It is positively related to the importance to the employer of (or the degree to which the employer's interests are affected by) the actions of employees in the job in question. Of special significance is the amount of damage which negligence or error on the part of the employees concerned would inflict on the employer's interests. (2) It is negatively related to the extent to which the actions of those in the job in question are subject to external control and supervision.

The crucial determinant of the responsibility level of a job is thus the importance to the employer of the (most important sorts of) decisions independently made by employees in the job concerned. In some cases these decisions are directly implemented by the employees in question (as where they operate equipment or are in direct contact with customers or clients). In other cases the decisions are implemented indirectly, often at several removes, by other employees over whom they are in authority. In all organisations above a certain size, indirect control is indispensable, and thus responsibility and authority tend to be closely associated. It is therefore common to measure the relative responsibility levels of jobs within particular organisations in terms of the numbers of employees directly and indirectly controlled.* But below the managerial hierarchy, in non-hierarchical organisations, and among specialist managers and independent professionals and craftsmen, responsibility and authority tend to be divorced, and thus measures of this type are inappropriate.

* Simon (1957), Marris (1964, pp. 89–99). For alternative measures of responsibility, see Lydall (1968, pp. 127–33) and Jaques (1967, p. 21).

More fundamental than the question of how responsibility should be measured, though, is the question of why it is that people believe that relative pay ought to reflect relative responsibility. In some cases, it is for reasons of economic efficiency; but in the present context it is the non-economic or moral arguments that are of particular interest.

One line of argument is that more responsible jobs should be more highly paid to compensate their incumbents for the worry and strain which responsibility entails, this being an expression of the principle of payment according to sacrifice coupled with the assumption that responsibility is burdensome and unattractive. But it is not clear that this assumption is generally correct.* Some sorts of responsibility are onerous, especially for certain kinds of people (Goldthorpe, 1968, pp. 123–4); and every sort of responsibility necessarily involves stress. Yet responsibility necessarily also involves independence, importance and power, which most people find attractive, and in most cases it would seem that responsibility is sought after for its own sake. Thus if sacrifice were the sole criterion, it would probably be more appropriate to argue for an *inverse* relationship between responsibility and pay.

Sacrifice, however, does not appear to me to be the sole, or even the main, foundation of the view that more responsible jobs ought, on moral grounds, to be more highly paid. Instead, most of those who put forward this view seem to feel simply that the relative pay of different jobs should *symbolise* their relative *importance* (in the particular sense outlined above). This attitude is especially salient with regard to authority; it is almost invariably felt that the hierarchy of pay within an organisation should symbolise and reinforce the hierarchy of authority.†

Before leaving the subject of secondary norms, it is perhaps worth explaining why, since the view that pay should be related to skill is frequently expressed, I have not introduced skill as a distinct secondary norm category. The problem is that skills are of very varied kinds; thus to assess the fairness of the pay of, say, doctors, airline pilots and welders, one must adopt some common denominator of skill. Most

---

* Both Smith and Mill, for example, treated the influence of trust on pay as something separate from the influence of 'ease or hardship' – see pp. 16–18 above. See also the empirical studies discussed on pp. 185–6 and 191–5 below.

† A point lucidly expounded by Marris (1964, p. 92). See also, for example, Boyle (1976, p. 39): 'the Lord Chancellor's salary...should be pitched at a level relative to the judicial pay structure that confirms the position and dignity of the office'.

moral (as distinct from economic) arguments for relating pay to skill appear to be based on two common denominators, both of which have already been considered. One is the amount of training required, which comes under the heading of sacrifice. The other is the degree of responsibility involved. For skill is essentially the ability to perform actions without external guidance. The more important the actions, and the smaller the amount of guidance, the greater, it would generally be agreed, is the level of skill. But greater skill in this sense is very similar to greater responsibility.

2.3 CHANGE

Ideas about what constitute fair or proper pay relativities do not alter rapidly. But it would be wrong to suppose that pay norms necessarily remain constant, and it is therefore important to consider the ways in which they may change over time.

(i) *Changes in primary norms alone*

It is convenient to divide the discussion into two parts. To begin with, I shall assume that secondary norms remain the same. For even if these general underlying criteria of fairness or propriety do not alter, primary norms regarding particular relativities may change for four sorts of reasons.

(1) *Information.* Given any specific set of secondary norms, opinions about what particular relativities ought to be are dependent on information about relevant attributes (such as the level of responsibility and the working conditions) of the employees or jobs concerned. Information of this kind is often imperfect, and changes in its quality, not necessarily in the direction of greater accuracy, may be sufficient to alter primary norms.

(2) *Attributes.* Primary norms may change independently of secondary norms also as a result of *actual* changes in relevant attributes of employees or jobs. In terms of sacrifice, for instance, the relative level of pay regarded as fair for a particular job might decline because of a technical innovation that improved working conditions, or because of a government subsidy to expensive training previously paid for by

employees. Likewise, in terms of responsibility, a reduction in the relative level of pay regarded as fair might occur if a job were subjected to closer supervision, or if automation transformed it from a skilled craft into a routine machine-minding operation (although certain sorts of automation, by raising the value of the equipment in the employee's charge, might have the opposite effect).

Similarly, primary norms may be changed by alterations in the attributes of jobs relevant to the category of secondary norms that I labelled social position. The social position of a particular job, whether in terms of sex or estate, depends not on the nature of the work as such, but on the characteristics of its typical incumbent. Since the relevant characteristics of individual people are largely formed (by birth, upbringing and education) before they enter the labour force, the relative social positions of particular jobs depend on the pattern of recruitment, and will thus remain unchanged so long as the same sorts of people continue to be recruited into them. This will tend to be the case in so far as employers (influenced by the sentiments of their existing employees) regard individuals whose personal attributes differ from those of the typical employees in the jobs concerned as being less suitable for employment. For example, women may be discriminated against if they attempt to enter male-dominated occupations.

As a result, there is probably quite a strong tendency for the social position of any given job, once established, to be self-perpetuating (which suggests that the relative social positions of particular jobs are largely a matter of historical accident). But alterations may be brought about by major autonomous changes in patterns of recruitment. Such changes might be caused by anti-discrimination legislation, or by reform of the educational system. But the most likely cause is large changes in supply and demand conditions in particular jobs. For example, a prolonged war, during which civilian employers were obliged to recruit women as replacements for conscripted men, might permanently transform some 'male' jobs into 'female' or 'neuter' jobs.

(3) *Taxation.* Insofar as secondary norms are framed in net of tax terms, primary norms concerning the gross pay relativities between particular jobs will be altered by changes in the progressivity of the tax system. For instance, increased progressivity (provided that it were not offset by greater use of fringe benefits and other avoidance devices) could cause people to feel that it would be fair to enlarge gross

pay differentials. It is thus of some interest to enquire which, if any, categories of secondary pay norms are likely to be couched in net of tax terms.

Need is a secondary norm which must usually refer to net relativities, since the needs in question are consumption needs, and consumption depends on net rather than gross pay. *Sacrifice* also must be a secondary norm which applies to net relativities; the just reward for greater exertion or unpleasant work is surely a greater level of consumption, not a greater tax liability. For the same reason, norms based on *social position* must for the most part refer to net pay. Indeed, the fundamental notion with regard to estate is that the maintenance of a particular social position requires a particular relative level of consumption. Similarly, one of the reasons why some people feel that women ought to be paid less than men is that the average woman's consumption is underwritten by her husband's income.

On the other hand, inasmuch as low pay for women is desired simply as a symbol of male dominance, differences in gross pay may be sufficient. Likewise, it may well be that *responsibility* is a secondary norm which refers to gross relativities. The relationship between responsibility and proper pay is, it was argued earlier, largely symbolic. What is more, it is symbolic of the relative importance and authority of different jobs within organisations in which people are associated as producers rather than consumers.

(4) *Relative prices.* If, as suggested above, some secondary norms refer to fair or proper levels of consumption, primary norms may also be altered by changes in relative prices, which (if consumption patterns vary) can alter the relationship between relative levels of consumption and relative levels of net of tax income. For example, Hirsch (1977, pp. 27–8) has argued that economic growth raises the relative prices of 'positional goods', on which, it may be supposed, richer people spend a larger proportion of their incomes. This might cause (especially these) people to feel that it would be proper to widen pay differentials.

(ii) *Changes in secondary norms*

In addition, primary norms can change without any alterations in information, job attributes, taxation or relative prices, simply as a result of changes in secondary norms. New secondary norms may develop, or old ones disappear. But in practice changes in the relative weights attached to existing secondary norms are probably of more importance. For instance, greater emphasis might be placed on the idea of payment in accordance with need, which could cause a general narrowing of what would be regarded as fair relativities. Or boredom might come to be thought a better justification than responsibility for high pay. Or there might be a change in attitudes concerning the role of women in society which affected beliefs about proper pay relativities between the sexes.

Secondary norms exist in the minds of individual people (and of course vary to a greater or lesser extent between one person and another). There are thus two ways in which the mix of secondary norms in society might be changed. (a) Particular individuals might change their minds. (b) Different age cohorts might have different ideas; if, say, people's views varied according to the decade in which they were born, the ideological composition of the population would alter over time even if no individual ever changed his mind.

In neither case is change likely to be fast. The first source of change is limited by the reluctance or inability of most adults to alter their ideas and values. The second is constrained by demographic factors – a complete turnover of the population takes more than a century. It is also, and this is more important, constrained by the fact that each age cohort derives its secondary norms very largely from preceding cohorts (children, that is, obtain their ideas mainly from their parents and teachers), which tends to reduce ideological differences between cohorts.

But new ideas and attitudes do arise in the minds of particular individuals, and some of them spread. It would thus be wrong to suggest that adults are completely incapable of changing their minds, either spontaneously or through discussion or as a result of various other sorts of external persuasion. The minds of the young, however, are much more plastic than those of the old. Thus the socialisation of recently born cohorts, and the creation of differences between their views and the views of their predecessors, play a crucial part in the diffusion of new ideas and the displacement of old ones.

This discussion of change raises the bigger question of the origins or determinants of secondary norms. Because change occurs only gradually, the mix of secondary norms in a society may be regarded as largely historically determined, the more so, the shorter the period under consideration. But from some points of view, and especially in a longer perspective, this is not altogether satisfactory, since it does not explain why changes occur or why secondary norms vary within and between societies.

Some people (for example, Hicks, 1955) argue that ideas about fair pay relativities reflect what pay relativities actually have been in the past, and in particular that custom hallows the consequences of former conditions of supply and demand or power; thus changes in pay norms are seen as a lagged function of changes in actual relativities which themselves are not normatively induced. Others go much further and argue that pay norms have no independent existence, being simply a species of pseudo-morality cooked up by particular groups to defend their established privileges or to legitimise their use of power in pursuit of financial advancement.

There is some truth in all this. The moral force of custom has already been noted; thus certain features of secondary norms (and the details of many primary norms) are undoubtedly fossils, some of which reflect the past influence of anomic pressures. It is also the case that people are more inclined to espouse moral values which favour their financial self-interests (for some evidence, see p. 24 above); and it would be naive to swallow whole all the moral arguments advanced in support of particular pay claims, or to suppose that these represent the sole motivation of the people concerned.

Nonetheless, moral values in general and ideas of fair pay in particular also lead lives of their own, independent of the current or past state of affairs, and to a considerable extent motivate people to behave in ways which cannot plausibly be accounted for in terms of financial self-interest. Not only do many individuals adhere to pay norms counter to their financial self-interests (p. 25); but also it is often in principle impossible to apply the concept of financial self-interest to groups (pp. 11–14). And indeed, if ideas of fairness had no independent force, it would be hard to explain why people bother to invoke them so frequently. In short, it seems to me incontrovertible that pay norms have some important roots in basic moral principles such as equality and hierarchy, although where such principles ultimately come from is a question which I cannot pretend to answer.

3

NORMATIVE AND ANOMIC PRESSURES

3.1 FAIRNESS, UTILITY AND BEHAVIOUR

In this and the next two chapters I shall explore at a theoretical level
the mechanisms by which pay norms can influence actual rates of pay.
I shall begin by discussing the motives (or utility functions) of
employers and employees, in order to clarify the similarities and
differences between my assumptions about motivation and those ordinarily made by economists.

(i) *Employers*

All sorts of people entertain pay norms, but in this book I shall
concentrate on the pay norms of employees, which in practice are very
much the most important kind. Although pay is sometimes influenced
also by the norms of employers, I shall assume for simplicity that
employers have no norms and that their motives are in this sense
entirely orthodox. There are of course various types of employer –
government, households, private firms – whose objectives differ, and
which operate under different sorts of constraints; there is also disagreement about what exactly are the objectives of the various types
of employer; but for the present purpose it is sufficient to assume
simply that each employer attempts to maximise *some* non-normative
objective function.

Whether or not they themselves entertain pay norms, employers are
a vital part of the mechanism by which norms influence pay. For it
is the employer (or his agent) who writes the pay cheque or fills the
pay packet, and thus all forces which govern pay, whatever their
nature, must in a proximate sense take effect by influencing the
behaviour of employers. The present chapter is therefore devoted
mainly to a discussion of the ways in which employees can exert
pressure on employers to set pay in accordance with their norms. I
shall also examine the pressures on employers not to comply with pay

norms, and the pressures which may cause employees not to want pay set in accordance with their norms.

(ii) *Employees*

Most employees have some definite ideas about fair or proper relative pay, especially where their own jobs are concerned, and the degree to which their pay conforms with their norms usually has a comparatively large effect on their happiness. But an employee's utility function is also likely to contain two prominent non-normative arguments. One is the nature of work itself. Other things being equal, that is, employees will gravitate towards jobs in which the work is interesting and light, and, when in a particular job, will attempt to make the work as pleasant as possible.

The other non-normative argument is money. Other things being equal, an employee will always prefer a larger income to a smaller income. This may appear incompatible with the idea that employees have specific pay norms. For it implies that employees want unlimited amounts of pay without regard to other people's pay, while pay norms imply that they want particular amounts of pay in relation to other people's pay. But the two things are not necessarily inconsistent.

First, one must distinguish between an individual's desires with respect to his own income and his desires with respect to the pay relativities between particular jobs. For instance, the belief that the job one presently occupies should be paid less than some other job is not incompatible with a strong desire to move into the better paid job.

Second, and even where employees lack the inclination or the opportunity to leave their present jobs, one can (as Pemberton, 1975, ch. 2, has pointed out) reconcile the existence of pay norms with the idea that people always prefer more pay to less by supposing that there is a discontinuity in the relationship between pay and utility at the normatively prescribed level of pay. More exactly, I shall assume that although an employee's utility is always increased by an increase in pay, the effect of a given pay increase is large when his relative pay is less than he considers fair and small when his relative pay is fair or more than fair. In other words, I shall assume that although an employee would not refuse an increase in pay above the norm, he would be unwilling to make much effort to attain it, whereas below the norm he would be willing to make a considerable effort to secure an equal increase in pay.

Employees want more money for the sake of its purchasing power. They thus also care about prices and taxes. Most employees seem especially sensitive to year to year changes in their real wages (particularly in a downward direction). I shall therefore assume that changes in real pay are an important determinant of the degree of resentment or militancy aroused by unfair relative pay. This assumption implies that employees, if they felt their pay to be fair in relative terms, would not be greatly concerned about changes in its absolute purchasing power, but that such changes influence the amount of effort they are willing to make to rectify unfairness in relative terms.

3.2 INDIVIDUAL NORMATIVE PRESSURES

In the next three sections I shall discuss the various ways in which employees can exert pressure on their employers to conform with their pay norms. I shall take it for granted that employees always want pay to conform with their norms and that employers always want to pay less than their employees would like. This is not invariably so. But for the moment it is convenient to concentrate on the very important class of cases in which employees must attempt to dissuade their employer from paying below their norm by imposing (or threatening to impose) sanctions on him. Collective action is evidently of great importance in this regard. But in this first section I shall examine only the methods by which individual employees, acting in isolation, might be able to bring normative pressure to bear.

(i) *Social sanctions*

An employer may be dissuaded from paying particular employees less than they regard as a fair wage by the fear that they will dislike, despise and ostracise him (Doeringer, 1971, pp. 24–5). Since what most people ultimately desire is affection and deference, the potential efficacy of this sort of pressure should not be under-rated. But for it to be effective there must be a good deal of social contact between employee and employer (or the agent of the employer who makes the pay decision). Thus it is unlikely to be of much importance for the great majority of employees in organisations above a certain, fairly small, size.

(ii) *Threat to quit*

One type of economic sanction available to the individual employee is the threat to quit (which is associated with the sort of individual monopoly power discussed on p. 9 above). A necessary condition for such a threat to be effective is that finding and training a suitable replacement should impose costs on the employer. In the context of the present argument, the *availability* of new recruits is unlikely to be the most significant factor, since the employer will have taken labour supply considerations into account in arriving at his preference for a wage below the employee's norm. Advertising and selection costs also are unlikely to be large. What may be important, however, is the cost of training.

What is relevant in this connection is employer-specific training, and especially on-the-job training (or experience). The largest costs of this sort of training arise from the slowness and inefficiency of, and the mistakes made by, inexperienced employees during the process of learning by doing. The size of these costs, as regards the replacement of a particular employee, depends in part on the nature of the job and in part on the degree of experience of the individual concerned. It also depends on the source of potential replacements – would they be recruited from outside the organisation, or would it simply be a matter of promoting a second-in-command? In most cases the costs will be fairly small, but in some they will be large.

Even when the costs are large, however, the effectiveness of the threat to quit also depends on the probability of the employee carrying it out. This will depend in part on the quality of the employee's alternative employment prospects and on the costs of changing jobs. But the employer will have taken this into account. Indeed, it is appropriate to suppose that at the wage preferred by the employer, the employee would make himself objectively worse off by quitting. This in itself need not nullify the threat to quit, since it is by no means unknown for employees to leave if they feel unfairly treated, even though their chances of obtaining another equally good job are small (for a striking example, see Corina, 1977).

But unless there is a genuine scarcity of labour (in which case the wage will tend to rise for very orthodox reasons), it is hard to believe that the individual employee's threat to quit will normally be a particularly potent method of coercing the employer into complying with his norm. Not only are the costs of replacing an individual employee usually small, but it would also be unrealistic to place too much weight on the willingness of individual employees to sacrifice their objective interests in defence of their norms, or on the readiness of employers to believe that their employees are willing to act in this way.

(iii) *Work intensity*

Another, more important, sort of economic sanction which the individual employee may be able to use against his employer is to remain in his job but work less hard. For the intensity, conscientiousness and enthusiasm with which an employee works usually makes an enormous difference to the value of his services to his employer. It governs the frequency with which he is absent or on sick leave; his willingness to undertake unpaid overtime; the amount of work he gets through in any given period of time; the quality of his work; the amount of care which he takes of the employer's equipment and reputation; his willingness to cooperate with the employer, especially in implementing technical and other changes; and his willingness to cooperate with other employees, which (as Thurow, 1976, pp. 81–5, 106–7, has noted) is especially important where employees must work as a team, or must impart skills to other employees.

Even so, considerations of this kind would be of little importance in the present context if it were possible (a) to specify in the (written or unwritten) contract between employer and employee exactly how conscientiously the latter was undertaking to work, and (b) to monitor accurately and cheaply the degree to which the employee was living up to his undertaking. For if this were so, although there might be hard bargaining over the terms of the contract, the employee could not work less hard than he had agreed to without being sacked.

Reality never conforms strictly with this model. There is always some vagueness and ambiguity about the extent of an employee's obligations, and thus some range within which he is free to vary the intensity with which he works. In some cases the range is small – for example, it is usually fairly simple to assess the performance of a semi-skilled production worker. But in many cases the range is large.

This is most conspicuously so in responsible jobs, since the essence of responsibility (as outlined on p. 30) is discretionary control over things which matter to the employer. The more responsible the job, the less closely is the employee's performance monitored, and the greater is the extent to which the employer's interests are affected by the quality of the employee's performance. Naturally enough, gross dereliction of duty will eventually come to the employer's attention (though perhaps not before a great deal of damage has been done) and will lead to the employee's dismissal. Even before this point, poor performance will jeopardise his promotion prospects. But above some minimum, which may be quite low (especially if it would be costly for the employer to replace him), the employee in a responsible job is free to choose how hard to work, and what he chooses to do in this regard may be of great importance to his employer.

An employee's choice of how hard to work will depend on many factors – it will vary according to the nature of the work, and from one individual to another. But other things being equal an employee will unquestionably work less hard if he feels that he is being treated unfairly by his employer – in particular, if he feels he is being underpaid. It is unlikely that this sort of gesture will take the form of a direct threat to the employer; it may even be the result of a subconscious impulse rather than a deliberate decision. But however it manifests itself, this sort of reaction gives the employer an incentive – in some cases a very big incentive – to pay in accordance with the employee's norm, even though he would otherwise choose to pay less.*

3.3 COLLECTIVE NORMATIVE PRESSURES (I)

By collective action one means not merely simultaneous action by a number of individuals, but coordinated action. Because coordination may be tacit, the line between individual and collective behaviour is not always easy to draw. But collective action in the sense in which I shall use the term is certainly a much broader concept than formal collective bargaining or union activity, since collective pressure is also exerted informally, both by groups of employees acting independently of their union and by non-unionised employees (some of whom may be able in addition to coerce their employers by threatening formally

* In a sense this simply generalises the old proposition about the 'economy of high wages' (e.g. Hicks, 1963, p. 94); it refers instead to the 'economy of *fair* wages' – cf. Thurow, 1976, p. 107.

to unionise). In the present section I shall restrict the discussion to collective action by employees in a single job against a single employer, postponing until the next section the subject of alliances between employees in different jobs and with different employers.

The most important type of collective pressure is an extension of one of the sorts of individual pressure discussed above, namely reduction (or the threat of reduction) of work intensity. This can take many forms, including general slowing of the pace of work, deterioration of the quality of output, wastage of inputs, damage to equipment, epidemic absenteeism, overtime bans, minor rule-breaking or (usually more effective) working strictly to rule, and refusal to cooperate in making innovations (sometimes known as 'productivity bargaining'). Its most extreme, though by no means its most common, form is the strike – a complete, but temporary, withdrawal of services.

The amount of pressure which can be brought to bear on an employer by these sorts of collective action depends on a number of things, of which I shall discuss five.

(i) *Degree of consensus*

Collective action presumes a measure of agreement on collective goals. But different employees in a given job may have different pay norms; they may disagree about what would be a fair structure of relativities within the job, or about what would be a proper rate of pay in relation to other jobs.

One should not exaggerate the likely extent of normative dissension, since the sorts of pressures which tend to generate consensus (discussed on pp. 25–6) are at their most effective within narrow groups such as the individuals in a single job. The efficacy of mutual persuasion is of course reduced if the employees in the job concerned are geographically dispersed, and the force of custom is diminished if employment is characteristically of a casual or short-term nature. But when the employees are concentrated in a few places and are typically employed for long periods, it is not implausible to suppose that a large proportion of them will come to share similar pay norms.

Nonetheless, there is always a certain amount (and sometimes a great deal) of disagreement among the employees in a given job as to what pay objectives they should pursue. At the same time, since the group will be weakened if it is divided, they usually have a strong incentive to try, by voting, negotiation and manoeuvring, to arrive at some compromise objective which can serve as the basis of a tactical alliance.

A high priority will attach to attempts to secure agreement on internal relativities. For if the employees in a particular job cannot agree on what they should be paid relative to one another, it will be extremely difficult for them to act collectively over external relativities. In this connection it is common for a single rate for the job to be advocated. This principle is simple, it appeals to many people on moral grounds, and it symbolises the community of interest essential to collective action. But for one reason or another it may be unacceptable – in which case it becomes necessary to seek an agreed-on pattern of internal inequality, which is usually more difficult.

Where the underlying disagreements over objectives are small, it will be possible to establish a broadly based and robust coalition. But the larger the disagreements, the smaller will be the amount of collective pressure that the group can exert, since the scope for forming coalitions will be narrower and the chances of them falling apart in action greater.

(ii) *Costs of action to employees*

The willingness of employees to undertake collective action, and the credibility of their threats to do so, will also depend on the size of the costs they would incur.

This will depend in part on the nature of the action contemplated. A general slow-down might entail no costs; physical violence or sabotage could lead to imprisonment; and a strike would involve a loss of earnings. The amount of hardship caused by loss of earnings would depend on the availability of alternative sources of income (such as social security benefits and strike pay) and of ways (such as tax rebates and borrowing) of financing essential consumption in the absence of current income. There is also the risk of being sacked for taking part in the action, and of promotion prospects being impaired; and the risk that collective action might cause redundancies by damaging the employer's commercial viability. In addition, there are the less tangible costs of collective action – the worry, the disruption of personal routine, and the emotional effort of confrontation.

The greater the costs, the smaller will be the amount of pressure which a group of employees can exert. But even large costs need not deter collective action, since they may be offset by the prospective gains. In part this is a purely objective tradeoff, the costs being set against the narrowly financial gains (being the appropriately discounted expected increase in pay above what it would otherwise have been). But the likelihood of employees taking collective action does not depend simply on whether or not the objective gains would exceed the objective costs, for two reasons.

(1) A simple financial reckoning may understate the subjective value of the gains. In particular, if employees have definite ideas about what would constitute a fair rate of pay, and if, without collective action, their pay would be less than this, then they may be willing to take action even though it would make them objectively worse off. Most people, that is, are prepared to make limited sacrifices in pursuit of matters of principle, and their resolution in this regard is usually much stronger when they are acting in concert with other people than it would be if they were acting alone.

(2) On the other hand, as Olson (1965) has emphasised, collective action may not succeed even if the objective costs are less than the objective gains, simply because the gains would be in the form of a public good – an increase in the pay of all the employees in the job concerned. Each individual employee, believing (in most cases correctly) that his participation will not materially affect the outcome of the action, has an incentive not to participate – thereby securing the benefits without incurring the costs. If enough individuals react in this way, the action is bound to fail.

To overcome this problem, the group must be in a position to impose sanctions on free riders. In some cases it may be able to deny them employment (by expelling them from the union in a closed shop). In other cases, free riders may be denied access to selective economic benefits provided by a union (such as sick pay or legal advice). They can also be subjected to odium and ostracisation: this is most effective in the context of relatively intimate groups; it also tends to be more effective when issues of principle (such as fair pay) are involved, since this increases both the willingness to impose social sanctions and the susceptibility of free riders to accusations of treachery.

45

(iii) *Replacement labour supply*

The amount of collective pressure which a group of employees can exert will depend inversely on the ease and cheapness with which their employer could sack and replace them all if they were to strike or misbehave in some other way.

One relevant factor in this regard is the state of the labour market, and especially the level of unemployment among those with the necessary skills in the same locality. More generally, a high degree of monopsony (i.e. an inelastic supply of labour), which would strengthen the employer's hand in an individualistic market, will weaken his position in the face of collective action. For if his labour supply is comparatively inelastic, it will be impossible for him to replace all his employees at short notice without greatly bidding up wages.

One must also consider the cost to the employer of losing the accumulated experience of his existing employees. In some cases, the required amount of employer-specific on-the-job training is small, but in others it is large. And the training cost of replacing most or all of the employees in a job would usually be disproportionately greater than the cost of replacing one or two, principally because there would be relatively fewer experienced employees to teach and supervise the new recruits.

The employees in the job concerned may be able to compound the employer's difficulty in replacing them. In professional and technical jobs, they may be able to do this through control of training facilities – although they must also be able to exert some (moral or economic) leverage on those who have received the relevant training. But in most jobs the employees can attempt to impede replacement only by some form of picketing. Physical violence against blacklegs is in general illegal; thus picketers must rely on verbal abuse and persuasion, both of which can be quite effective.

(iv) *Costs of action to employer*

The amount of pressure which a group of employees can bring to bear through collective action depends a great deal on the size of the loss that the action would inflict on their employer, either by reducing his output or by increasing his costs.

The size of the loss depends in part on the nature of the collective action – a strike will have a bigger effect on output than a go-slow, and blocking a major innovation will have a bigger effect on costs than wasting materials. It also depends on the place of the job concerned in the process of production – is it of vital importance, or could it be by-passed by having the work done by employees in other jobs, or external sub-contractors, or temporarily not done at all?

In private enterprises, losses of output are significant only insofar as they cause losses of sales revenue. In some cases (for example, a manufacturing firm with large stocks), the loss of sales will be less than the loss of output. In others, it will be greater – as for example where a firm's customers transfer permanently to other suppliers. In many cases, though, the loss of sales revenue overstates the cost of collective action to a private employer, since certain expenses are usually also reduced – it being unnecessary, for example, to pay the wages of striking workers.

Government agencies and public enterprises evaluate losses of output in a somewhat different way. Most government agencies do not sell their output, and must therefore make some direct assessment of the value of the lost output to their clients or the general public. Even in the case of a public enterprise which does sell its output, account will be taken not only of the loss suffered through collective action by the enterprise itself, but also of the losses imposed on its customers and on the society as a whole.

(v) *Tactical skill*

The factors discussed above are those which fundamentally determine the amount of pressure which a group of employees can exert on its employer. If these factors combine to put a particular group into an extremely strong position, the astuteness of its leaders is unlikely to be of much importance. And if a group is fundamentally impotent, no amount of diplomatic virtuosity will change matters. But in other cases tactical skill may have a significant effect on the amount of pressure which a group can bring to bear.

3.4 COLLECTIVE NORMATIVE PRESSURES (2)

The preceding section was focussed on collective action by employees in a single job against a single employer. But in practice alliances between employees in different jobs, and between the employees of different employers, are also of considerable importance.

(i) *One employer, several jobs*

The possibility of joint action by employees in several different jobs against their common employer requires no more than minor modifications to the argument of the previous section, especially since the definition of a job has been left vague and the possibility of pay differentials within a single job has been admitted.

One of the things which distinguishes the case of several jobs from the case of a single job is the greater likelihood of systematic disagreement over objectives, especially with regard to the pay relativities between the jobs concerned. Disagreement of this kind will be lessened insofar as having a common employer leads to the sort of sustained social connections from which shared norms tend to emerge. But employees may still be separated by the fact of working in different establishments, or by differences in the nature of their work. Thus among the employees of a given employer there will be pockets, large and small, of close social contact, within which there may well be something approaching a normative consensus, but between which there is a greater chance of disagreement over relativities.

Whether or not, however, the employees in a particular set of jobs agree on what relativities ought to be, there is often a strong incentive for them to form some sort of coalition, tacit or overt. In some cases this is because financial resources can be pooled, in some because a variety of external allies can be united, and in others because joint action precludes sacking or other retaliation by the employer against small or weak groups. In most cases, however, the advantages of such coalitions arise because joint action would inflict greater damage on the employer.

This is most marked where the work of those in one job is to some extent substitutable for the work of those in another job. For example, engineers and supervisory staff can sometimes temporarily operate an automated plant (such as a power station) if its manual workers go on strike. On a longer term basis, the employees in one job may be able to train permanent replacements for the employees in another job. But whatever its specific causes, substitutability evidently enhances the advantages of forming a coalition, especially for those employees whose services are most easily dispensed with. For the damage which simultaneous and coordinated action would inflict on the employer would exceed the sum of the various bits of damage that each member of the coalition could inflict by acting alone.

Complementarity has the opposite effect. This occurs where the jobs concerned are the specialised parts of a complex production process, such as a vehicle assembly line. If the employees in one job were, for example, to strike, there would be less work (and in the limiting case of strict complementarity, no work) for those in other jobs to do. This would render those in other jobs less powerful, since if they also were to strike the additional loss to the employer would be comparatively small (in the limit, it would be zero). Thus the damage inflicted on the employer by joint action is less than the sum of the various bits of damage that would be inflicted by separate action, and the incentive to form alliances is diminished.

Even in the case of strict complementarity, though, there may be another kind of incentive for the employees concerned to form an alliance. For a reduction of output by those in one job could cause those in other jobs to lose part or all of their pay through being laid off or put on short time; it might even inflict greater damage on other employees than on the employer. As a result, for example, a single coordinated strike might entail lesser costs for the employees involved than a series of independent strikes in different jobs.

Thus where the employees in a number of jobs are more or less in agreement about what relativities ought to be, they will often act jointly rather than separately against their common employer. Indeed, where there is agreement of this kind, one group may support another even though it stands to gain nothing itself by so doing, simply because it believes the cause to be just (this sort of alliance being especially important as a potential source of power for otherwise weak groups).

Even where there is disagreement about relativities, the mutual advantages of joint action may still be sufficient to cause a coalition to be formed, based on some sort of compromise. The nature of the compromise will depend partly on the relative bargaining skills of the parties involved, and partly on how deeply they are attached to their respective norms, but mainly on their relative contributions to the strength of the alliance, as measured by the difference between the power of each group on its own and its power as a member of the alliance. Thus a weak group which allies itself with a strong group must expect the compromise objective to lie closer to its partner's norms than to its own.

Tactical alliances based on compromises of this kind may prove durable and successful. In some cases, indeed, the social contact created by such a marriage of convenience may gradually breed internal normative consensus. But where the gains from cooperation are small in relation to the disagreements about what relativities ought to be, any compromise must be fragile, and in most instances joint action against the employer will be impossible. For this to be so, the differences of opinion need not be objectively large – even small differences can be the subject of passionate feeling.

In some cases, disagreement over relativities, while too great to permit joint action, will not be so great as to preclude some looser type of alliance. For example, if one group of employees were to strike, others might give passive support by refusing to do the work of the striking employees on either a temporary or a permanent basis, or by refusing to train external replacements for them, or by refusing to cooperate with the employer in sub-contracting or other arrangements for by-passing their work. Such tacit support, or even an attitude of neutrality rather than hostility on the part of other employees, can often markedly increase the amount of damage which collective action inflicts on an employer. The motives of other employees for giving such support, even in the absence of detailed agreement on objectives, are usually partly tactical, in expectation of reciprocal help on subsequent occasions, and partly based on vague precepts of solidarity, or on a general feeling that the employer is a common enemy.

(ii) *Several employers*

Employees can sometimes exert substantially more pressure on their employer by making alliances with the employees of other employers. Alliances of this sort are usually based on economic or organisational links between employers which put those who work for one employer in a position to impose sanctions on other employers.

One such sort of linkage arises where different employers form part of a single diversified company, or are all connected by the fact of being in the public sector. Similarly, a firm's employees may be able to exert pressure on its customers or suppliers by threatening to deprive them of some vital input or refusing to handle their outputs. A coal miners' strike, for instance, is more damaging if railwaymen refuse to move existing coal stocks to power stations or if dockworkers refuse to unload imported coal.

Another way in which employers may be connected is by the fact of being product market competitors – producers of outputs which are close substitutes for one another. In this type of case, the employees concerned have two reasons for making alliances. First, they have a strong incentive to force all the employers to conform to a common standard of wages. For if some employers are made to adhere to a specific norm, while others are allowed to pay lower wages, the latter may be able to undercut the former in the product market, thereby causing employment in the firms which adhere to the norm to decline. Second, in trying to enforce a common standard, the employees of the firms in question can often gain by adopting a coordinated strategy of striking each employer in turn. This raises the cost of a strike to the individual employer, since he loses trade to his competitors, who are still producing. It also reduces the cost of a strike to his employees, who can be supported from the pay of his competitors' employees.

Even where there are no economic or organisational links between employers, alliances between their employees may be fruitful for other reasons. In particular, a large union embracing the employees of many disparate employers enjoys economies of scale with regard to the provision of finance, information, legal advice and negotiating expertise. Employees in a single firm, who might have little success if they acted alone, can often exert more pressure on their employer with the financial backing of a large union and the professional assistance of its officers. They may also gain advantageous publicity from demonstrations of sympathy by those who work for other employers.

As with alliances among the employees of a single employer, there are various kinds and degrees of alliance between the employees of different employers. In some instances, the strong will help the weak for purely normative reasons, without any expectation of objective gain. In others, the alliance will depend strictly on the provision of reciprocal assistance, sometimes of an active kind, sometimes in the form of benevolent neutrality. In some circumstances, the members of an alliance will adopt common pay objectives (as, for example, where their employers are product market competitors), in which case internal differences of opinion must be resolved in the same sort of

51

way as in a coalition among the employees of a single employer. In other circumstances, alliances may flourish without specified common objectives, held together by a mixture of mutual advantage and solidaristic rhetoric.

Not all tight alliances between the employees of different employers operate by attempting straightforwardly to coerce each of the employers into conforming with the relevant norms. In a small but significant class of cases, they operate by restricting the supply of labour to an extent such that the normatively prescribed wage is established by competition between the various employers. This is an attractive strategy where the employees in question would otherwise be in weak bargaining positions vis-à-vis their individual employers, or where the number or geographical dispersion of employers is so great as to make coordinated direct action against them a difficult or costly exercise. It is only possible, though, where essential skills (either genuinely necessary or legally required) must be acquired by a programme of training whose scale of operation is controlled by the employees themselves – examples being a professional school with a limited number of places, or an apprenticeship scheme with a limit on the number of apprentices per craftsman.

Supply restriction is a strategy which, in its pure form, has a number of limitations. First, it requires a good deal of competition between employers; a monopsonist (or a monopsonistic cartel), if confronted with a restricted supply of labour, would simply pay the minimum wage necessary to prevent the employees concerned from turning to alternative work. Second, it requires an accurate knowledge of demand to gauge the degree of restriction needed to bring about the desired wage. And third, it is not possible by this means to enforce the rate for the job principle; although supply restriction may cause the average wage in the job concerned to attain a specific level, it cannot prevent employers bidding the pay of exceptionally able individuals above that of their less talented colleagues. As a result of these various limitations, supply restriction is often coupled with direct efforts to make pay conform with the relevant norms, for example by establishing standard or minimum (time or piece) rates.

3.5 NORMATIVE AND ANOMIC PRESSURES

In the last three sections I have considered the pressures which employees can exert on an employer to coerce him into conforming with their pay norms. In this section I shall begin to explore the ways in which these normative pressures conflict with anomic pressures, being the various forces (described in sections 2 and 3 of chapter 1) which tend to cause employers *not* to conform with the pay norms of their employees. I shall also begin to consider the influence of anomic pressures on employees themselves.

I should perhaps explain why I use the term 'anomic', rather than 'economic', to describe these orthodox pressures. The reason is simply that virtually all the normative pressures discussed in the previous three sections are also economic. (It would be strange, for example, to characterise striking as a non-economic activity.) The crucial distinction, it seems to me, lies not between economic and non-economic pressures, but between those pressures which arise from desires to enforce fair pay and those which do not.

Some anomic pressures on pay relativities, incidentally, are wholly or partly caused by the existence of norms of a different kind, namely *employment* norms. The freedom of action of employers and employees, that is, is commonly constrained by conventions – enforced by the same sorts of pressures as pay norms – about how certain sorts of work should be done, and by whom (see, for example, Doeringer, 1971). In some cases these employment norms reinforce pay norms; but in others they may directly or indirectly cause employers or employees to wish to deviate from pay norms.

(i) *External anomic pressures*

By *external* anomic pressures (on an employer) I mean those which bear on the relationship between the wages which he pays and the wages paid by other employers.

Not all jobs, of course, are filled by recruitment from the external labour market. Some, for reasons of efficiency or convention, are usually filled from among an employer's existing employees. But it would be wrong to suppose, as is sometimes suggested, that external anomic pressures can affect pay only in jobs which are filled by external recruitment. For what is crucial as regards these pressures is the expected present value of the total earnings of an employee during his period of service with an employer, which depends not only on the level of pay in the 'port of entry' but also on the structure of internal pay relativities (as well as on the pattern of internal mobility and the expected length of the period of service). What is true, however, is that a given level of 'career earnings' may be consistent with more than one pattern of internal relativities. Thus where there are comparatively few ports of entry into an organisation, external anomic pressures need not exert a very precise influence on its internal pay structure (Doeringer, 1971; Mackay, 1971).

There are two, very familiar, sorts of external anomic pressure – surplus and shortage.

(1) *Surplus*. If an employer were to set pay in accordance with the norms of his employees, he might be paying more than was necessary to secure the amount of labour he required. Even taking a long view, that is, he might at a lower wage (or set of wages) obtain a sufficient supply of labour of adequate quality, without an excessively high rate of turnover. In such a situation of excess supply, it is clear that the employer could gain if he were able to pay a lower wage. This is so regardless of the nature of the employer – a government department, just as a private firm, would benefit from this sort of reduction of its costs.

If, however, the employer is for one reason or another obliged to pay the normatively prescribed wage, he will pursue an optimal course of action subject to this addition to the large set of constraints under which he already operates. In view of the excess supply of labour, he will spend very little on advertising for employees, or on improving working conditions. From among the queue of applicants, he will hire the best qualified, rejecting the less suitable (even though, were he free to choose, he might prefer to hire some of the less well qualified applicants at a lower wage). Given the level of the wage, he will adopt more mechanised techniques than he would otherwise have done, and, if the excess supply is confined to specific jobs, he will keep the numbers of employees in those jobs to a minimum by replacing their services where it is economical to do so with the services of extra employees in less well paid jobs.

In some circumstances, the difference between a second best solution along these lines and the employer's preferred solution with a lower wage will be small – adherence to the pay norm causing only slightly reduced sales or profits, or (in the case of a government department) only slightly higher taxes or poorer service. But in other circumstances the difference will be large – for example, the second best solution might lead to the complete extinction of a firm operating in a highly price-competitive product market, especially if its competitors were not constrained to pay the normatively prescribed wage.

Another sort of surplus, which does not involve excess supply in the usual sense, would arise where adherence to a pay norm was inconsistent with taking full advantage of a monopsonistic position. Even, that is, if an employer were not paying more than the minimum wage necessary to secure a particular supply of labour, he might prefer, if he were free to do so, to pay a lower wage and employ the resulting smaller supply of labour. Similarly, adherence to the normative principle of a common rate for the job might prevent an employer acting as a discriminating monopsonist, keeping his wage bill down by paying the employees in any given job different amounts, according to the quality of their alternative employment prospects.

(2) *Shortage*. On the other hand, conformity with a particular pay norm might cause an employer to experience a scarcity of labour. This need not take the form of a simple deficiency of numbers. There might instead be an adequate (and quite possibly an excessive) number of applicants for jobs, but of poor quality; or a sufficient number of good recruits, but an undesirably rapid rate of turnover. The employer might thereby be prevented from producing a sufficient quantity of output; or the quality of his output might deteriorate, for example through lack of ability or experience on the part of his employees; or his costs might rise, for example because low quality labour was inefficient or because a high rate of labour turnover increased his expenditure on training. Thus he would prefer to set pay in excess of the norm in order to attract a larger, better, and less transitory supply of labour. He might wish to increase the pay of all the employees in particular jobs, or he might wish to breach the rate for the job principle by offering higher pay only to employees of superior calibre.

If, though, the employer is not free to deviate from the pay norm, he will, as in the case of a surplus of labour, take steps to minimise the adverse effects of having to conform with it (Doeringer, 1971, pp. 94–5). To begin with, there are various means by which he may be able to increase his labour supply without raising the wage: he can spend more on advertising and recruitment (including more careful screening to reduce the risk of rejecting suitable applicants); he can improve working conditions and in other ways increase the attractiveness of the job concerned (though I am regarding fringe benefits as an integral part of pay); and, if the problem is a shortage of qualified labour, he can start or expand his own training scheme. Even if he cannot sufficiently increase his labour supply in this fashion, there are a number of ways in which he may be able to circumvent or reduce the need for the labour in question. These include increasing the amount of overtime worked by his existing employees, and employing sub-contractors. It may be possible to mechanise or reorganise the work so that it can be done by a smaller number of workers, or by workers with less ability and experience, or by other categories of employees which are not in short supply. This may be a matter of using known (but more expensive) techniques, or it may involve the development of new techniques specifically to cope with the scarcity of labour.

How disadvantageous it would be for an employer in a situation of labour shortage to adopt this sort of second best strategy, rather than straightforwardly to pay a higher wage, will vary widely from case to case. In some circumstances there will not be a great deal in it – the shortage may simply tip the balance in favour of a more automated technique, or cause a marginal deterioration in the quality of a service (such as a rise in class size in a school). Indeed it is perfectly possible that not being able to raise the wage may force the employer to invent new techniques of production that actually make him better off than he would otherwise have been. But there are also circumstances in which there is no alternative way of increasing the labour supply and in which the costs of having to do without the labour concerned would be very large, involving perhaps the loss of crucial orders, or even the complete stoppage of production.

(ii) *Internal anomic pressures*

There are also certain pressures on employers to deviate from pay norms which do not arise in the external labour market. They are relevant mainly to the structure of internal pay relativities.

(1) *Mobility*. It may be in an employer's interest, for anomic reasons, to pay job A more than job B in order to facilitate the transfer of employees from one to the other. Such transfers might be desirable because experience in B was an essential prerequisite of good performance in A (which might perhaps be a supervisory role), or because a period of service in B was the best way of evaluating

potential recruits for A; and it would be necessary, in order to accomplish the desired transfers, to pay A more if it were less attractive in non-pecuniary terms than B and if internal mobility were effectively a voluntary matter.

To pay A more than B, however, might conflict with pay norms. In such a case the employer, if he were to conform with these norms, would have to suffer the cost in terms of employee morale of forcing workers to switch jobs against their will, or the disadvantages of direct external recruitment into job A, or the expense of reorganising production so as to reduce the need for this particular pattern of internal mobility.

(2) *Incentives.* Internal anomic pressures may arise also from an employer's desire to provide financial incentives for his employees to work harder or more conscientiously.

For example, even if, at the normatively prescribed rates of pay, there were no reluctance to move from job B to job A, the employer might wish to increase the relative pay of A in order to intensify competition for promotion among the employees in job B – the competition taking the form of showing who can do the best work. This sort of conflict between pay norms and anomic pressures would not arise, of course, if employment norms dictated that promotion should be based on seniority rather than merit. It might also be avoided or lessened (as might conflicts concerning internal mobility) by increasing the attractiveness of job A in terms of non-pecuniary privileges.

Payment by results is another sort of incentive scheme which is liable, in ways to be discussed in the following chapter, to conflict with pay norms; ordinary piecework, for example, since it involves higher pay for more industrious and efficient individuals, is inconsistent with the rate for the job principle. The strength of the employer's desire to pay by results, regardless of conflict with pay norms, varies from job to job. In some, payment by results has a very beneficial effect on productivity – especially where the contribution of individual workers or groups is easily assessed, and where the work itself is distasteful or boring. But most payment by results systems have certain incidental disadvantages (for instance, they tend to be abused by workers seeking to stabilise their earnings over time), and in many jobs the potential benefits to the employer of payment by results are small or non-existent.

(iii) *Anomic pressures on employees*

Thus far in this section I have considered the pressures on employers to disregard the pay norms of their employees. But the discussion in the first section of this chapter of the motives of employees suggests that there are two sorts of reasons why, in certain circumstances, an employee might not *want* pay relativities to conform with his (or anyone else's) norms.

(1) *Money.* Other things being equal, an employee would always be better off with higher pay. Thus, for example, a worker in a category of labour of which there was a shortage would benefit from a rise in pay, even if the pay of the job concerned were already at a level he considered fair. Similarly, the harder-working and more productive individuals in a particular job would usually gain from the abandonment of the rate for the job principle (by which they in effect subsidise their less efficient colleagues) and the introduction of some form of payment by results.

(2) *Jobs.* The other potential source of anomic pressure on employees is their desire to occupy the best possible job. Specifically, in situations in which adherence to a pay norm results in an excess supply of labour, there will be a pool of employees who would like to be, but are not, taken on, some of whom might have been offered (and would have been happy to accept) employment had the level of pay been below the norm. For lower pay might on the one hand have increased the number that employers wished to hire and on the other hand have decreased the number of applicants for employment. Thus some employees might be better off if the common rate of pay in a job were below what they considered a fair level. Others, especially those of inferior quality, might benefit if the rate for the job principle were abandoned, so that they could compete with better quality applicants by offering their services for a lower wage.

In this connection it is worth distinguishing between two different sorts of excess supply. One is that in which the employees who are surplus to requirements have never worked in the job concerned. The other is that in which existing occupants of the job are threatened with redundancy. The distinction is relevant for two reasons. First, existing employees are commonly better placed than potential employees actually to cause a reduction in pay below the norm. Second, they are usually in a better position to try artificially to increase the demand for labour, for example by blocking technical innovations, thus diminishing or eliminating the excess supply without a reduction of pay (although even existing employees are likely to fail in this regard if the cause of the redundancies is, or if the blocking of innovations would lead to, a decline in external demand for the employer's product).

If, for whatever reason, pay is not reduced below the norm, and insofar as direct action on the demand for labour is not possible, those who fail to get employment in the job concerned will (like an employer forced to conform with a pay norm) choose a second best solution. Specifically, they will take work in the most attractive of the jobs in which they can actually obtain employment, which in some cases will be with the same employer – perhaps on a lower rung of the same promotion ladder.* If no such job exists, or if none is sufficiently appealing, they will be unemployed. The second best situation (be it another job or unemployment) may be only marginally less attractive than the preferred job, or it may be a great deal less attractive. In general, the greater the gap in attractiveness between the preferred job and the second best situation, the more willing will an employee be for pay in his preferred job to fall below the level he considers fair.

It remains to consider what, in such a situation of excess supply, determines which employees are hired and which are rejected (since this also may affect the strength of the pressure for pay to fall below the norm). In a world without employment norms, selection would be on the basis of quality. The applicants for a job could be regarded as a queue arranged in order of suitability (including, as Thurow, 1976, has stressed, trainability) for the work in question, of whom, given the normatively prescribed rate of pay, the employer would hire the first so many, turning away the rest. The threshold level of qualifications necessary to obtain employment would depend on the size and quality of the supply of applicants and on the level of demand, both of which would be affected by the normatively prescribed rate of pay.† Moreoever, although it would obviously not be possible for employees

---

* Those who find alternative jobs may be termed 'subemployed' – employed, but not in the jobs which, at prevailing rates of pay, they would prefer to occupy.

† In particular, other things being equal, a higher pay norm would cause a higher threshold quality level.

to compete for jobs in the orthodox manner by bidding down pay, they could and would compete in terms of quality, striving to acquire or display characteristics which put them nearer to the front of the queue (this being what Thurow calls 'job competition').

In practice, of course, the process of selection would be complicated by the employer's ignorance and uncertainty about the true capacities of the various individuals in the queue (see Thurow, ch. 7, and Blaug, 1976, pp. 845–50). It would be affected also by various sorts of employment norms. For example, the prejudices of employers or employees against women or racial minorities might push members of these groups further back in the queue than their abilities would warrant. Similarly, because workers regard their jobs as a form of property, it is often impossible for an existing employee to be displaced by an outside applicant of higher quality. And selection among existing employees in situations of excess supply is frequently influenced by considerations of seniority: for instance, 'custom and practice' may require that any vacancy in job A be automatically filled by promotion of the most senior employee in job B; convention may likewise dictate that when there is a contraction of demand, the most recent recruits must be laid off, regardless of their ability.

4

DIRECTLY DETERMINED RELATIVITIES

In this and the following chapter I shall look more closely at the effects of the various pressures on pay discussed in the previous chapter. In doing this, I shall make a fundamental distinction between *directly determined* and *indirectly determined* pay relativities.*

The essential feature of directly determined relativities is that they are the subject of a single decision. To put it another way, they are relativities within *pay groups*, a pay group being defined as a group of employees whose pay is settled jointly. Indirectly determined relativities, by contrast, are those between pay groups. Their essential characteristic is that they are the result of many separate (though interdependent) decisions. The decision makers in a single pay group, by altering the absolute money level of its pay, can exert a partial influence on the relativities between it and other groups; but they cannot completely control these external relativities, since they cannot control the absolute money pay of other groups.

A modern capitalist economy is made up of a very large number of pay groups of various shapes and sizes. Some of them contain tens, even hundreds, of thousands of employees; the pay of all teachers in England and Wales, for example, is the subject of a single decision. At the other end of the scale, there are pay groups which contain only one employee; where, for example, a single domestic servant is hired, or where the fee of a film star is fixed on an individual basis. In between lies a continuum of different sized pay groups: the small firm in which everybody's pay is decided unilaterally by the employer; the managerial employees of a large company who are paid on a standard scale established by job evaluation; the skilled manual workers in a particular plant who collectively negotiate a separate pay settlement; and so on.

As these examples imply, there is not a one-to-one relationship between pay groups and employers: in many instances, the employees

* This is similar to the distinction made in Pay Board (1974) between 'differentials' and 'relativities'.

of a single employer are split into several pay groups, with the pay of (say) manual, clerical and managerial employees being separately determined, perhaps with further divisions between different establishments; and in some instances, a single pay group spans many employers, as in the case of the teachers (whose employers are the various local education authorities). Neither is there a one-to-one correspondence between pay groups and alliances of the sort discussed in the preceding chapter: the members of an alliance, whether or not they all have the same employer, may give each other a great deal of support without their pay being jointly determined; and joint negotiations may cover categories of employees between whom there is considerable antagonism. Nor are pay groups the same thing as negotiating groups: representatives of several different negotiating groups (several unions, say) may jointly bargain over the pay of their various members; and a single negotiating group may make a number of genuinely separate pay deals with different employers.

In most circumstances, the boundaries between pay groups, and thus the distinctions between directly and indirectly determined relativities, are pretty obvious. But institutional arrangements are not always a good guide. For example, an employer may make nominally separate pay deals with different categories of employees, but virtually dictate the outcome in each instance. In which case, unless the employer in making each pay deal gives no thought to its implications for his other pay deals, his employees constitute one pay group, not several, since the relativities between the various categories of employee are effectively the subject of a single decision. Likewise, where the employees of different employers have a tight alliance, and are powerful enough to have a large influence on pay, the relativities between those employers may in effect be directly determined, even in the absence of overt joint negotiations.

There are also, as these examples may suggest, some ambiguous cases. How much collusion over pay negotiations must there be within an alliance of employees before the alliance is regarded as a single pay group? And how much of a common influence must an employer have on the pay of his various categories of employee, and how sensitive must he be to the linkages and repercussions between their various pay settlements, before the pay relativities between them are to be regarded as directly determined? Inevitably, the dividing line must to some extent be arbitrary, and to this extent the boundaries between pay groups are blurred and the distinction between directly and indirectly determined relativities is less sharp in reality than (for purposes of exposition) I shall make it seem.

It is important to ask what determines the shape of the pattern of pay groups within an economy, since this affects both the structure of pay relativities and the pace of wage inflation. Several different influences are at work. Clearly, the boundaries between pay groups are to a considerable extent governed by boundaries between employers. To some extent they are governed also by other conventional economic demarcation lines, as for example where the employees of firms which are product market competitors form an alliance to pursue a common wage policy, or where employers who are labour market competitors collude to gain a monopsonistic advantage, or where employees who do roughly the same sort of work, whether for one or for many employers, band together to negotiate collectively. But the distribution of power (and thus the factors which influence the distribution of power) is also extremely important, for example in determining whether or not an alliance between the employees of different employers can enforce a single pay strategy, or whether or not a single employer can impose a common pay policy on all his employees.

The form of pay groups is sometimes also affected by the nature of, and the pattern of adherence to, pay norms: some pay groups are based on alliances between employees which in turn are wholly or partly the product of normative consensus; rather differently, a strong desire to make certain relativities conform with specific norms may lead one set of employees to insist on the enlargement of their pay group to include some other set of employees, with or without the consent of the latter; similarly, the existence of conflicting norms among his employees may induce an employer to introduce company-wide wage negotiations to eliminate internal leap-frogging. In addition, the shape of pay groups, both in the public and in the private sector, is often influenced by considerations of administrative convenience and economy.

Over time, the pattern of pay groups in an economy alters in response to changes in these various influences, although there is a good deal of inertia, which means that the pattern at any moment of time is to some degree arbitrary. In the long term, the trend in most capitalist economies has been towards fewer, bigger pay groups, partly because of an increase in the concentration of employment in large firms and public organisations, and partly because of the spread of collective bargaining. But there are occasionally movements in the opposite direction, as where a pay group splits up because of the breakdown of an alliance, or where a particular government increases the freedom of different agencies in the public sector to pursue separate pay policies. And of course the picture is perpetually being altered by the birth of new firms, industries, and public organisations, and by the decay and death of old ones.

In what follows, though, I shall for convenience take the pattern of pay groups as given, in two senses. First, I shall assume that it does not change. Second, I shall assume that it is exogenously determined, even though the forces which govern the boundaries between pay groups are to some extent the same as those which govern the pay relativities within and between these groups. To relax these two assumptions would complicate the argument, but would not affect its substance.

4.2 A BASIC MODEL

For the remainder of this chapter I shall focus on the determination of pay in a single isolated pay group, assuming pay (and other relevant variables) in all other pay groups to be arbitrarily given. In the following chapter I shall abandon this partial equilibrium approach and investigate the consequences of interdependence between pay decisions in different pay groups.

In later sections of the present chapter I shall consider directly determined relativities – those which are internal to particular pay groups. But it is convenient to begin by assuming such internal differentials away and analysing the case in which all the employees in the pay group with which we are concerned happen to be paid at a single rate, which I shall label w.

The level of this wage rate is proximately determined by the employer, whose pay decision I shall regard as the solution of a constrained optimisation problem. One basic ingredient of the decision must therefore be a utility function which specifies the employer's objectives. These may be complex, and will vary according to the nature of the employer. But the fundamental principles of the pay decision can be captured, and exposition kept to a minimum, by assuming that the employer runs a private firm and wishes simply to make (the present discounted value of) his profits as large as possible. The essence of the argument below, it should be reiterated, does not depend on the assumption that the employer is a private firm, let alone a profit-maximiser; the term 'profit' is simply a convenient proxy for *all* types of non-normative objectives.

Given his goals, the employer's pay decision will depend on the character of the opportunities or constraints with which he is confronted, which I shall divide into two sets, anomic and normative.

(i) *Anomic constraints*

In choosing a wage rate, the employer will be influenced by various familiar factors which have nothing to do with pay norms, including the preferences of his customers or clients, the behaviour of his competitors in the product market, the technology of production (as modified by employment norms), and the availability of labour – which depends on the behaviour of his competitors in the labour market and on the preferences of employees. These constraints, in conjunction with the employer's desire to increase his profits, generate the anomic pressures on him discussed in the last section of the previous chapter.

There are, it may be recalled, several different sorts of anomic pressure. The most important in the context of the present argument are those which I called surplus and shortage. In other words, given that the employer is constrained by assumption to choose a single wage rate, his principal objective (normative considerations aside) will be to set it at that specific level at which he is paying the minimum amount necessary to secure a sufficient supply of labour of adequate quality. I shall call this specific level the *anomically optimal wage*, and I shall label it $\hat{w}$.

The anomic constraints mentioned not only determine the value of $\hat{w}$; they also determine the consequences of deviating from $\hat{w}$. These consequences are most conveniently summarised in the *anomic pressure function*, $A(w)$, which specifies what, in the absence of all normative pressures, the highest attainable level of the employer's profits would be at all possible values of the wage rate. Such a function is depicted in figure 4.1. Clearly, (the discounted sum of all future) profits, P, attains a maximum at $\hat{w}$; when the wage is above $\hat{w}$, the employer's profits are eroded by the fact that he is paying unnecessarily much for his labour; when the wage is below $\hat{w}$, the employer's profits are reduced because he is short of labour.

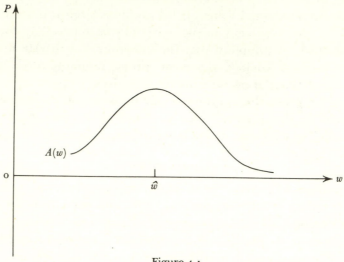

Figure 4.1

The shape of $A(w)$, and especially the steepness of its slopes above and below $\hat{w}$, reflect the details of the anomic constraints on the employer. For example, if profits drop off very sharply below $\hat{w}$, this may imply that the employer is in a very competitive labour market, in which he cannot pay less than the 'going wage' without losing a good deal of his labour force. Similarly, if profits fall very rapidly above $\hat{w}$, this may imply that the employer is in a very competitive product market, in which he cannot raise his prices to cover increased wage costs without losing a lot of sales. In addition, of course, one must not forget that the shape of $A(w)$ also depends on the levels of pay prevailing (or expected imminently to prevail) in other pay groups, which we are taking as given. Were these other wage rates different, so in general would be the form of $A(w)$ and the value of $\hat{w}$.

(ii) *Normative constraints*

Let us suppose provisionally that all the employees in the pay group in question share common pay norms and a common reference set. The level at which, on normative grounds, they will want the wage to be set will thus evidently depend on the rates of pay prevailing (or expected imminently to prevail) in those other pay groups with which they compare themselves, and on the normatively prescribed relativities between their own pay and the pay of these other groups.

66

In this connection, one must recognise that multiple comparisons will usually yield inconsistent results. More specifically, it is unlikely, where the reference set of a particular group of employees contains more than one other group, that normative comparisons with these various other groups will all imply the same desired rate of pay for the group in question. Suppose, to take the simplest example, that the employees in a particular group think that they ought to be paid the same as those in two other groups, but that these two other groups are in fact paid differently. At what level will the employees in the group concerned want their pay to be set? The answer, since people always tend to prefer more money to less, is that they will want their pay to match that of the higher-paid of the two other groups. More generally, given the relativities prescribed by the norms of a particular group between its own pay and the pay of the groups in its reference set, and given the pay of these other groups, which between them imply a number of possible desired rates of pay for the group concerned, the employees in the group concerned will prefer the highest of these possible desired rates. This I will call the *most favourable comparison* principle. Its importance will become apparent in the next chapter.

I shall call the rate of pay associated with the most favourable comparison the *normatively prescribed wage*, and I shall label it $\bar{w}$. (I shall also assume for the moment that there are no reasons why the employees in question might want to be paid less than this.) The impact of the normatively prescribed wage on the employer's pay decision will depend crucially on how much pressure the employees in the group concerned can exert on him.

The most important type of normative pressure is the threat to act in such a way as to deprive the employer of some or all of his profits.* There are many different ways – discussed in the previous chapter – in which employees may be able to reduce output or raise costs, in some cases temporarily (as with a strike), in others permanently (as where an innovation is blocked). Some of these measures can be implemented by individual action; others require more or less formal collective action. The total amount of pressure which can be exerted on the employer in these various ways depends on a range of considerations discussed in the previous chapter.

The influence of these pressures on the employer's pay decision can conveniently be expressed in the *normative pressure function*, $N(w)$,

* I shall for simplicity ignore the social sanctions discussed on pp. 39–40 above.

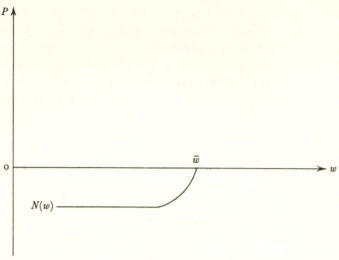

Figure 4.2

which specifies the amount of profits that the employer would lose as a result of normative action by his employees at each possible level at which he might set the wage. Such a function (which relates, of course, to the discounted sum of the various temporary and permanent costs of normative action) is drawn in figure 4.2. At wage rates below the normatively prescribed wage, $\bar{w}$, the employer would lose some profits through employee action, and thus the normative pressure function lies below the horizontal axis. It intercepts the horizontal axis at $\bar{w}$, and then disappears; this is because the loss of profits through employee action would be zero if the wage were at or above the normatively prescribed level (which reflects my earlier assumption that employees will not object to being paid more than a fair rate, but will not take action to force their wage above this rate).*

The shape of $N(w)$ in the range below $\bar{w}$ reflects three things. (1) The most important is the amount of damage which the employees could, if they chose, inflict on the employer; the greater this is, the further below the horizontal axis will the function lie. (2) Taking certain sorts of action would inflict costs also on the employees. The larger these costs, the smaller will be the likelihood of normative action, and thus the closer to the horizontal axis will the normative pressure function lie. (3) The militancy of the employees concerned – their

* One possible exception to this rule is that if the wage were initially above the fair level, the employees concerned might be prepared to fight any move to reduce it.

sensitivity to unfair relative pay – is also important. The greater their militancy, the readier will they be to incur the costs of normative action; thus the greater is the likelihood of such action, and the further below the horizontal axis will the normative pressure function lie. One important determinant of the degree of militancy of a given group is what has recently happened (or is expected to happen) to the purchasing power of its wages. Another is the degree of unfairness (in relative terms) involved; employees may well wish , is suggested by the particular way in which figure 4.2 is drawn) to limit their response to small deviations of pay below the normatively prescribed level, reserving their maximum possible response for large deviations.

(iii) *Outcomes*

An employer's pay decision is always governed by the relative strengths of a number of conflicting pressures, some anomic, others normative. Given the various constraints pushing him in one direction and another, he will choose the line of least resistance – the pay strategy which promises the greatest (though not necessarily a great) degree of success in achieving his goals.

More precisely, given the anomic and normative constraints on him (of whose nature, I shall provisionally suppose, he is accurately informed), the employer will under the present assumptions choose that wage rate which maximises his profits. His profits at any particular wage rate are by definition equal to the sum of the anomic pressure function, which specifies what profits would be in the absence of all normative pressures, and the normative pressure function, which specifies the reduction of profits caused by normative pressure. In formal terms, that is,

$$P(w) \equiv A(w) + N(w),$$

and the employer accordingly selects that value of w which maximises $A(w) + N(w)$.* This is illustrated in figure 4.3: the $A(w)$ and $N(w)$ functions are drawn in much the same way as in the two previous diagrams; their sum is depicted by the heavy line labelled $A(w) + N(w)$; the employer chooses the wage at which this heavy line reaches its highest point.

Depending on the exact character and strength of the anomic and

* The form of $N(w)$, incidentally, is unlikely to be strictly independent of the form of $A(w)$, but this does not affect the essentials of the argument.

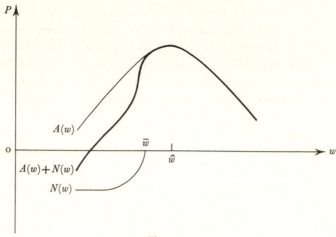

Figure 4.3

normative pressures on the employer, which are reflected in the shapes of $A(w)$ and $N(w)$, there are four different possible types of outcome.

(1) The employer may wish for anomic reasons to pay more than his employees desire on normative grounds, the most likely reason being that at the normatively prescribed wage he would suffer from a shortage of labour. His employees, not objecting to being paid more than a fair wage, will passively go along with his wishes, and thus the outcome will be governed solely by anomic forces. This is the situation in figure 4.3; clearly, the employer will set the wage at the anomically optimal level, $\hat{w}$, and $N(w)$, whose value is zero over the relevant range, will have no influence on his decision.

(2) Another type of case in which the outcome is strictly anomic is that in which the employees would like the employer to set the wage above the anomically optimal level, but are not powerful enough to force him to do so. Such a case is depicted in figure 4.4; evidently, even with the full force of employee sanctions deployed against him, it is more profitable for the employer to set the wage at $\hat{w}$ than at any wage above $\hat{w}$.

(3) A third type of outcome is that in which the wage rate is completely determined by normative pressures. In this sort of case, the employer is forced to conform strictly with his employees' norm, even though on anomic grounds alone he would have preferred to pay less. An outcome of this kind is shown in figure 4.5; although the anomic incentives for the employer to set the wage at $\hat{w}$ are substantial,

70

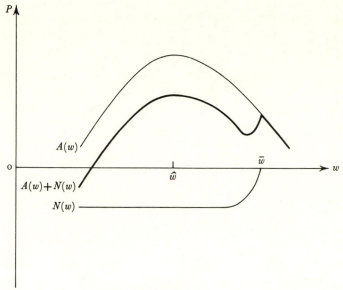

Figure 4.4

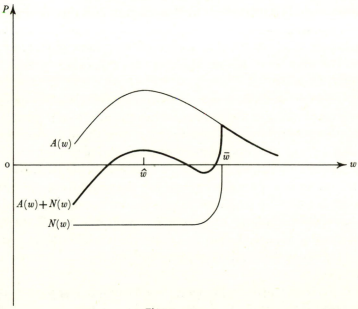

Figure 4.5

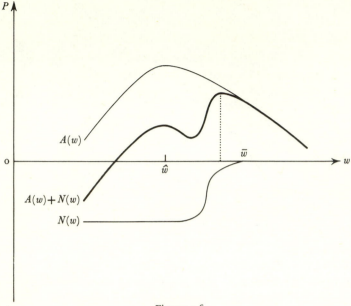

Figure 4.6

they are swamped by the cost of the reaction that this would provoke from employees, as indeed is the case at every value of w below the normatively prescribed wage, $\bar{w}$. Thus it is in the employer's interest to set the wage at $\bar{w}$, despite the fact that this causes him to have a surplus of labour.

(4) In the three types of outcome so far considered, the wage chosen by the employer has always been either the anomically optimal rate, $\hat{w}$, or the normatively prescribed rate, $\bar{w}$. But there is also a range of possible hybrid (or compromise) outcomes. These occur where the wage desired by employees exceeds that which the employer would prefer on anomic grounds, and where the employees are powerful enough to force the employer to pay more than his preferred wage, but not powerful enough to make him comply strictly with their norm. Such a case is depicted in figure 4.6; precisely where the chosen wage lies in the range between $\hat{w}$ and $\bar{w}$ depends on the exact shapes of $A(w)$ and $N(w)$.

It is perhaps worth emphasising the asymmetry apparent in these four cases: if the normatively prescribed wage happens to be greater than the anomically optimal wage, the outcome may be $\bar{w}$ or $\hat{w}$ or anywhere in between, depending on the relative strength of normative and anomic pressures; but if the normatively prescribed wage is less than the anomically optimal wage, then $\hat{w}$ always prevails. It is also worth noting a fifth, rather different, type of outcome, namely that in which, as the result of an artificial restriction of the labour supply, the anomically optimal wage is equal to the normatively prescribed wage. In this sort of case the normatively prescribed wage prevails without any direct normative presssure being exerted on the employer.

4.3 COMPLICATIONS

I shall now consider the consequences of relaxing some of the simplifying assumptions made in setting up the basic model of the employer's pay decision.

(i) *Misperceptions and errors*

It is probably reasonable to assume that the employer has a fairly accurate picture of the anomic constraints to which he is subject. It may be, though, that he will not accurately perceive the form of the normative pressure function, at any rate to begin with. He will probably be well aware of the extent of the costs which he could suffer through employee action, and indeed of the costs which such action would inflict on his employees. But he may misjudge the militancy of his employees. This will affect, among other things, the chances of normative action being not merely threatened but actually taken. For example, if the employer underestimates militancy, he may precipitate a strike which, had he been better informed, he could (and would) have avoided by a prior change in his wage offer. By the same token, of course, employees, through not accurately perceiving the form of the *anomic* pressure function, may take actions which are unnecessary or which unexpectedly fail.

These sorts of information or communication failures are quite common, especially since concealing one's true position is often a good bargaining strategy. And it is possible (in cases where the normatively prescribed wage exceeds the anomically optimal wage) for them to affect the level of the wage chosen by the employer. For instance, an employer who overestimates employee militancy may concede an unnecessarily high wage, and never be aware of the fact. Likewise, employees who overestimate their employer's incentive to resist may fail to press for a wage increase that they could in fact have secured.

But employers and employees are fully aware of these particular dangers. Thus unless large irreversible costs are involved, an employer will tend to err on the side of underestimating militancy. Similarly, employees will deliberately tend to err on the side of underestimating the employer's incentive to resist. Both sorts of underestimate tend to provoke the kind of confrontation which causes the estimates to be revised in the direction of greater accuracy. As a result, information and communication failures of this general type do not usually have a large effect on the wage ultimately chosen by the employer. What they mainly affect instead is the cost, in terms of time and conflict, of arriving at the final outcome.

(ii) *Anomic pressure from employees*

In the previous section it was taken for granted that the employees in the pay group with which we are concerned will always want the wage to be set at (or above) the normatively prescribed level, $\bar{w}$. But when $\bar{w}$ exceeds the anomically optimal wage, $\hat{w}$, there would in general be an excess supply of labour if the wage were set in accordance with the norm.* The potential employees of whom this surplus is composed may prefer to work in another job or be unemployed rather than work in the job concerned for less than the norm. But where their attachment to the norm is weak or their second best option is relatively unattractive, they will want pay to be set below the norm, and thus their interests will be in direct conflict with the interests of those actually employed in the job in question.

On the whole, though, potential employees are less well placed than actual employees to influence the employer's pay decision. For although they may be very numerous, they are usually dispersed among other jobs or unemployed. This deprives them of many sources of direct leverage on the employer in question, and makes it very difficult for them to act collectively. It also means that they have no social ties with those actually employed in the job concerned, who will therefore almost certainly be unwilling to accept a reduction in pay in order to increase the level of employment.

Thus whereas the actual employees in a job are commonly in a position to impose a variety of sanctions on their employer to coerce him into conformity with their norm, potential employees can usually

---

* The exception being cases in which (a) the employer is a monopsonist and (b) $\bar{w}$ is less than or equal to the 'perfectly competitive' wage.

do no more than offer on an individual basis to work for a wage below the norm – an influence on pay which is simply one of the ingredients of the anomic pressure function. As we have already seen, this will be sufficient to cause the wage to be set below the norm if the employer's gains from abandoning the norm would be large, or if his actual employees are weak. But in other circumstances such attempts by potential employees to undercut the norm will fail.

In some cases, however, the set of people who could obtain work only if pay were below the norm will include some (or all) of those currently employed in the job concerned. One such case is that in which the surplus of labour is associated with a contraction of demand faster than the rate of natural wastage. Redundancies among existing employees (and possibly the total collapse of the firm) might be caused also by the enforcement of a norm for the first time, pay having previously been below the norm. In this sort of situation, even if they have the power to force the employer to conform with the norm, the employees in the pay group concerned may prefer to allow their pay to be below the norm in order to keep up the level of employment. Even those whose jobs are not threatened may be willing to sacrifice some pay in order to safeguard some at least of the jobs of their friends and colleagues. This is especially likely if a large number of jobs are at risk or if alternative jobs are so scarce that most of those who would be made redundant would become unemployed.

This possibility is easily incorporated into the formal framework outlined above. It would affect the shape of the normative pressure function, causing it to hit the horizontal axis at a wage below the normatively prescribed level, $\bar{w}$ – though not necessarily so low as the anomically optimal wage, $\hat{w}$, nor necessarily so low as to prevent *all* redundancies. The wage chosen by the employer would then, as before, lie at the level preferred by the employees, or at the anomically optimal level, or somewhere between the two, depending on the relative strength of normative and anomic pressures.

(iii) *Multiple norms*

Let us now drop the assumption that all the employees in the pay group concerned share the same norm (retaining, however, the assumption that they are all paid at a single rate). Different employees may have different reference sets, not least because of differences of view about

75

the proper scope of comparisons, and they may have different norms concerning particular pay relativities. For both sorts of reason, there may be a considerable spread of opinion among the employees in a given pay group about the level at which the wage, on normative grounds, ought to be set, although there will also be pockets of agreement, especially among those who are in close social contact with one another.

In so far as his employees negotiate collectively with him, the full extent of the disagreement among them is unlikely to impinge directly on the employer's pay decision, since, for reasons explained earlier, they will tend to form coalitions based on compromise objectives. In some cases, indeed, and especially if the raison d'être of the pay group is an alliance between employees, the employer may have to reckon with only one employee norm, the battle between different norms having been fought out behind the scenes. But it is quite possible for there to be two or more different coalitions of employees within a single pay group, as well as individuals whose norms are such that they cannot bring themselves to join any coalition. And of course there are pay groups in which there is no collective bargaining at all.

When there is more than one *bargaining unit* on the employee side in a single pay group, one must conceive of there being as many normative pressure functions (let us label them $N_1(w)$, $N_2(w)$, etc.) as there are bargaining units, each of which specifies both the normatively prescribed wage of the unit concerned and the loss of profits that it could impose on the employer. These various functions are unlikely to be independent of one another, because the amount of damage that a bargaining unit could inflict on the employer is often dependent on the actions of other units. Moreover, some bargaining units will be more powerful than others (and those which are isolated individuals will often be unable to exert any normative pressure).

But all that is relevant from the employer's point of view is the *sum* of these various normative pressure functions, which we shall label $N(w)$, for it is this which specifies the total loss of profits that he would suffer through normative action by the various bargaining units at any given wage rate. This total loss, it should be noted, is unlikely to be equal to the loss that he would suffer through normative action at the same wage rate in the event of all the employees in the pay group uniting in pursuit of a compromise objective, since the power of a coalition is usually greater than the sum of the powers of its constituent elements.

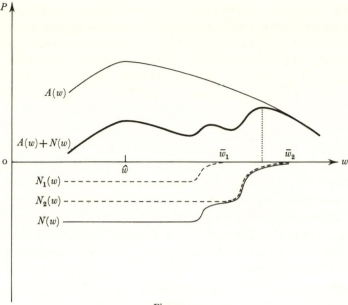

Figure 4.7

Once the $N(w)$ function is seen in this light, as being the sum of a number of separate normative pressure functions (which need not, incidentally, all be associated with different norms), no further modifications to the formal model are required; it remains the case that the employer will choose that value of w which maximises $A(w) + N(w)$. Figure 4.7 illustrates this; it depicts a situation in which there are two bargaining units, whose normatively prescribed wage rates are $\bar{w}_1$ and $\bar{w}_2$. The amount of pressure that each of these units individually will exert on the employer at various wage rates is reflected in the two dashed lines labelled $N_1(w)$ and $N_2(w)$. The sum of these two dashed lines, which reflects the total amount of pressure that these bargaining units will exert, is the continuous line labelled $N(w)$; it intercepts the horizontal axis at the higher of the two normatively prescribed wage rates. The employer then selects, as before, the wage rate at which the heavy line labelled $A(w) + N(w)$ attains its highest point.

When there is more than one employee norm, there exists the possibility of a type of outcome which we have not yet considered, namely one in which the wage chosen by the employer is a compromise between different employee norms. This may occur even if the norm of a single bargaining unit unambiguously prevails, since the bargaining unit may be a tactical alliance of people with differing norms.

77

But outcomes which represent a compromise between the norms of separate bargaining units can also occur, this being the sort of case shown in figure 4.7. One should add, though, that the more numerous are the different norms, the more divided (and hence the weaker) will the employees in the pay group be, and thus the smaller will be the likelihood of *any* of their norms affecting the outcome.

(iv) *Government intervention*

Much government intervention in the process of pay determination is of an indirect character – including aggregate demand management policy, and legislation affecting such things as closed shops, picketing, unfair dismissal, liability for breach of contract, compulsory arbitration, and the level and availability of unemployment benefits. But the government in one form or another may also intervene directly in the employer's pay decision. For example, the employer may be obliged by law not to pay less than some minimum wage, or to restrict the size of pay increases, or to conform with a rate of pay prescribed by some tribunal or review body. Orders of this kind, which may reflect the government's (or a tribunal's) pay norms, are usually backed up by penalties for non-compliance.

This sort of intervention can easily be incorporated into the formal model by means of a function, $G(w)$, which specifies both the particular level at (or above or below) which the government wants the wage to be set, and the expected size, at any given wage level, of the penalties for non-compliance, measured in profit-equivalent units. (To translate the penalties into these units one must know, among other things, the size of any fines involved, and whether or not they would be tax-deductible, as well as the probability of non-compliance being detected, and the employer's attitude towards risk.)

In the case of a minimum wage order, $G(w)$ looks something like $N(w)$ in figure 4.2: that is to say, it hits the horizontal axis at the minimum wage, and disappears above this wage, since there is no objection to the employer paying more than the minimum; at wage rates below the minimum, the function lies below the horizontal axis by an amount which reflects the size of the penalties for breach of minimum wage orders and the chances of a breach being discovered. A limit on the size of pay increases, by contrast, given the existing wage of the pay group concerned, is effectively a *maximum* wage order; in this case $G(w)$ runs along the horizontal axis (i.e. has a value of zero) until the maximum allowable wage is reached, whereafter it lies below the horizontal axis to an extent which measures the expected size of the penalties for exceeding the pay limit. In the case of an order to pay the wage prescribed by a tribunal, no more and no less, $G(w)$ hits the horizontal axis at the prescribed wage rate (since conformity with the order entails no penalties), but at wage levels above and below the prescribed rate the function lies below the horizontal axis by an amount which reflects the expected size of the penalties for disobeying the order.

But whatever the specific character of the government intervention, the general rule is that the employer chooses that wage rate which maximises $A(w) + N(w) + G(w)$. The impact of the government's orders on the chosen wage will therefore evidently depend not only on the exact nature of the orders and on the exact size of the penalties for non-compliance, but also on the amount of pressure on the employer from other quarters, anomic and normative, to disregard the government's orders.

Anomic pressures, for example, may lead the employer to pay more than the statutory minimum wage, which will therefore have no influence on the outcome. The same would be true if the chances of the employer being prosecuted for paying less than the minimum wage were small, relative to the amount by which this would enable him to increase his profits. Similarly, the employer may choose to exceed the limit for pay increases because the penalties for doing so are less damaging than the sanctions which his employees would impose on him if he were to abide by the limit and pay them less than their normatively prescribed wage.

On the other hand, there are instances in which a government order completely determines the pay decision, as where harsh penalties and strict policing cause an employer to comply with the statutory minimum wage, even though he would otherwise have paid substantially less. And there are also a variety of possible hybrid outcomes, in which anomic or normative pressures lead an employer to disobey a government order, but in which the fear of penalties causes him to limit his transgression and to choose a wage rate different from that which he would otherwise have preferred.

4.4 INTERNAL RELATIVITIES: GENERAL PRINCIPLES

In this and the next two sections I shall continue to analyse the determination of pay in a single pay group, assuming pay (and other relevant factors) in all other groups to be arbitrarily given. But I shall abandon the assumption that all the employees in the group with which we are concerned are paid at a single rate.

Where there are different jobs within a single pay group, or different categories or qualities of employee within a single job, the employer must choose not one wage rate, w, but a set or structure of wage rates, w^1, w^2, ..., w^k, one for each category or quality of employee in each job. This is not to say that the employer will necessarily decide to make all these distinct wage rates *unequal*; he may choose to pay two or more occupations, or several different qualities of labour, at the same rate. (And it should certainly not be supposed that a decision to make two or more distinct wage rates equal is any less interesting or significant than a decision to make them unequal.)

The set of wage rates, w^1, w^2, ..., w^k, may conveniently be written as a (k-component) vector, $\mathbf{w}$. This may in turn be regarded as consisting of a set, or vector, of ($k-1$) *internal* pay relativities, say

$$\frac{w^2}{w^1}, \frac{w^3}{w^1}, \ldots, \frac{w^k}{w^1},$$

plus one absolute rate of pay, say w^1, which, given the pay of other groups, governs the *external* pay relativities between this group and other groups. This decomposition of $\mathbf{w}$ is important, because we have defined the concept of a pay group in such a way that relativities within pay groups differ crucially from relativities between pay groups, the former being directly determined by a single decision, the latter being the product of many separate decisions.

(i) *The basic model*

Before entering into a discussion of those details of the employer's pay decision which are peculiar to pay groups within which there are several distinct wage rates, it is vital to emphasise that the general principles involved are identical to those set out in the two previous sections with regard to a single wage rate. The formal model is also exactly the same, save for the substitution of the vector $\mathbf{w}$ for the scalar

w in functions such as $A(w)$, as may be seen from the following outline.

In choosing a set of wage rates, the employer will be subject to certain anomic pressures. The most important of these will usually be surplus and shortage – the need, in order to increase profits, to attract appropriate amounts of labour of various different types into various different jobs, while not paying out more in wages than the minimum necessary to accomplish this. In addition, it may be in the employer's interest to promote certain patterns of internal mobility and to build various kinds of financial incentive into the wage structure. These considerations alone, given the state of affairs in other pay groups, would cause the employer to choose a particular vector of wage rates, $\hat{\mathbf{w}}$. The consequences of adopting any other strategy can be summarised in a function, $A(\mathbf{w})$, which specifies the best attainable level of profits, ignoring all normative considerations, at any given vector of wage rates.* The strength and character of the anomic pressures on the employer are reflected in the speed with which this function declines as $\mathbf{w}$ departs from the anomically optimal wage vector, $\hat{\mathbf{w}}$, by different amounts and in different directions.

The employer will also be subject to normative pressures from his employees. Specifically, he will face one or more employee bargaining units, each of which, given the rates of pay prevailing in other groups, will want him to adopt some particular normatively prescribed vector of wage rates, $\overline{\mathbf{w}}_i$. If he does not, the bargaining unit will impose sanctions on him, whose character can be expressed in a normative pressure function, $N_i(\mathbf{w})$, which specifies the loss of profits that the employer would suffer as a result of normative action by the ith bargaining unit at any given vector of wage rates. Where there is more than one employee bargaining unit, the employer will be subject to an assortment of normative pressures, pushing him in various directions, whose combined impact can be summarised in a function, $N(\mathbf{w})$, which is the sum of all the $N_i(\mathbf{w})$ functions. It specifies the total loss of profits that the employer would suffer through normative action at any given configuration of wage rates.

Confronted with these anomic and normative constraints, the employer will, as before, take the line of least resistance, choosing that set of wage rates which offers the greatest prospective degree of success

---

* $A(\mathbf{w})$ is a scalar-valued function of a vector.

in achieving his objectives. In formal terms, the employer will select that $\mathbf{w}$ which maximises his profits, $A(\mathbf{w}) + N(\mathbf{w})$.

As was the case with the choice of a single wage rate, there are several possible types of outcome, depending on the particular nature and relative strengths of the various pressures on the employer. In some cases all employee bargaining units will be so weak that the employer will choose the anomically optimal outcome, $\hat{\mathbf{w}}$. In others, one specific bargaining unit will be powerful enough to force the employer to implement its particular normatively prescribed vector, regardless of all other considerations. And in others, the chosen outcome will represent a compromise, either between the anomically optimal outcome and the norms of some specific employee bargaining unit, or between the norms of two or more different bargaining units, or both.

Finally, one must not forget that if rates of pay in other pay groups were different, so in general would be the anomic and normative pressure functions, and thus the vector of wage rates chosen, in the particular pay group with which we are concerned.

(ii) *Government intervention*

As before, various types of direct intervention by the government in the employer's choice of a set of distinct wage rates can be accommodated in the model by means of a function, $G(\mathbf{w})$, which specifies, in profit-equivalent units, the expected size of the penalties, at any given vector of wage rates, for failing to comply with the government's directives. The argument of the preceding section thus requires extension in this regard only inasmuch as government intervention may affect a pay group's internal relativities.

The simplest instance of this is where a tribunal or review body lays down a particular structure of wage rates for different jobs in a pay group, or requires that all workers in a given job be paid the same, regardless, for example, of their quality, or of their sex or race. Internal relativities may also be affected when a limit on pay increases is imposed. This is especially likely if the limit applies only to certain categories of employee (for example, the higher paid), or if it bears unevenly on different categories of employee (for example, because it imposes an absolute rather than a proportional ceiling on pay increases). But it may also happen if the limit applies uniformly to all employees, since this may prevent a change in internal relativities which would otherwise have occurred. Similarly, the effect of a minimum wage order on internal relativities will depend on the exact nature of the order – how high the minimum is, whether it applies to all workers or only to categories such as full time males, and whether there is only one minimum or several different minima for different jobs.

As in the case of a single wage rate, the employer chooses $\mathbf{w}$ to maximise $A(\mathbf{w}) + N(\mathbf{w}) + G(\mathbf{w})$. Thus the impact, if any, of these various kinds of government directive on his decision concerning internal relativities will depend not only on the exact nature of the directive but also on the size of the penalties for non-compliance, in relation to the character and strength of other pressures, normative and anomic, on internal relativities. For instance, strong normative counter-pressure, by making it worth the employer's while to disobey, might nullify a government order to pay men and women the same. Likewise, an across the board minimum wage high enough and sufficiently strictly enforced to increase the pay of some of the workers in a group might, if normative or anomic pressures to preserve a particular structure of internal relativities were strong enough, simply cause an equal increase in the pay of all the workers in the group; if such pressures were weak, on the other hand, the effect of the minimum wage order might be to compress internal relativities.

(iii) Diagrammatic illustration

The use of diagrams to illustrate the present model of the determination of several wage rates in a single pay group is in general precluded by the impossibility of multi-dimensional draughtsmanship. But in the special case in which there are only two distinct wage rates within a pay group, one can (as for example on page 87) draw an appropriate type of diagram, namely a contour map. The axes of the diagram measure the two wage rates, w^1 and w^2. Any given point in the diagram is accordingly associated with a particular value of w^1 and a particular value of w^2. The slope of a ray from the origin through any point measures the value of the single internal relativity, w^1/w^2, at that point. The distance of the point from the origin reflects the state of external relativities; the greater the distance along any particular ray, the higher are both w^1 and w^2, and thus, given the pay of other groups, the better off is this group as a whole relative to other groups.

Profits or losses at any point must be thought of as distances above or below the surface of the page, their magnitude being indicated in the diagram by the number of the contour line on which the point lies. Thus if the surface of the page is regarded as sea level, the function $A(\mathbf{w})$, for example, is a mountain whose upper slopes are dry and whose summit is at $\hat{\mathbf{w}}$. The function $N(\mathbf{w})$, by contrast, is an underwater reef of complex form, which may in places just break the surface. The function $A(\mathbf{w}) + N(\mathbf{w})$ is a mountainous terrain, mostly below sea level, whose highest point (if one ignores the possibility of government intervention) corresponds with the particular pair of wage rates chosen by the employer.

The sort of diagram used earlier to illustrate the choice of a single wage rate, incidentally, may be thought of as a section or slice through the contour map diagram along a ray from the origin. For as one moves along such a ray, the internal relativity between the two wage rates does not change, and thus one can treat them as if they were a single wage rate.

4.5   INTERNAL RELATIVITIES: NORMATIVE PRESSURES

In the two remaining sections of this chapter I shall enlarge on the model outlined in the preceding section, looking in more detail at certain matters peculiar to pay groups within which there are several distinct wage rates. I shall start, in the present section, with a closer examination of normative pressures.

(i) *Agreement (1)*

Let us initially restrict our attention to one hypothetical employee bargaining unit, which I shall label X, all of whose members both share the same norms (and the same reference set) and are paid at one particular wage rate, say w^1.

The employees in this bargaining unit will want the employer to adopt some specific normatively prescribed vector of wage rates, $\overline{\mathbf{w}}_X$. To begin with, they will want internal relativities to be set precisely and directly in accordance with their norms concerning these relativities (regardless, it should be noted, of what wage rates are prevailing in other pay groups). They will also have a preference concerning external relativities which, given the pay of other groups, can be expressed as a preference concerning the absolute level of one (it does not matter which, given their preferred internal wage structure) of the wage rates in their pay group, which I shall for convenience take to be w^1. Their preference with regard to the level of w^1 is arrived at in much the same way as in a pay group containing only one wage rate; given the rates of pay prevailing in their reference set, and given their norms with respect to the relativities between w^1 and the wage rates in the reference set, there will usually (because of the problem of inconsistent comparisons) be several possible levels of w^1 which might be desired on normative grounds by the employees in bargaining unit X, of which, according to the most favourable comparison principle, they will prefer the highest.

Their attitude towards wage vectors which differ from $\bar{w}_X$ will depend on the exact nature of the difference. One possible type of difference would involve no deviation from their preferred internal wage structure, but a different level of w^1. The employees in bargaining unit X would not complain if w^1 were above their preferred level – if, that is, they were paid at more than a fair rate relative to other pay groups. But they would object, and would impose sanctions on the employer, if he were to set w^1 below their preferred level.

Another possible type of difference would involve no deviation from the preferred level of w^1, but a different set of internal relativities. Once again, the employees in the bargaining unit in question would not protest at being paid more than they considered a fair amount relative to other employees in the same pay group, but they would object, and would respond with sanctions, to being paid less. The degree of objection (and thus to some extent the level of sanctions) would depend both on the size and on the character of the deviations from their preferred internal wage structure. For example, they might feel more strongly about some internal relativities than about others; or they might attach more importance to the rank order of wage rates than to the exact size of differentials; or their objection to being paid unfairly relative to one category of employees within the pay group might be lessened if at the same time they were paid more than fairly relative to some other category.

In addition, there is a whole range of situations in which both internal and external relativities differ from those implied by $\bar{w}_X$. In

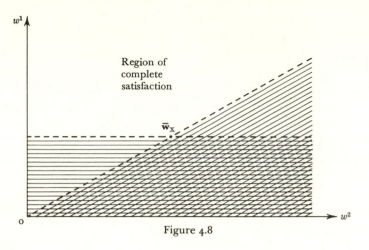

Figure 4.8

such cases, the same general principles apply – no objection to payment at more than a fair rate relative to any other given set of employees, but resistance to being paid less. However, the feelings of those in bargaining unit X about deviations from their preferred internal wage structure are unlikely to be independent of the state of external relativities (a higher level of w^1, say, compensating to some extent for an unfavourable change of internal relativities); and vice versa.

All of which may be illustrated in the case of a pay group containing only two wage rates by a diagram such as figure 4.9. Consider first, however, figure 4.8. The normatively prescribed wage vector of bargaining unit X is indicated by a point labelled $\overline{w}_X$. Any outcome which involves this unit being paid unfairly in external terms – relative, that is, to other pay groups – must lie in the shaded region below the horizontal line through $\overline{w}_X$ (which indicates the normatively prescribed level of w^1). Any outcome which involves this unit being paid unfairly in internal terms must lie in the shaded region below the ray from the origin through $\overline{w}_X$ (which indicates the normatively prescribed value of w^1/w^2). Outcomes in the cross-hatched region of the diagram are unfair in both external and internal terms; outcomes in the single-shaded regions are unfair either in external or in internal terms; while outcomes in the unshaded region (which I shall label the *region of complete satisfaction*) are fair or more than fair in both external and internal terms.

86

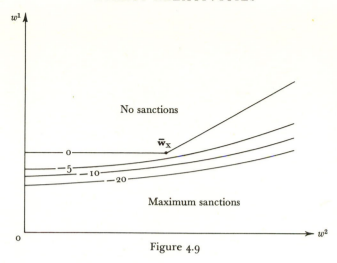

Figure 4.9

The loss of profits that bargaining unit X would inflict on the employer through normative action at any given wage vector – the form of its particular normative pressure function, $N_X(\mathbf{w})$ – is then shown in figure 4.9, a contour map. Evidently, no sanctions would be imposed in the region of complete satisfaction. The level of sanctions imposed in other regions (as measured by their effect on profits) is shown by the contour lines. These attain a minimum value (-20 in the diagram) associated with the maximum possible amount of damage that this bargaining unit could inflict on the employer. The position and shape of the contour lines reflect the strength of feeling of the employees in bargaining unit X about different amounts and different sorts of deviation from $\overline{\mathbf{w}}_X$.*

(ii) *Agreement (2)*

Let us now consider another hypothetical bargaining unit in the same pay group, Y, whose members happen to share the same norms and reference set as the employees in bargaining unit X, but (because they are in a different job, or are a different quality of labour in the same job) are paid at a different wage rate, w^2.

Clearly, the normatively prescribed wage vector of the employees in Y, $\overline{\mathbf{w}}_Y$, will be the same as that of the employees in X, $\overline{\mathbf{w}}_X$. However,

* Note that the slope of any given contour line cannot at any point be greater than or equal to the slope of a ray from the origin through that point (since this would imply indifference between points with the same internal relativities but different levels of w^1). Nor can it be less than or equal to zero (which would imply indifference between points with the same level of w^1 but different values of w^1/w^2).

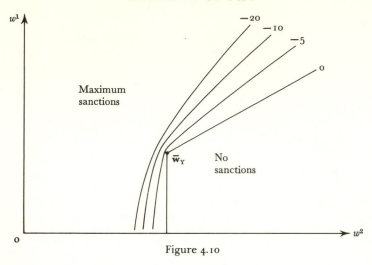

Figure 4.10

because they are paid at a different wage rate, the attitude of the employees in Y towards wage vectors which differ from $\overline{\mathbf{w}}_Y$ will not be the same as the attitude of the employees in X towards wage vectors which differ from $\overline{\mathbf{w}}_X$. For example, the employees in Y would not object if the internal relativity w^1/w^2 were below the normatively prescribed value (which would mean that they were being paid more than fairly in internal terms), and would impose sanctions on the employer if w^1/w^2 were above its normatively prescribed value; whereas the employees in X would react in exactly the opposite way. And as regards fairness in external terms, the employees in Y, unlike those in X, will be far more concerned about the level of w^2 than about the level of w^1.

Thus despite the fact that the employees in both bargaining units share the same norms and reference set, the forms of their normative pressure functions, $N_X(\mathbf{w})$ and $N_Y(\mathbf{w})$, are different. This is illustrated in the case of a pay group containing only two wage rates by figure 4.10, which depicts $N_Y(\mathbf{w})$ as a contour map. It has been drawn according to the same principles as the map of $N_X(\mathbf{w})$ in figure 4.9. Moreover, $\overline{\mathbf{w}}_Y$ is in the same place as was $\overline{\mathbf{w}}_X$. But the shapes of the two maps are quite different. In particular, in figure 4.10 the region in which no sanctions would be imposed lies in the lower right hand part of the diagram (where w^2 is relatively high), whereas in figure 4.9 the region of no sanctions lay in the upper left hand part of the diagram (where w^1 is relatively high).

88

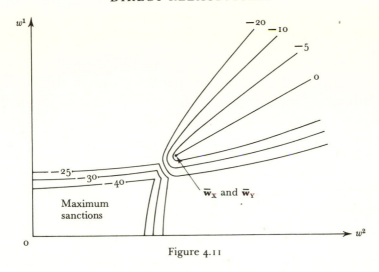

Figure 4.11

An employer confronted with bargaining units X and Y must reckon with the reactions of both of them. In choosing a wage vector, that is, he must concern himself not so much with the individual normative pressure functions, $N_X(\mathbf{w})$ and $N_Y(\mathbf{w})$, as with their sum. Figure 4.11, a contour map drawn by superimposing figure 4.10 on figure 4.9, illustrates this. Plainly, if the employer wishes to avoid sanctions from either bargaining unit, he must conform strictly with the shared norm concerning the internal relativity w^1/w^2 – in diagrammatic terms, he must choose an outcome on the ray from the origin through $\overline{\mathbf{w}}_X$; in addition, he must satisfy the aspirations of both bargaining units with regard to external relativities, which restricts him to that part of the ray (labelled with a zero in the diagram) which lies in the quadrant north-east of $\overline{\mathbf{w}}_X$.

There is evidently also a wide range of wage vectors which would completely satisfy one but not both bargaining units (and which would therefore provoke sanctions from only one of them); in the diagram, these outcomes lie in the quadrants north–east, north-west, and south-east of $\overline{\mathbf{w}}_X$. Finally, there is a range of wage vectors which would satisfy neither bargaining unit (and would thus provoke sanctions from both of them); in the diagram, these outcomes lie in the quadrant south-west of $\overline{\mathbf{w}}_X$, in which the pay of both bargaining units is unfair in external terms.

The interests of bargaining units X and Y are clearly not identical. Nonetheless, the mutual advantages of forming a coalition, in conjunction with the fact of sharing the same norms, might be sufficient to cause them to merge together into a single bargaining unit. Were they to do this, the form of their joint normative pressure function would be similar to the sum of their individual normative pressure functions, in that they would impose their severest sanctions in response to outcomes which involved both of them being paid unfairly, while their reaction to outcomes which treated only one of them unfairly would be less drastic. But the joint normative pressure function would differ from the sum of the individual functions inasmuch as the cost to the employer of choosing any particular deviant wage vector would tend to be larger– were this not so, there would be no point to the alliance.

(iii) *Disagreement* (*1*)

Let us now examine the implications of differences of norms (and reference sets) among the employees in a given pay group, considering first disagreements between employees who are paid at one particular wage rate, say w^1. Many of these disagreements will concern external relativities; but of special interest in the present context are differences of opinion about internal relativities. In this respect, some of the employees concerned will be unambiguously more militant than others, favouring a higher level of w^1 relative to all the other categories of employees in the pay group. But there will usually also be some less clear-cut disagreements – one skilled worker, say, favouring a lower wage relative to unskilled workers, but a higher wage relative to supervisors, than another.

But although they may entertain different norms, the reactions of employees paid at a given wage rate to deviations from their normatively prescribed wage vectors will exhibit a certain similarity. In particular, all such employees will be better off (and will thus tend to impose lesser sanctions on the employer) if this wage rate is increased relative to other wage rates, internal and external. Thus the normative pressure function of any bargaining unit whose members are paid, for example, at the rate w^1 will have the same general form as $N_X(\mathbf{w})$; and the corresponding diagram (in the case of a pay group containing only two wage rates) will have the same general shape as figure 4.9, with a region of no sanctions in the upper left hand corner. The same will be true, of course, of the sum of all such normative pressure functions, which expresses the combined impact of all the bargaining units in question on the employer's pay decision.

Normative disagreements among employees paid at a common wage rate, if they are the subject of passionate feeling, may preclude alliances between the employees concerned, even if such alliances would afford a substantial increase in power over the employer. But in general the likelihood of coalitions among those paid at the same wage rate is very high, because of their common interest in raising this rate, regardless of differences of view about the precise level at which it ought to be set in relation to the pay of other employees. Indeed, where the advantages of joint action are at all significant, most of the employees in question will usually combine into a single bargaining unit. To do so, however, they must agree on some compromise objective, which as was explained in the previous chapter will tend to be a weighted average of their individual norms, the weights being proportional to their contributions to the power of the alliance. Their joint response to deviations from this compromise objective will reflect the general nature of their individual reactions to deviations from their individual norms, the normative pressure function of any alliance among those paid at the rate w^1, for example, having broadly the same form as $N_X(\mathbf{w})$.

(iv) *Disagreement* (2)

Finally, let us consider the consequences of normative disagreements between employees paid at different wage rates. The simplest way of doing this is to revive our hypothetical bargaining units X and Y, but to assume that their members entertain different norms, and thus that the normatively prescribed wage vectors $\overline{\mathbf{w}}_X$ and $\overline{\mathbf{w}}_Y$ are no longer the same. This does not affect the general form of the normative pressure functions $N_X(\mathbf{w})$ and $N_Y(\mathbf{w})$, but it does affect the nature of their sum, which is what is important as regards the employer's pay decision.

The fact that those in bargaining units X and Y entertain different norms does not necessarily mean that they are in conflict. For example, they may agree on the relativity between them, w^1/w^2, and disagree only about other internal relativities and external relativities – about how high, that is, w^1 and w^2 should be set in relation to the pay of other employees. Moreover, they need not be in conflict even if they do disagree about w^1/w^2, since X's normatively prescribed value of w^1/w^2 may be less than Y's, which implies that there is a range of values of w^1/w^2 that would satisfy both of them – as, for example, where the minimum skill differential acceptable to skilled workers is less than the maximum acceptable to unskilled workers. In this sort of case, the

91

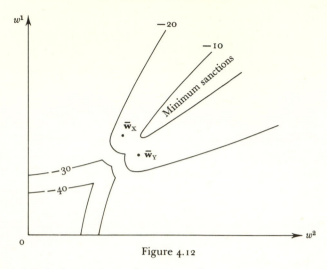

Figure 4.12

employer clearly has greater freedom of choice with regard to w^1/w^2 than in cases in which X and Y are strictly in agreement, although to avoid sanctions from either bargaining unit the employer must also set w^1 and w^2 at levels which satisfy the (not necessarily identical) aspirations of X and Y with regard to external and other internal relativities.

But it is also possible that X and Y will disagree about w^1/w^2 in such a way as to bring them into conflict – the minimum value of w^1/w^2 acceptable to X being greater than the maximum acceptable to Y. In this sort of situation, there is clearly no wage vector that would satisfy both bargaining units, and thus there is no way in which the employer can avoid normative sanctions altogether – the best he can do in this respect being to choose an outcome which provokes the minimum possible level of sanctions. The nature of the sanctions-minimising outcome will depend on the size of the difference between X's and Y's preferred values of w^1/w^2 and on the intensity of feeling among the members of these bargaining units about deviations from their preferred values. If the difference of opinion is small, and if neither X nor Y would react violently to minor deviations, the employer's best strategy, other things being equal, will be to choose a compromise outcome somewhere between the two preferred values, which neither completely satisfies nor completely outrages either of the bargaining units. A case of this sort is illustrated in figure 4.12.

If, on the other hand, the difference of opinion is large, or if X and

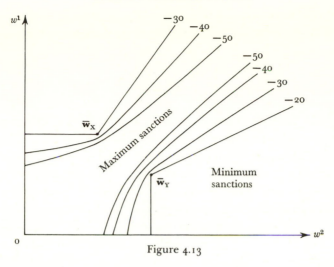

Figure 4.13

Y are very sensitive to deviations from their norms concerning w^1/w^2, then (as may be seen from figure 4.13) to choose a compromise solution would be a mistake, since it would merely infuriate both bargaining units. Instead, the employer will be better off if he plumps squarely for the preferred solution of that bargaining unit which could inflict the greatest damage on him (Y, in figure 4.13), even though this provokes all-out action by the other, less powerful, bargaining unit. At the same time, however, if he wants to minimise the level of normative sanctions, the employer must choose a wage vector which satisfies the more powerful bargaining unit's aspirations concerning external and other internal relativities. Moreover, he may in some cases (though not in that depicted in figure 4.13) be able partially to pacify the less powerful unit by setting its pay at what it regards as more than a fair level relative to other categories of employees within and outside the pay group. For the bitterness of the struggle between X and Y over w^1/w^2, and thus the level of sanctions imposed on the employer, will usually be diminished if both w^1 and w^2 are set at relatively high levels.

Disagreement between X and Y about w^1/w^2 will also have an important influence on the chances of them allying or merging into a single bargaining unit – a far more important influence, at any rate, than disagreements with respect to other relativities. For as far as these other relativities are concerned, X and Y have a common interest in increasing both w^1 and w^2 relative to the pay of other employees, whereas they may be in conflict over w^1/w^2. If they are *not*

93

in conflict in this respect, and if forming an alliance would enhance their power over the employer even to a modest extent, the likelihood of them combining into a single bargaining unit is evidently high. Indeed, such a merger may occur even if X and Y are in conflict over w^1/w^2, since the gains from the alliance may be sufficient to outweigh their disagreement.

If such an alliance is to be made, compromise objectives must be thrashed out with regard to both w^1/w^2 and other relativities. And, as before, the location of the compromise in relation to the individual preferences of the parties to the alliance will depend on the relative sizes of their contributions to its collective power. But given some such compromise, the joint normative pressure function of the alliance will be of much the same form as in the case in which X and Y shared the same set of norms (and in diagrammatic terms it will have much the same shape as figure 4.11). That is to say, the employer will be able to escape sanctions altogether only by conforming with the compromise value of w^1/w^2 and setting both w^1 and w^2 high enough to satisfy the aspirations of the coalition concerning other relativities. If he chooses a wage vector which both parties to the alliance regard as unfair in this latter respect, the employer will suffer the maximum level of sanctions that the alliance can impose. If, however, while paying both parties fairly in this latter respect, the employer were to deviate from the compromise value of w^1/w^2, thus annoying one but not both of the parties to the alliance, he would provoke some lesser level of sanctions.

4.6 INTERNAL RELATIVITIES: NORMATIVE AND ANOMIC PRESSURES

In this final section I shall make a closer examination of the conflict between normative and anomic pressures within a single pay group containing several distinct categories of employee. All discussion of this type of conflict, it should be noted, is complicated by the simultaneous existence of another type of conflict, that between different norms. Thus in order to keep the exposition simple, I shall assume in this section either that all the employees in the pay group concerned share the same norms or that the balance of power between bargaining units is such that one particular set of norms dominates all others.

This assumption, it should immediately be pointed out, is a

somewhat dangerous one. (a) The outcome of the conflict between different norms is not necessarily independent of the character of the anomic pressures on the employer. Even if, for instance, the employer's choice of a wage vector is strictly determined by a particular set of employee norms, these may not be the norms of the bargaining unit (or aggregate of bargaining units) which can inflict the greatest damage on him. For the wage vector preferred by this most powerful bargaining unit may happen to be one which is extremely unattractive to the employer on anomic grounds, and he may therefore choose instead to conform with the norms of some other, weaker, bargaining unit. (b) Conversely, the outcome of the conflict between normative and anomic pressures is not necessarily independent of the conflict between different norms. For example, anomic forces might triumph because normative disagreements prevented the formation of a strong alliance between several weak bargaining units, or because the conflicting preferences of two powerful bargaining units cancelled one another out.

It is convenient to divide the discussion into two parts. First, I shall consider conflicts between pay norms and surpluses and shortages – although this part of the discussion is to some extent relevant also to conflicts involving (a) internal mobility patterns and (b) incentive schemes based on the principle of encouraging competition for promotion (see pp. 56–7). Second, I shall consider conflicts between normative pressures and incentive schemes of the payment by results variety.

(i) *Surpluses and shortages*

In cases where the wage rates in the anomically optimal vector are either all greater or all smaller than the corresponding wage rates in the normatively prescribed vector, the way in which normative and anomic pressures interact in a pay group containing several distinct wage rates is somewhat similar to the way (discussed in section 4.2) in which they interact in the case of a single wage rate. For example, if each anomically optimal wage rate exceeds its normatively prescribed counterpart (i.e. if, at the normatively prescribed vector of wages, there would be a shortage of every category of labour), then the employer will, with the acquiescence of his employees, set each wage rate above its normatively prescribed level.

Even in this particular example, though, there is an important difference. For in the corresponding case of shortage with a single wage rate, the employer would have set the wage exactly at its anomically optimal level. But in the present case he may be inhibited from setting all the wage rates at their anomically optimal levels because the resulting pattern of internal relativities would conflict with the normatively prescribed pattern. As a result, the most profitable strategy for him may be to set all the wage rates above their normatively prescribed levels, but to set some of them above, and others of them below, their anomically optimal levels.

This is, in fact, but one instance of the type of interaction between normative and anomic pressures which is peculiar to pay groups containing several distinct wage rates, namely that in which anomic pressures cause the employer to want to set some wage rates higher, and others lower, than his employees on normative grounds desire. I shall explore the consequences of this type of mixed conflict in two stages.

(1) *One job.* I shall consider first the case where the pay group in question contains only one job, but where employees (actual and potential) vary in quality, because of differences in innate ability or formal training or experience. I shall assume, moreover, that employees adhere to the rate for the job principle (i.e. that their norm concerning internal relativities is that the wage rates of the different qualities of labour should all be equal); and that in addition, given pay in other groups, they want this common rate to be set at some specific normatively prescribed level.

Because labour quality varies (and assuming for simplicity that the administrative savings from wage standardisation may be neglected), the employer always has an anomic incentive to breach the rate for the job principle. For wherever he sets the common rate, there will be either a shortage of good quality labour, or a surplus of low quality labour, or (in most cases) both. He would therefore prefer, on anomic grounds alone, to pay different qualities of labour differently, setting each of their wage rates at the minimum level necessary to attract a sufficient amount of each quality of labour to make up an optimal mix of employees of varying quality (thus eliminating both shortages and surpluses).

Such an anomically optimal strategy would not be opposed by the top quality of employees, provided that their pay was set at more than a fair rate relative to other jobs, and provided that there was no danger of the existing employees among them being displaced by cheap low quality labour. The second best quality of labour, however, would oppose this strategy, although their resentment at being paid less than fairly relative to the top quality would be somewhat reduced by the fact of being more than fairly paid relative to other qualities and perhaps also relative to other jobs. And descending further down the hierarchy of quality, the intensity of the opposition would mount, especially below the level at which the anomically optimal wage rates are regarded as unfair in both internal and external terms, and especially if low quality existing employees feared displacement by the increased supply of good quality labour. There would usually also be, of course, many low quality potential employees who would gain from wage differentiation according to quality, since it would improve their chances of employment in the job concerned; and there might in addition be some low quality existing employees, already threatened with redundancy, in a similar situation. But apart from this last category, and apart from the top quality of labour, all the existing employees would more or less vigorously oppose wage differentiation according to quality.

The employer's response, given the adherence of his employees to the rate for the job principle, will depend on the strength of his anomic incentive to pay according to quality, in relation to the amount of normative pressure that his employees (particularly his low quality employees) can exert on him. If the gains from attracting and retaining more high quality workers and the savings from reducing the pay of low quality workers are great, or if his employees are weak, the employer will take no notice of the rate for the job principle and will adopt the anomically optimal solution. In other cases, though, it will be more profitable for him to choose a less than anomically optimal degree of wage differentiation according to quality; and in some cases it will be best for him to pay all the employees in the job concerned at the same rate.

This last type of outcome appears to me to be in practice rather common – so common, in fact, that it is often taken for granted.* It is therefore worth pursuing some of its implications. (I shall concen-

---

* Which is not to say that *all* observed instances of a single wage rate in a particular job necessarily reflect the influence of the normative rate for the job principle. Some tendency towards uniformity may also arise, for anomic reasons, from the administrative convenience of standardising wages. It is also possible, though less likely, that in certain jobs anomic pressures are such that employers, while free to employ several qualities of labour at different wage rates, choose to employ only one.

trate for simplicity on the case of strict compliance with the rate for the job principle, although the analysis below is relevant also to less extreme degrees of anomically sub-optimal differentiation.) In particular, it is worth enquiring about the level at which, given that he is normatively constrained to comply with the rate for the job principle, the employer would on *anomic* grounds prefer to set the common wage.

In this regard, much will depend on how important it is for him to have (at least a certain proportion of) high quality employees. For compliance with the rate for the job principle, by reducing the heterogeneity of the employees in the job concerned, makes the tradeoff between cheapness and quality much cruder than it would otherwise be. If the employer wants to attract or retain some good quality labour, he must pay all his employees a rather high wage, at which it will not be worth his while to employ more than a limited amount of low quality labour. Conversely, if he sets the common wage low enough to make it profitable to employ a lot of poor quality labour, he must expect to attract very few good quality employees.

If it is not vital to the employer to have many able or experienced employees (i.e. if low quality employees are a reasonably close sub-stitute), he will want to set the wage rather low – though not necessarily so low as to eliminate all surpluses – despite the fact that this would make him very short of good quality labour. For the loss that he suffers through lack of good quality labour is less than the loss that he would suffer through paying unnecessarily high wages to his low quality labour. One may thus observe the paradoxical, but not unfamiliar, spectacle of an employer who claims to have many unfilled vacancies in a particular job (albeit only for the 'right men'), but who does not wish to increase its rather low wage.

Many employers, however, are in quite the opposite position. Low quality labour is for them a poor substitute for able and experienced employees. They will therefore want to set the common rate in the job concerned at a rather high level (though not necessarily so high as to eliminate all shortages), even though this results in a very large excess supply of low quality labour, since the gains from hiring more low quality labour at a reduced wage would be more than offset by the costs of losing high quality labour. Thus one may observe another paradoxical but familiar spectacle – the employer with a large (and perhaps increasing) surplus of applicants for a particular job who wishes to maintain (or even increase) its wage.

Where the employer actually decides to set the common rate in the job concerned, of course, does not necessarily depend only on his anomic preferences. It may also depend, in very much the manner discussed in section 4.2, on where his employees want it to be set on normative grounds, and on how much pressure they can exert on him. In particular, he may be forced to set the wage above his anomically preferred level. But it is worth reiterating that even if (because his employees are too weak to do more than enforce the rate for the job principle, or are very worried about redundancies, or because the anomically preferred wage exceeds the normatively prescribed wage) the employer chooses to set the common wage at his anomically preferred level, there will still usually be both shortages (of high quality labour) and surpluses (of low quality labour)* in the job concerned.

Normative pressures on internal relativities may thus, contrary to the implications of the simple model in section 4.2, stop certain wage rates rising in response to shortages. Even more important, though, is the fact that there are two distinct ways in which normative pressures may stop the wage in a particular job falling (either absolutely or relatively) in the face of a queue of applicants willing to work for less than the prevailing wage. One is by (more or less strict) enforcement of normatively prescribed inter-job pay relativities. The other is by enforcing the rate for the job principle (or, more generally, by causing a less than anomically optimal degree of wage differentiation according to quality). For this means that the advantages of attracting and retaining some good, or even moderately good, employees will usually deter the employer from setting the wage low enough to eliminate excess supply, even if he is free to do so.

The preceding discussion, incidentally, also illuminates the relationship between the model of the choice of a single wage rate in sections 4.2 and 4.3, and the model of the choice of a set of wage rates in sections 4.4 to 4.6. In particular, it suggests that there are two quite different ways in which the former model may be interpreted as a special case of the latter – and I shall continue to assume that we are dealing with a pay group containing only one job.

The first interpretation is that there is a single wage rate in the former model because labour is homogeneous in quality (at any rate within the job concerned, and allowing for the administrative economy of wage standardisation). The other interpretation, which is in my

---

* Although the existence of employment norms (pp. 53, 60) may mean that not all the surplus labour at a given moment is of low quality.

opinion of greater practical relevance, is that the employees in the job concerned force their employer to adhere to the rate for the job principle (even though they cannot always prevent him from setting the common rate below what they regard as a fair level relative to other jobs). If this second interpretation is to be adopted, however, it must be recognised that what was described in section 4.2 as the anomically optimal wage, $\hat{w}$, is in fact a hybrid product of anomic and normative forces. Specifically, it is the level at which the employer would on anomic grounds prefer to set the wage, given that he is normatively constrained to pay all the employees in the job concerned at the same rate.

(2) *Several jobs.* Let us now consider the interaction of normative and anomic pressures in the case of a pay group containing several different jobs, each of which, I shall assume for simplicity, is for normative reasons paid at a common rate. I am also assuming, it should be recalled, that there is a single dominant norm regarding both the internal pay relativities between these jobs and the level of this set of wage rates relative to pay in other groups.

The employer is liable to face problems similar in principle to those discussed above in the context of a single job with heterogeneous labour. In particular, if he were to conform with the normatively prescribed pattern of internal relativities, he could not in general eliminate both shortages and surpluses of labour in the various jobs in question. If he were to raise all the wage rates to the point where there was no job in which he was short of labour of adequate quality,* he would be paying unnecessarily much (and attracting unnecessarily good labour) in most of the other jobs. If, on the other hand, he were to reduce all the wage rates to the point where there was no job in which he was paying an unnecessarily high wage, he would be short of labour of adequate quality in most of the other jobs. Anywhere in between, he would experience shortages in some jobs, while paying unnecessarily much in others.

If his employees (especially those in jobs where there tends to be a surplus of labour) are weak, or worried about redundancies, or if the purely anomic gains from abandoning the normatively prescribed

---

* There might, incidentally, be no such point. For if a shortage reflected failure to achieve the desired pattern of *internal* mobility (see p. 56), it could be eliminated only by changing *internal* relativities. The same applies to internal surpluses.

structure of internal relativities would be large, the employer will abandon it, and will adopt instead a structure whereby in each job he pays the minimum wage necessary to secure a sufficient supply of labour of adequate quality. But if the anomic gains would not be very great (perhaps for the sorts of reason mentioned on p. 54), or if his employees are in a position to inflict a good deal of damage on him, he will find it more profitable either to stick strictly to the normatively prescribed internal wage structure or to deviate from it only to some anomically sub-optimal extent.

If the employer is constrained to conform (at any rate more closely than he would otherwise have wished) with the normatively prescribed internal wage structure, he must consider the general level at which, on anomic grounds, it would be best for him to fix this set of wage rates. This will evidently depend on the costs of going short of labour of adequate quality in jobs paid at less than the anomically appropriate rate, in relation to the costs of paying unnecessarily much in jobs whose wage would be above the anomically appropriate rate. Specifically, the employer would on anomic grounds prefer to fix the set of wage rates at that general level at which these two sorts of costs would be in balance.

He may not in fact be allowed to do this, since his employees may for normative reasons want their wages to be fixed, and may be powerful enough to coerce the employer into fixing them, at some higher level. But even if this is not so, and the employer freely chooses the general level (though not the internal structure) of this set of wage rates, one must recognise that he will usually still suffer from shortages of labour in some jobs and surpluses of labour in others. Once again, then, normative pressures specifically on internal relativities may prevent certain wage rates rising in response to excess demand, and may prevent other wage rates falling in response to excess supply.

(ii) *Payment by results*

Incentive schemes of this general type are in many pay groups an important source of conflict between normative and anomic pressures. When implemented on an individual basis, they tend to fall foul of pay norms for two reasons.

The first is their inconsistency with the rate for the job principle. If the employees in a particular job are strongly wedded to this idea, and if they are in a position of power, the employer may be forced to introduce a more restricted form of individual payment by results than he would otherwise have desired – perhaps only as a relatively minor supplement to a common basic time rate. Or he may be driven to eschew individual payment by results altogether and to rely instead on straightforward time rates or on a group bonus scheme relating pay to some measure of the total output of the employees in the job concerned (which would provide less of an incentive to individual workers).

The second (and conceptually distinct) reason why individual payment by results systems tend to clash with pay norms is that they are liable to cause less productive employees to earn less than what is regarded as a fair rate for the job concerned, relative to other jobs. The employer may therefore be obliged, if the employees in question are powerful, to contemplate setting the system up in such a way that all those in the job concerned can be reasonably confident of earning at least the normatively prescribed rate (which implies that most of them will earn more).*

The disadvantages of this solution are twofold. One is that it is expensive in itself, the need to pay an average rate above the norm offsetting some of the gains from providing incentives to employees. The other is that such a payment by results system, if introduced in one job, would cause a reaction from employees in other jobs in the same pay group, demanding higher pay to keep inter-job relativities in line with prevailing norms. To accede to these demands would be expensive, and would regenerate opposition among the less productive employees in the job paid by results, whose earnings would again be depressed below what they considered a fair rate relative to other jobs in the pay group.

Similar problems arise because it is impossible accurately to predict or control average earnings in most (individual or group) payment by results systems. Thus, especially where several jobs are paid by results, internal relativities are liable to keep accidentally drifting out of line with pay norms, provoking sanctions from those who happen to lose out in relative terms. If most of his employees are in weak bargaining

* This, incidentally, should not be confused with the straightforwardly anomic proposition that an employer may have to pay a higher average rate in a job paid by results than in an identical job paid on a simple time basis because the uncertainty and variability of earnings make employees reluctant to work in jobs paid by results.

positions, and if the gains from providing incentives are large, these various sorts of problems will not deter the employer from payment by results. But if many categories of employees in a pay group are powerful, the costs involved in frequent battles to restore internal relativities distorted by payment by results may be sufficient to cause the employer to abandon payment by results altogether.

As an alternative, he may contemplate some scheme whereby all the employees in the pay group receive a bonus which varies with the performance of the group and is proportional to basic pay. This would not affect internal relativities, and would thus avoid the problems mentioned above. But the incentive effect of such a scheme would be limited by the fact that the size of the bonus would be only dimly related to the activities and efforts of individual employees. Moreover, such a scheme might come into conflict with norms concerning *external* relativities. In particular, if his employees were powerful, the employer would have to ensure that the scheme did not operate in such a way as to depress their pay below what they considered a fair level relative to other pay groups. This would probably involve adopting a system that consistently kept pay above the external norm, which might make the whole scheme too expensive to be worthwhile.

(iii) *Change*

By way of a brief conclusion to the discussion of these last three sections, it is worth emphasising that internal pay relativities need not remain constant. At any given moment in a particular pay group, of course, the character of anomic and normative pressures will be such as to cause the employer to choose some specific internal wage structure. All the relativities concerned may be governed by particular pay norms, or all may be dictated by anomic considerations, or the outcome may be a mixture of some sort.

Over time, however, the nature of the employer's constrained-optimal internal pay strategy may change. Alterations in conditions of demand or supply, for example, might intensify anomic pressures to the point where the employer ceased to take any notice of pay norms. Or a change in technology might confer on some category of employees the ability to inflict great damage on the employer, or might make the services of some other category less essential. Such a change in the balance of power could alter the compromise objectives of a dominant coalition of employees, or could cause the norms of one bargaining unit to be wholly or partly superseded as an influence on the employer's pay decision by the norms of another bargaining unit. Moreover, there are various ways (discussed in section 2.3) in which pay norms themselves can change over time, which, if such changes were to occur among members of a powerful bargaining unit, could cause internal pay relativities to alter without changes in the balance of power and without the influence of anomic pressures.

5

INDIRECTLY DETERMINED
RELATIVITIES

In the previous chapter I dealt with the determination of pay in a single pay group, taking pay in all other groups as given. In the present chapter I shall allow pay in all groups to vary, and I shall analyse the nature and consequences of interdependence between pay decisions in different groups, with special reference to (a) the determination of external (or indirectly determined) relativities and (b) the behaviour of the general money wage level.

To simplify the exposition, I shall for most of this chapter neglect internal relativities, assuming that all the employees in each group are paid at a common rate. I shall also provisionally assume that the employees in any given group all share a single pay norm. These, it may be recalled, were the assumptions made in section 2 of the previous chapter, and indeed the model of the pay decision propounded in that section is the basis of the analysis in the present chapter.

I shall restrict most of the formal analysis to a hypothetical economy containing three pay groups, whose wage rates I shall label A, B and C. This is the minimum number of groups needed to illustrate the general principles of the model. It is also the maximum consistent with diagrammatic representation of the model (which is important because the algebraic alternative is much clumsier). For in a three-group economy there are only two independent external relativities, say A/B and A/C, plus a third distinct but dependent relativity, say C/B. Thus one can make use of a two-dimensional diagram (such as that on p. 106) with A/B and A/C measured along the axes. Each point in the diagram represents a particular pair (or vector) of values of A/B and A/C, while the slope of the ray from the origin through that point implies a particular value of C/B.

In this and the next two sections I shall further simplify the model by excluding all anomic pressures on pay, assuming, that is, that rates of pay are always set strictly in accordance with normative consider-

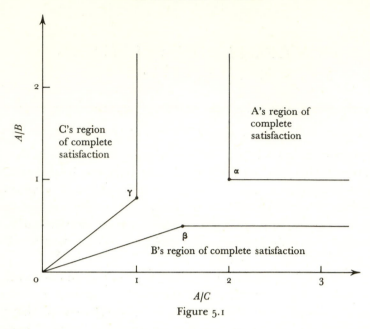

Figure 5.1

ations. In addition, I shall temporarily suppose that the pay settlements of the three groups occur in a fixed sequence, ABCABC...,
and that the employees in each pay group, though fully informed
about previous settlements, make no attempt to anticipate subsequent
settlements.

(i) *The model*

The pay norms of groups A, B and C will be labelled **α**, **β** and **γ**
respectively. Three such norms are represented in figure 5.1, in which
I have also marked a region of complete satisfaction for each group.
Consider, for example, group B. In order for group B to be at least
fairly paid relative to group A, relativities must lie on or below a
horizontal line through **β** (since at all points above this line the
relativity A/B exceeds the maximum value acceptable to B). Similarly,
in order for group B to be at least fairly paid relative to group C,
relativities must lie on or below the ray from the origin through **β** (since
at all points above this ray, which must lie on steeper rays, the
relativity C/B exceeds the maximum value acceptable to B). These two
requirements jointly define the region in which group B is at least fairly

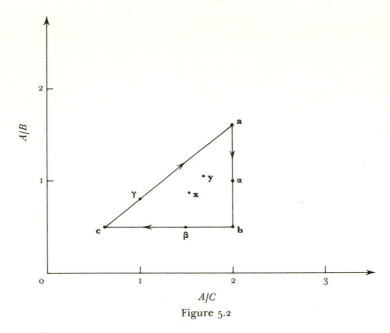

Figure 5.2

paid relative to both group A and group C. Similar requirements define the regions of complete satisfaction of groups A and C.

The evolution of pay settlements is illustrated in figure 5.2, in which the same three norms are marked, but in which for clarity the regions of complete satisfaction are omitted. Let us suppose arbitrarily that relativities initially conform with group C's norm, γ, and that A is the first group to make a settlement.

Since the pay of B and C, and thus the relativity C/B, is fixed, group A's choice is confined to the ray from the origin through γ (each point on which, given the pay of B and C, corresponds with a particular level of A's money wage rate). This restriction is important because no point on the ray, since it does not pass through A's norm, α, can precisely satisfy A's preferences with regard to both the relativity A/B and the relativity A/C – this being what I described on page 67 as the problem of inconsistent comparisons. As explained earlier, group A will resolve this problem by choosing the *most favourable comparison* – the highest of the various wage rates (or the most distant from the origin of the corresponding points on the ray) implied by its normative comparisons. In the present example, group A will accordingly choose the wage which corresponds with the point **a**, where it is paid at what it regards as a fair rate relative to C, but at more than a fair rate relative to B. To put the matter another way, group A will proceed along the ray corresponding to the given value of *C/B until it comes to the boundary of its region of complete satisfaction.*

The second group to make a pay settlement is, by assumption, B. Since the pay of groups A and C, and thus the relativity *A/C*, is fixed, group B is constrained to choose some point on the perpendicular through **a**. No point on this perpendicular, which does not pass through **β**, can exactly satisfy B's preferences regarding both the relativity *A/B* and the relativity *C/B*. Thus group B, in the same way as group A, applies the most favourable comparison principle and chooses the wage corresponding to point **b**, where it is paid at what it regards as a fair rate relative to A, but at more than a fair rate relative to C. In other words, group B simply increases its money wage, thereby moving down the given perpendicular, until it comes to the boundary of its region of complete satisfaction.

It is now group C's turn to make a pay settlement. Because the pay of groups A and B (and thus the relativity *A/B*) is given, group C is constrained to choose a point on the horizontal line through **b**. In much the same fashion as groups A and B, C increases its money wage, thereby proceeding leftwards along this line, until it comes to the boundary of its region of complete satisfaction at the point **c**.

The next group to make a settlement is A. Clearly, A will again choose point **a**, while groups B and C will subsequently again choose points **b** and **c**, and so on. Thus pay relativities will on the present assumptions perpetually oscillate between the three values **a, b** and **c**, following the triangular path denoted in figure 5.2 by a line with directional arrows. What is happening on this path, it may be helpful to recall, is that relativities are bouncing in a particular way between the regions of complete satisfaction of the three groups concerned.

(ii) *Properties of the model*

(1) The triangular path in figure 5.2 is unique and stable, in the sense that the system converges to it regardless of initial conditions, and tends to return to it if dislodged by extraneous shocks. In other words, to arrive at this particular pattern of oscillation of relativities it is not necessary to start the system off, as was done above, from **γ**. Any

starting point would eventually have led to the same result (as the reader, especially if he wishes to test his understanding of the diagram, may care to verify by experiment).

(2) Thus far, although the sequence in which settlements occur has been specified, nothing has been said about the length of the intervals between them. But this is important, since (regarding a complete circuit of the triangle as one period of time) the *average* value of pay relativities in any period, which governs the relative affluence of the three groups, is a weighted average of the relativities generated by the three individual settlements, the weights being the relative lengths of time (or fractions of the period) for which each of the settlements prevails before being superseded by the next.

For example, the point **x** in figure 5.2 shows what this average would be if the settlements occurred at equal intervals, while the point **y** shows what the average would be if **a** prevailed for half the period and **b** and **c** each for one quarter of the period.* In the latter case, not surprisingly, the average lies closer to group A's region of complete satisfaction. It is also clear that if the relative intervals between settlements, whatever they are, remain constant from period to period, then so on average do relativities, even though within each period they fluctuate around the average.

The periodic average value of pay relativities cannot lie outside the triangle **abc**, whose coordinates alone thus place certain limits on the relative affluence of the three groups. But these limits may be quite wide, as is the case in figure 5.2, and hence it is also vital to understand what governs the relative lengths of the intervals between settlements. A proper investigation of this point must await abandonment of the fixed sequence assumption in the next section, but it is evident that the explanation lies in the relative speeds with which the various groups react to situations in which they are unfairly paid, and that this in turn depends on, among other things, their relative power.

(3) The final observation to be made about the triangular circuit of relativities in figure 5.2 is that the process of going round it pushes up the general money wage level – as is obvious from the fact that each settlement results in an increase in the absolute pay of one group, while no group's absolute pay ever decreases.

* As usual, there are several possible methods of calculating the average, none of which is unambiguously the best. The examples in figure 5.2 and in later figures are (weighted) arithmetic means of **a**, **b** and **c**.

In any given period (i.e. in the course of each complete round of settlements) the money wage rates of all three groups increase by the same proportion. This must be so, since the relativities which result from each group's individual settlements (the points **a**, **b** and **c**) remain the same from period to period. Thus to ascertain the rate of increase of the general money wage level it is sufficient to ascertain the rate of increase of any one of the three wage rates.

Consider, for example, group A. Each of its pay settlements, given the pay of groups B and C, moves relativities from point **c** to point **a** along the ray from the origin through **c**. The proportional increase in group A's absolute money pay from one period to the next must therefore be equal to the distance **ca** divided by the distance oc (which in the particular instance depicted in figure 5.2 is 220 per cent).

The rate of increase of the general money wage level thus depends on the positions of **a** and **c** (which between them imply the position of **b**), in relation to the origin. Roughly speaking, the larger is the triangle of which these three points are the coordinates, the greater is the rate of wage inflation; but the further the triangle lies from the origin, the smaller is the rate of wage inflation. The positions of **a**, **b** and **c** depend in turn on the positions of α, β and γ. In particular, the size and distance from the origin of the triangle **abc**, which reflects the rate of wage inflation, depends (in ways to be explored in later sections) on the degree of conflict between the pay norms of the three groups.

In this simple wage–wage spiral model, the rate of wage inflation evidently remains constant from period to period. This, however, does not necessarily imply that the rate of wage inflation remains constant in calendar time, since the length of the periods may alter. This depends on what happens to the absolute lengths in calendar time (as opposed to the relative lengths) of the intervals between individual settlements. For instance, if the intervals between settlements were all four months, the annual rate of wage inflation in the case depicted in figure 5.2 would be 220 per cent. If, however, each of the intervals were to decline to two months, the annual rate of wage inflation would rise to 924 per cent.

(4) Before studying in detail the consequences of varying and abandoning the assumptions of the present simple model, it is worth reiterating that its essential characteristics are not dependent on the assumption that the economy contains only three pay groups. It is not

difficult, especially with the aid of a computer, to construct models involving more groups which exhibit the same properties, namely that from any arbitrary starting point relativities converge to a particular stable pattern of oscillation, which is associated with a particular constant periodic rate of wage inflation.

5.2 NORMATIVE PRESSURES: SEQUENCE AND TIMING

(i) *Sequence*

In the previous section it was assumed that pay settlements occur in a particular sequence, ABCABC... To have assumed a different sequence, with the same norms, would have altered the outcome, though not the general character of the model. For example, had I assumed the sequence to be ACBACB..., the result would have been perpetual oscillation of relativities around a different triangular path (depicted in figure 5.3) and a different periodic rate of wage inflation.

The reason why the process is sequence-dependent is that each group's pay decision depends not only on its norm, but also on the state of relativities at the juncture at which its decision is made, since this affects which of the various comparisons is the most favourable and thus which *aspect* of its norm is crucial in determining the size of its pay settlement. And the state of relativities at any particular moment is usually dependent on the sequence in which previous pay settlements have occurred.

For example, in the ABC sequence considered in the preceding section, the most favourable comparison for group A is always that with group C, and thus it is A's norm with regard to the relativity A/C (i.e. the vertical face of A's region of complete satisfaction) that determines the size of its settlement. In the ACB sequence, by contrast, the most favourable comparison for group A is that with group B, and thus it is A's norm with regard to the relativity A/B (i.e. the horizontal face of A's region of complete satisfaction) that determines the size of its pay settlement. This explains, of course, why the resulting rate of wage inflation is different. For the rate of wage inflation is determined by the degree of conflict between the norms of the various groups, and this is in general bound to depend on which aspects of the norms actually govern pay settlements.

The fact that the outcome is to some extent sequence-dependent is significant because in models of this kind there are many possible

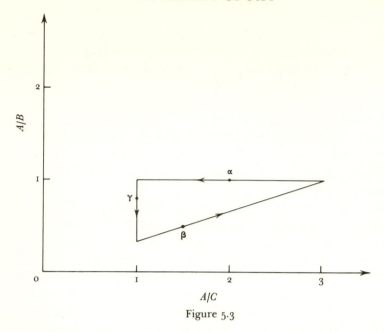

Figure 5.3

different sequences. Even with only three groups, the number of plausible sequences can be made quite large by allowing individual groups to make more than one settlement in each complete round and by permitting pairs of groups to make simultaneous settlements (although the path around which relativities oscillate ceases to be triangular in shape). And in more realistic cases, with far more than three pay groups, the number of possible different sequences is very large.

(ii) *Sequence and intervals*

It is thus important to explain what determines the sequence in which pay settlements occur. At the same time, since the two sets of causes are tangled together, it is appropriate to explain what governs the length (both relative and absolute) of the intervals between settlements, whose effects on the average value of relativities from period to period, and on the rate of wage inflation in calendar time, were explored in the previous section. The most convenient way to go about this is to suppose that relativities are initially in some arbitrary state, and to ask what determines which group will be the next to make a settlement, and how soon this settlement will take place. There are three main types of influence.

(1) *Militancy.* One extremely important factor is the strength of feeling among the membership of each pay group about the need, if any, for a new pay settlement. This will depend largely on the proximity of the prevailing state of relativities to the region of complete satisfaction of the group in question, and on the sensitivity of members of the group to unfair pay in relative terms.* It will also depend on how long the various aspects of the current state have prevailed, which in turn will depend on the nature and timing of previous pay settlements.

The militancy of a given group in the face of a given set of relativities will also depend, it was suggested earlier, on what has recently happened to its real wage – its purchasing power over goods and services. This is bound to be greatly affected by changes in its relative wage, since the wages of other groups, being costs of production, influence prices (and in the case of government employees, taxes). But it is also affected by changes in such things as profit margins, productivity and the terms of trade, and by autonomous changes in taxes. Factors of this sort may affect the timing of pay settlements even if their size is determined by norms with regard to relativities. Moreover, one would expect factors of this sort to affect the militancy of all groups to a roughly equal degree, and therefore to influence mainly the absolute or average intervals between settlements (and hence the rate of wage inflation in calendar time), rather than the sequence of settlements or the relative intervals between them.

There are various other considerations which may influence the militancy of particular pay groups, including the temperaments and political philosophies of their leaders and members. But in any event, other things being equal, it will be the group that is most militant at any given moment that makes the next pay settlement, and its degree of militancy will determine the amount of time that elapses before it does so.

(2) *Power.* Other things, however, are in general not equal. In particular, an exceedingly militant but weak group may react more slowly than a less aggrieved but more powerful group, even though, on present assumptions, both ultimately make settlements which (temporarily) completely satisfy them. There is all the difference in the world, that is, between a group which can force a settlement in a week

---

* One might represent this by drawing indifference maps (similar to those in section 4.5), one for each group, showing the strength of their feelings about any given 'unfair' set of relativities.

and have it backdated several months, and a group which must fight a six-month battle to achieve a settlement which, even then, does not come into effect at once. Not least, the periodic average value of relativities is likely to lie much closer to the region of complete satisfaction of the former group, even if it is less sensitive to unfair treatment than the latter group.

Differences in power between groups are bound to have an important effect on the relative intervals between settlements, and will usually also influence the sequence in which they occur. In this regard it is worth noting that the relative power of different groups at any moment is unlikely to be independent of the amounts of time that have elapsed since their pay was last changed. Specifically, a group will tend to be weaker, the more recent was its last settlement, especially if it involved a struggle which depleted its financial reserves and its stock of goodwill with its allies. This factor tends both to impart stability to the sequence of settlements and to increase the average interval between them. The average interval between settlements (and thus the pace of wage inflation in calendar time) is also influenced by factors which have a common effect on the power of most or all groups, such as laws on picketing and the provision of welfare state benefits to strikers' families.

(3) *Contract and custom.* One must also take account of legal and conventional considerations with regard to the length of the intervals between the successive wage settlements of individual groups. In the United States, for example, pay settlements are often legally binding contracts of specified duration, whereas in Britain settlements are in principle open-ended, although it is customary to renew them about once a year. Institutional rigidities of this kind are inevitably an important influence on the sequence and timing of pay settlements in any short period; at any given moment, they may effectively pre-determine the pattern of settlements for a year or two ahead. As a result, the path around which relativities oscillate, since it will be affected by initial conditions, may be to some extent arbitrary.

But in the longer term, in which all contracts are renewed and their lengths may be varied, legal and customary considerations are less important. Their main role is to impart some stability to the sequence of settlements and the relative and absolute intervals between them, which depend fundamentally (on present assumptions) on the power, the norms and the sensitivity to unfair pay of the various groups in the economy.

(iii) *Anticipation*

Up to this point it has been assumed that pay groups, though fully informed about prior settlements, do not attempt to anticipate subsequent settlements. Anticipation, however, can alter (and in some circumstances radically alter) the character of the present model. The extent and nature of the alterations will depend on which (and how many) groups anticipate the future, which settlements they anticipate, and what their expectations are based on. But most species of anticipation have two important effects in common.

First, anticipation increases the magnitude of the periodic oscillation of relativities and the associated rate of wage inflation. The reason for this is that any group which anticipates (and which believes that in the future other groups will obtain wage increases) will, at each settlement, insist on a larger wage increase than it would otherwise have done. For it will wish to ensure that it is fairly paid not merely (as I have assumed up to now) at the time when the settlement is made, but also subsequently, when the groups with which it compares itself have also obtained wage increases.

Second, any group which fails to anticipate the future, or which underestimates future wage increases, will be at a disadvantage in the sense that the periodic average value of relativities will be further from its region of complete satisfaction than would otherwise have been the case. The relative affluence of more far-sighted or pessimistic groups, by contrast, will tend to increase. (There is thus clearly an incentive to err on the side of overestimating future wage increases, especially where a long period is expected to elapse before a group's next settlement.)

To illustrate these general points, let us consider the specific effects of two familiar types of anticipation.

(1) *Rational expectations.* By rational expectations I shall mean expectations which are based on attempts at understanding the principles that govern the behaviour of other groups. To provide an example, let us revert to the case illustrated in figure 5.2 (in which settlements occur in the sequence ABC), but with the difference that group A, and only group A, rationally and accurately anticipates the future. A thus

recognises that between the time it makes one settlement and the time it makes the next there will be two sub-periods in which A/B conforms with B's norm and one sub-period in which A/C is governed by the interaction of B's and C's norms. Group A will accordingly compensate for this by making its own settlement so large that *on average over the whole period* it will not be paid at less than it regards as a fair rate relative to either B or C.

Let us assume for simplicity that the intervals between settlements are equal. In this case, A (although still constrained to choose a point on the ray from the origin through **c**) will choose not point **a** but point **a'** in figure 5.4, with the result that the periodic average value of relativities is not **x** but **z**, which lies on the boundary of A's region of complete satisfaction. Plainly, anticipation makes group A better off. It also raises the periodic rate of wage inflation – as is apparent in the diagram from the fact that **ca'** is longer than **ca**.

There are various ways in which this example could be modified and still yield a determinate result. For instance, B might understand and anticipate the behaviour of C, but not of A. In this case, one could assume either that A fully understood B's behaviour or that A, while understanding certain aspects of B's behaviour, failed to grasp that it was anticipating C. But what one cannot do, without (on present assumptions) destroying the model altogether, is to suppose that more than one group fully comprehends and anticipates the behaviour of both other groups. For since no constraint on the power of groups to raise wages has yet been introduced into the model, and since (given the norms in figure 5.4) there is no way in which more than one group can be completely satisfied with the periodic average value of relativities, all truly far-sighted groups would always insist on infinitely large wage settlements.

(2) *Adaptive expectations.* In reality, the number of pay groups in the economy and the amount of mutual ignorance of motivation are such that the rational expectations version of the present type of model is rather implausible. It is more likely that expectations will be *adaptive* – based, that is, on some sort of extrapolation of past events, and adjusted in response to non-fulfilment of past expectations. It is therefore of considerable importance to note that under most assumptions the introduction of adaptive expectations into the present type of model causes wage inflation to tend continually to accelerate.

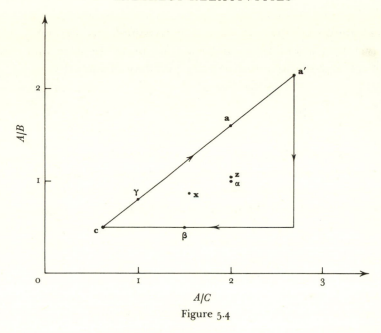

Figure 5.4

The general reason for this is readily apparent. When norms conflict, there is no periodic average value of relativities which can satisfy
all groups. Thus whatever rates of wage increase are expected when
settlements are made, the outcome is bound to disappoint some
groups – which in itself implies that other groups must have obtained
larger-than-expected wage increases. The disappointed groups will
therefore revise their expectations of future wage inflation upwards,
and will accordingly obtain larger wage increases than at their previous
settlements. But this will cause other groups to be disappointed and
to revise *their* expectations and wage increases upwards, and so on.
Thus, since there must always be some disappointed groups, and since
any disappointed group will obtain a larger wage increase than it
obtained in the previous period, the general money wage level must
tend to rise forever at an increasing rate.

For this to be so, at least two conflicting groups must anticipate (since
otherwise one would eventually attain a stable outcome similar to that
depicted in figure 5.4, in which the single anticipating group was
completely satisfied). Moreover, the *speed* with which wage inflation
accelerates will usually depend on the number (or proportion) of
groups which anticipate. It will also evidently depend on the rapidity

and sensitivity with which groups adapt their expectations in the face of disappointment; the quicker and more completely they react, and the more they attempt to learn from (or to compensate for) their previous mistakes, the faster will wage inflation accelerate.

5.3 NORMATIVE PRESSURES: NORMS AND REFERENCE SETS
(i) *Consensus, disagreement and conflict*

The examples in this chapter so far have been based on one hypothetical set of pay norms. I shall therefore now investigate the way in which the outcome in the present type of model is dependent on the nature of the norms of the pay groups involved.

(1) *Satiation.* In this regard the most fundamental distinction is that between cases in which there is a *region of satiation* and cases in which there is not. By a region of satiation I mean one or more sets of relativities which would completely satisfy all the pay groups in the economy. Such a region would clearly exist if all groups shared a common norm – this being what I shall call the case of *consensus*. But it is also possible for a region of satiation to exist if pay groups disagree about what relativities ought to be, provided that the nature of the disagreement is such that they are not in conflict – for example, if A's desired value of A/B is less than B's.

In diagrammatic terms, a region of satiation exists whenever the regions of complete satisfaction of all the groups in the economy overlap or intersect. It is obvious from figure 5.1 that this is not the case with regard to the particular set of norms considered in the examples in the last two sections. But it is also clear from figure 5.1 that with a different set of norms the regions of complete satisfaction might intersect, as in the case of the norms represented in figure 5.5, where the region of satiation is cross-hatched.

When a region of satiation exists, the character of the model is transformed. From any arbitrary starting point (and ignoring for the moment the possibility of anticipation), relativities converge to the region of satiation, and there the whole process stops. Consider, for example, figure 5.5, in which it is assumed that settlements occur in the sequence ABC. The first group to settle, which is assumed to be A, is as usual constrained to choose an outcome on the ray from the origin through the arbitrary starting point (which is circled in the

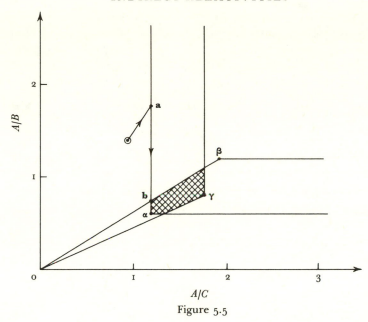

Figure 5.5

diagram). It accordingly chooses point **a**, which lies on the boundary of its region of complete satisfaction. Group B, which is as usual constrained to choose an outcome on the perpendicular through **a**, chooses point **b**, which lies on the boundary of its region of complete satisfaction. It is now group C's turn to make a settlement. But at point **b** relativities are already within the region of complete satisfaction of group C, which will therefore not want any change in its pay. The same will subsequently be true of groups A and B. There will thus be no further alteration of wages, and relativities will remain at the point **b**.

As this example suggests, the terminal state of relativities (the position of the point where the process stops) depends on the starting point and on the sequence in which settlements occur – except in the special case of consensus, when one always ultimately arrives at the point corresponding to the shared norm. In other cases, if the starting point lies outside the region of satiation, the terminal point must lie somewhere on its boundary; if one starts within the region, there is no movement at all.

The example in figure 5.5 implies that the existence of a region of satiation prevents continual wage inflation of the sort discussed in the

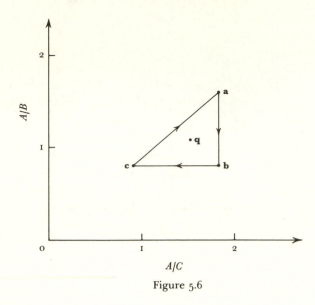

Figure 5.6

last two sections. This conclusion, however, may be vitiated by the introduction of adaptive expectations. In particular, if two or more groups anticipate the future, and form their expectations adaptively, there can be a self-sustaining wage–wage spiral even in the absence of normative conflict.

Such a case is illustrated in figure 5.6. It is assumed that all three groups share a common norm, **q**, and that settlements occur at equal intervals in the sequence ABC. Wage inflation is proceeding at a constant periodic rate, and the periodic average value of relativities is equal to the common norm. Each group expects the other two groups to obtain wage increases in the coming period equal to those which they obtained in the previous period, and therefore increases its own wage by the same amount in order to keep the periodic average value of relativities on the boundary of its region of complete satisfaction. The expectations of each group are thus always exactly fulfilled.

The periodic rate of wage inflation in this sort of case (unlike the cases discussed in the two previous sections) is in an important sense indeterminate. It depends primarily on what the rate of wage inflation happens to have been in the past, and it can be permanently altered by extraneous shocks. Figure 5.6, in other words, tells one not why the rate of wage inflation is what it is, but merely why it is maintained from one period to the next.

(2) *Total and partial conflict.* If the norms of the various groups in the economy are such that there is no region of satiation, which must be presumed to be the usual case, then relativities are bound (on present assumptions) to oscillate perpetually, and thus there will be continual wage inflation, regardless of the presence or absence of anticipation. Moreover, the further the system is from having a region of satiation, the more rapid a periodic rate of wage inflation will it generate.

The particular set of norms on which the examples in the previous two sections were based exhibits what might be called *total* conflict, there being (as is evident in figure 5.1) no overlap between any of the regions of complete satisfaction. Furthermore, the assumed degree of conflict is very large, as is indicated by the very high periodic rates of wage inflation that it produces. But it is clear that one could devise other examples of total conflict in which the degree of conflict was much smaller (i.e. in which the points α, β and γ were much closer together), and in which the rate of wage inflation was correspondingly much lower. There are clearly also many possible types of *partial* conflict – situations in which the various norms are such that there is some conflict and some agreement (or non-conflicting disagreement). Let us consider two examples, assuming in both cases that there is no anticipation and that settlements occur in the sequence ABC.

(1) In figure 5.7, groups B and C share a common norm, βγ. Group A, while agreeing with groups B and C about the relativity *B/C*, wants to be paid more than B and C would prefer; thus α lies on the same ray as βγ, but further from the origin. As a result, relativities tend to oscillate around a triangle whose size (and hence also the rate of wage inflation) is governed straightforwardly by the extent of the disagreement about A's position relative to B and C, this being the sole conflict in the system.

(2) In figure 5.8, groups B and C have different but non-conflicting norms, and thus there is a region of outcomes (shaded in the diagram) that would satisfy both of them. But β and γ both conflict with group A's norm, α. Once again the result is that relativities tend to oscillate perpetually around a particular triangular path, thereby increasing the general money wage level at a particular constant rate.

(ii) *Coat-tail settlements*

Figure 5.8 also happens to exemplify another general feature of the present type of model, namely that the periodic rate of wage inflation

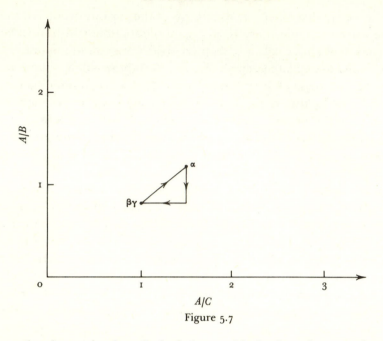

Figure 5.7

may be determined exclusively by a *critical subset* of pay settlements, the remainder being what I shall call *coat-tail* settlements. For it is evident from the diagram that the value of the ratio **ca/oc** (which is the rate of wage inflation) is determined exclusively by the conflict between groups A and C over the relativity *A/C*. Were the magnitude of this particular conflict different (i.e. if **α** or **γ** were horizontally displaced by a small amount), then so, to an exactly commensurate degree, would be the rate of wage inflation. Group B's settlements, by contrast, although they cause *B* to increase over time at the same rate as *A* and *C*, do not contribute to the determination of the common rate of increase; group B is thus riding on the coat-tails of groups A and C. This can be seen in figure 5.8 from the fact that group B's norm, **β**, which governs the size of its pay settlements, could be displaced by a small amount in any direction without affecting the periodic rate of wage inflation.

Any vertical displacement of **β** would of course shift the triangular path of relativities bodily upwards or downwards. Thus figure 5.8 also makes it clear that coat-tail settlements, although they do not affect the rate of wage inflation, do affect certain relativities. More specifically, a coat-tail settlement always affects the pay of the group con-

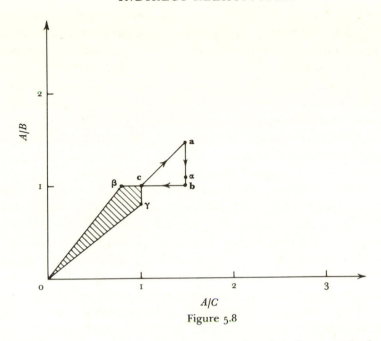

Figure 5.8

cerned relative to other groups; but unless it influences the intervals between critical settlements, it does not affect pay relativities between groups whose settlements are in the critical subset. In figure 5.8, that is, B's settlements affect the values taken by A/B and B/C on the triangular path around which relativities oscillate, but not the values taken by A/C – although the *timing* of B's settlements, by influencing the timing of A's and C's settlements, may nonetheless affect the *periodic average* value of A/C.

The reason why coat-tail settlements exist is that the degree of mutual conflict which underlies the settlements within the critical subset is greater than the degree of conflict between the groups in this subset and other groups. As a result, the conflicts within this subset dominate the outcome and determine the rate of inflation, while the other conflicts are mere side-shows. For the size of a critical settlement is never influenced by the size of coat-tail settlements; the most favourable comparison for a group in the critical subset is never with the pay of a group outside it (which, by the way, reduces the likelihood of coat-tail settlements affecting the *timing* of critical settlements in the way mentioned above).

These general propositions are borne out by the example in figure

123

5.8. The size of group A's settlements is based on comparisons with group C's pay, and vice versa; in neither case do comparisons with group B affect the outcome (although the size of group B's settlements is based on comparisons with the pay of group A). This is because the conflict between groups A and C over A/C is greater in degree than any of the conflicts between them and group B. For there is by assumption no conflict between B and C over B/C; and the conflict between A and B over A/B (reflected in the vertical distance between α and β) is comparatively small.

The possibility of coat-tail settlements is not confined to cases of partial conflict of the sort depicted in figure 5.8; such settlements can occur also when there are no overlaps between any of the regions of complete satisfaction. As it happens, there have been no coat-tail settlements in the particular instances of total conflict so far considered, such as that depicted in figure 5.2. But consider the case illustrated in figure 5.9, in which the assumptions are identical to those of figure 5.2, except that the position of α is somewhat different. As a result, the periodic rate of wage inflation is governed solely by the conflict between groups B and C over B/C (which therefore oscillates between the rays from the origin through β and γ). The conflicts in which group A is involved are all smaller than that between B and C, and thus its settlements are coat-tail settlements, whose influence on the triangular path of relativities is confined to the values taken by A/B and A/C. Indeed, given this sequence of settlements and the positions of β and γ, it is not difficult to demonstrate that group A's settlements would be coat-tail settlements if α lay anywhere within the rectangle bordered by a heavy line (regardless of whether the result was partial or total normative conflict).

In addition, it should be emphasised that whether or not a particular settlement is a coat-tail settlement may depend not only on the nature of the various pay norms but also on the sequence in which settlements occur. For instance, with the same norms as in figure 5.9, but with settlements in the sequence ACB, group A's settlements are no longer coat-tail settlements, as may be seen from the fact that in figure 5.10 the oscillation of the relativity B/C is no longer confined between the rays from the origin through β and γ. The reason why a change of sequence may have this effect is that, as explained earlier, sequence often determines which aspect of a group's norm determines its pay decision, and hence which of the various conflicts latent in a given set of norms are actually exposed. (But given the membership of, and the

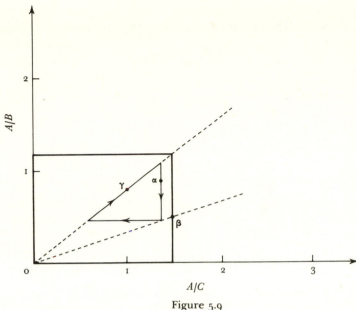

Figure 5.9

sequence of settlements within, the critical subset, the sequence in which coat-tail settlements occur has no effect on the periodic rate of wage inflation).

Another factor which may influence whether or not a particular group's settlement lies in the critical subset is anticipation. In particular, if a group anticipates the future to a greater degree (or more pessimistically) than most other groups, and thus makes disproportionately large settlements, it may well have an influence on the periodic rate of wage inflation even though its settlements would otherwise have been of the coat-tail variety. In figure 5.9, for example, if group A alone anticipated, and by an amount sufficient to cause its settlements to lie outside the rectangle bordered by heavy lines, its settlements would enter the critical subset and the periodic rate of wage inflation would increase.

Moreover, when two or more conflicting groups whose settlements (for whatever reason) are in the critical subset anticipate the future on the basis of adaptive expectations, the periodic rate of wage inflation will tend, for reasons given earlier, continually to accelerate. Anticipation of this sort by coat-tail groups alone, however, so long as they remain coat-tail groups, will not have this effect.

Finally, it is worth correcting one possible misapprehension con-

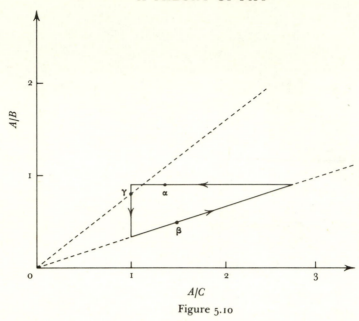

Figure 5.10

cerning coat-tail settlements. In a three-group economy, the existence of a coat-tail settlement necessarily implies that the periodic rate of wage inflation is governed by simple bilateral conflict between the other two groups, rather than by more complex multilateral conflict of the sort illustrated in, say, figures 5.2 and 5.10. But with more than three groups this equivalence evaporates; in reality, that is, there may be both multilateral conflict in the critical subset and coat-tail settlements outside it. There may well also be another phenomenon which cannot exist in a three-group economy (in which coat-tail settlements must directly imitate settlements in the critical subset), namely groups which ride on the coat-tails of coat-tail groups, and which perhaps have other groups riding on their coat-tails.

(iii) *Incomplete comparisons*

In all the hypothetical cases so far considered in this chapter I have assumed that each group, before making a settlement, compares its own pay with the pay of *every* other group in the economy (and then selects the most favourable of these comparisons). This assumption, though not implausible with only three groups, is, as was noted in chapter 2, utterly untenable in practice, since the economy contains a very large number of pay groups and since information about pay is far from freely available. Thus it is important to ascertain the consequences of incomplete comparisons – which are the same, incidentally, regardless of whether reference sets are restricted through deliberate choice or through lack of information.

For obvious reasons, incompleteness will have no effects at all if the omitted comparisons would not otherwise have been the most favourable for the groups concerned. In figure 5.10, for example, nothing would be changed if group B were unaware of group A's existence, since the size of B's settlements is based on comparisons with the pay of group C. Likewise, in figure 5.9 it would not affect the outcome if groups B and C were both ignorant of group A's coat-tail settlements. But in cases in which incompleteness does make a difference, it is liable to have two sorts of effects.

(1) *Wage inflation.* It may cause the periodic rate of wage inflation to be less than it would otherwise have been (and it can never have the opposite effect).* For it is *perceived* conflict over relativities which generates inflation in the present type of model, and the failure of some groups to compare themselves with others may obscure important disagreements between them. Not least, it may cause settlements which would otherwise have been in the critical subset to become coat-tail settlements.

Figure 5.11, for example, which is simply an adaptation of figure 5.2, illustrates a case in which C is a hidden group – in which, that is, groups A and B do not know how much C is paid, even though C is fully informed about their pay. The outcome is perpetual oscillation around the triangle marked in the diagram. Groups A and B, however, do not perceive that relativities are in two-dimensional motion; they are aware only of the relativity *A/B*, which accordingly oscillates between their respective norms. Group C's invisibility has thus caused its settlements to leave the critical subset; the result is wage inflation of 100 per cent per period, which is less than half the rate that would be generated if each group's comparisons were complete.

Conversely, the omission of an otherwise-most-favourable com-

* This is not true, though, of certain other types of imperfect information. Exaggerated information about the size of pay settlements, for example, is likely to increase the rate of inflation.

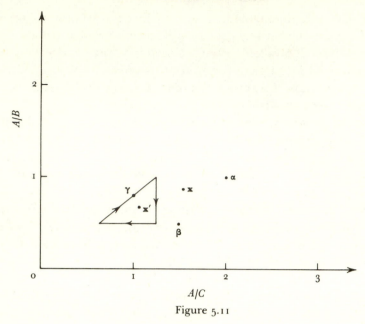

Figure 5.11

parison will obviously not reduce the periodic rate of wage inflation if it does not affect the critical subset – if, that is, the group whose comparisons are restricted would otherwise have made a coat-tail settlement. Figure 5.12, for example, is a variant of figure 5.9 in which group A (which would otherwise have made a coat-tail settlement) is ignorant of group C's pay and thus bases the size of its settlements instead on comparisons with group B. But the periodic rate of wage inflation, being governed exclusively by the conflict between groups B and C over B/C, is unaltered.

(2) *Relativities.* As far as any particular group is concerned, it is always an advantage (in cases in which incompleteness makes a difference) to be excluded from the comparisons of other groups, and especially to be in a position where others cannot find out what one is paid. For this will cause the periodic average value of relativities to lie closer to one's region of complete satisfaction than would otherwise have been the case. In figure 5.11, for example, where C is a hidden group, the periodic average value of relativities (assuming for simplicity equal intervals between settlements) is x', which is unambiguously closer to C's region of complete satisfaction than x, which is what the periodic average would have been had all comparisons been complete.

128

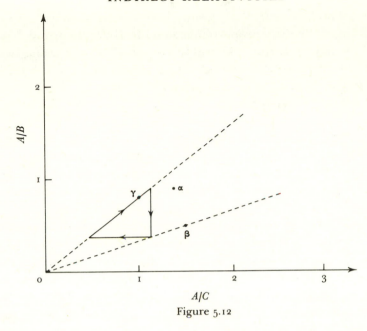

Figure 5.12

Conversely, it is always a disadvantage (in cases in which incompleteness makes a difference) for other groups to be excluded from one's own comparisons, and especially not to know how much other groups are paid. In figure 5.12, for instance, group A evidently suffers as a result of its ignorance of group C's pay, since (as may be seen by comparison with figure 5.9) this causes the triangular path around which relativities oscillate to shift towards the origin, away from A's region of complete satisfaction.

5.4 NORMATIVE AND ANOMIC PRESSURES: SIMPLE MODELS

All anomic influences on pay were excluded from the three preceding sections by the assumption that settlements are invariably made strictly in accordance with normative considerations. In the four remaining sections of this chapter I shall explore, in stages, the consequences of relaxing this useful but extremely unrealistic assumption.

(i) *Local shortages*

Let us first suppose that pay is governed solely by normative forces in all pay groups but one, in which, as a result of excess demand, the

anomically optimal wage persistently exceeds the normatively prescribed wage by a given proportional amount. In such a group, it was
argued in chapter 4, the wage will always be set in accordance with
anomic considerations, simply because employees have no objection
to being paid at more than they consider a fair rate. This can have
three sorts of repercussions.

(1) *Wage inflation.* It may cause the periodic rate of wage inflation to
be higher than it would be if all settlements were normatively
determined. Whether or not it does so depends, of course, on whether
or not the pay settlements of the group concerned are in the critical
subset.

One possibility is that the settlements of the group concerned,
perhaps because it is invisible, are coat-tail settlements regardless of
whether they are normatively or anomically determined. In this case
the rate of wage inflation will evidently be unaffected. The group
concerned, however, will be a coat-tail group of a type different from
those considered earlier, in that it will be carried along not by normative but by anomic pressures.

A second possibility is that the settlements of the group concerned
would be in the critical subset even if they were normatively determined – in which case any settlement in excess of the normatively
prescribed wage is bound to increase inflation. This possibility is
illustrated in figure 5.13, an adaptation of figure 5.2, in which a
shortage causes group A's pay to be set at the anomically optimal level,
$\hat{a}$, rather than at the normatively prescribed level, $\bar{a}$.

A third possibility is that the shortage in question may cause a
settlement which would otherwise have been a coat-tail settlement to
enter the critical subset, which again is bound to increase the rate of
wage inflation (though by less than if the settlement had been in the
critical subset to begin with). This last possibility is illustrated in figure
5.14, which is an adaptation of figure 5.9. Had group A's pay been set
at $\bar{a}$, its settlement would have been a coat-tail settlement. But $\hat{a}$
exceeds $\bar{a}$ by so much as to cause group B's most favourable comparison
to be with the pay of group A (rather than group C), thus bringing
A's settlement into the critical subset and raising the periodic rate of
wage inflation.

In the cases of the sort illustrated in figures 5.13 and 5.14, wage
inflation is generated, and its speed is governed, by the interaction of

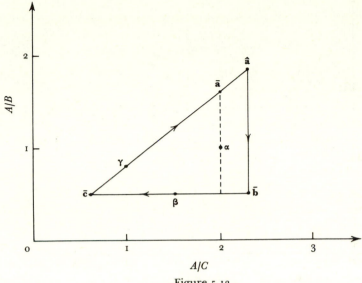

Figure 5.13

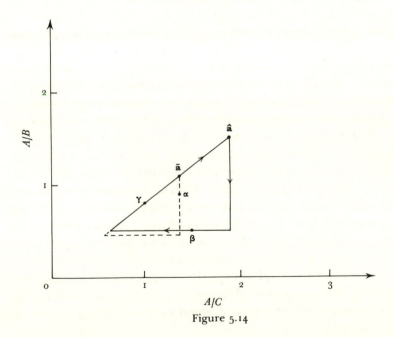

Figure 5.14

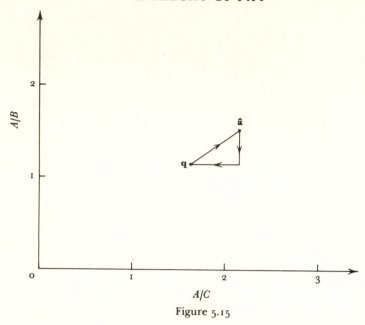

Figure 5.15

two quite different types of conflict over pay relativities. One is conflict between different norms. The other is conflict between normative and anomic pressures. It was shown in earlier sections of this chapter that the former type of conflict alone is sufficient to generate wage inflation. The same is true of the latter. Shortages of labour in one or more pay groups could cause enduring wage inflation even if pay norms were such that a region of satiation existed, and even if there were no anticipation.

Consider, for example, figure 5.15, in which all three groups are assumed to share the same norm, **q**, but in which a persistent shortage of labour in group A causes its pay settlements to exceed their normatively prescribed level. In each period, with a view to restoring fair relativities, groups B and C also obtain wage increases. The result (given the sequence ABC) is that relativities oscillate around the triangle marked in the diagram, and that the general money wage level rises at a periodic rate governed straightforwardly by the extent of the conflict between normative and anomic forces over group A's relative pay.

It was mentioned earlier that when wage inflation is generated by conflict between different norms, adaptive expectations tend to cause the process continually to accelerate, provided that at least two conflicting groups in the critical subset anticipate the future in this way. The same conclusion holds for conflict between normative and anomic pressures, and for the same basic reason. Consider, for example, the case illustrated in figure 5.15. There is no periodic average value of relativities which can satisfy both the employer in group A and the employees in (say) group B. Thus even if both parties anticipate future wage increases, one of them is bound to be disappointed each period; the disappointed party will adapt its expectations upwards and will enlarge the proportional size of its next pay settlement; wage inflation will therefore (on present assumptions) persistently accelerate.

(2) *Relativities.* Whether or not a shortage of labour in one pay group increases the periodic rate of wage inflation, it will always (assuming the sequence of, and intervals between, settlements to be given) increase the periodic average relative wage of the group concerned. This effect will be more pronounced in cases in which the periodic rate of wage inflation is unaffected, for the obvious reason that there are fewer (and in a three-group economy, no) induced and potentially offsetting changes in the behaviour of other groups.

If, say, group A's pay settlements are 20 per cent larger than they would otherwise have been, and no other group's settlements are altered, A must at every stage of the proceedings be 20 per cent better off relative to every other group. But group A will gain even if, as in figure 5.13, its 20 per cent larger settlements cause every other group's settlements to increase by 20 per cent. For at the stage at which all other groups have retaliated (point c̄ in the diagram), A is no worse off than it would otherwise have been, and at every other stage (points â and b̄) it is better off, relative to at least one other group. On average, however, the gain is less than 20 per cent (although group A's employer may have anticipated this in fixing the size of its settlements).

(3) *Sequence and intervals.* In addition, this type of labour shortage may cause the settlements of the group concerned to occur sooner than they would otherwise have done – and it is important to emphasise that in general the sequence and timing of settlements is affected not only by normative pressures of the sort discussed on pp. 113–15 but also by anomic pressures.

In so far as the pay of the group concerned does not affect the size of the settlements made by other groups, a change in the timing of its settlements is unlikely to affect the timing of their settlements; thus the result will simply be an alteration of relative intervals (and perhaps sequence) which tends to enhance the periodic average position of the group in question. But to the extent that the timing of other groups' settlements also changes, and especially if the group concerned is in the critical subset, the particulars of the outcome are less easy to predict – although one possible consequence is a reduction in the average interval between settlements, which would increase the calendar rate of wage inflation relative to the periodic rate.

It is also worth noting that the sequence in which settlements occur, which usually affects the intensity of conflict between differing norms (and hence the periodic rate of wage inflation), may in addition affect the degree of conflict between normative and anomic pressures. For the size of the proportional excess, in a group in which there is a labour shortage, of the anomically optimal wage over the normatively prescribed wage may depend on the state of relativities at the point at which its settlement is made, which is likely in turn to depend on the sequence in which previous settlements have occurred.

(ii)   *Local surpluses*

Let us now consider cases in which the anomically optimal wage is *less* than the normatively prescribed wage. In any such case, it was argued in chapter 4, there are several possible types of outcome. One is that the normatively prescribed wage will prevail. But it is also possible that pay will be set below the normatively prescribed level (though not necessarily so low as the anomically optimal level), for one of three reasons. (a) The employees in question may be too weak to offset the anomic pressures on their employer. (b) Though in principle sufficiently powerful to enforce the normatively prescribed wage, the employees may be insufficiently militant – insufficiently sensitive to unfairness in relative terms (perhaps because their real wages are for other reasons rising rapidly). (c) Though both sufficiently powerful and sufficiently militant, the employees may choose to keep their pay below the normatively prescribed level in order to avoid redundancies.

All three causes have similar effects, which I shall analyse in the same

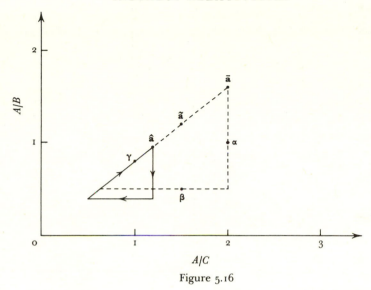

Figure 5.16

way as with local shortages, assuming that pay is set strictly in accordance with normative considerations in all pay groups but one, where it is set below the normatively prescribed level at each settlement by a given proportional amount.

(1) *Wage inflation.* If, in the absence of anomic pressures, the group in question would have made coat-tail settlements, then whether or not its pay is below the normatively prescribed level will not affect the periodic rate of wage inflation. A second possibility, however, is that anomic pressures will cause the group to make coat-tail settlements, although it would otherwise have been in the critical subset. In this case, the periodic rate of wage inflation will clearly be lower than it would be if all settlements were strictly normatively determined, although not by so much as might be supposed from the size of the difference between the actual wage settlements of the group concerned and its normatively prescribed settlements.

This second possibility is illustrated in figure 5.16, another adaptation of figure 5.2, in which it is assumed that group A's pay is set at the anomically optimal level, $\hat{a}$. The periodic rate of wage inflation is therefore determined solely by normative conflict between groups B and C over the relativity B/C, while group A is another example of a species mentioned earlier – a coat-tail group carried along by anomic,

135

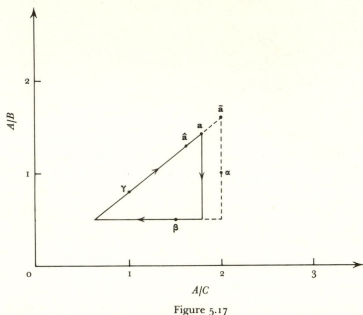

Figure 5.17

rather than normative, pressures. Group A would in fact be a coat-tail group if its pay were set at any level below that corresponding to point **ā** in the diagram; but in the range between **ā** and **â**, group A would become an example of yet another species of coat-tail groups – those carried along partly by normative and partly by anomic pressures.

A third possibility is that, even though reduced by anomic pressures, the settlements of the group concerned remain within the critical subset – in which case the periodic rate of wage inflation will be not only reduced but reduced in direct proportion to the size of the gap between the actual settlements of the group in question and its normatively prescribed settlements. Such a case is illustrated in figure 5.17, another variant of figure 5.2, in which group A's pay is set roughly midway between its anomically optimal and its normatively prescribed level. The rate of wage inflation is still determined entirely by conflict between different norms, but the *intensity* of the conflict has been damped by anomic pressures. Figure 5.17 is thus an example of a very important class of cases – those in which surpluses reduce the rate of wage inflation by causing the actual degree of conflict between groups with different norms to be less than the maximum potential degree of conflict.

136

The character of the outcome would have been rather different had it been assumed that group A in figure 5.17 was so weak (or apathetic or afraid of redundancies) that its pay was set not merely below the normatively prescribed level but actually at the anomically optimal level. Group A's settlements would still have been in the critical subset; but there would have been an element of conflict between normative and anomic pressures (as well as between different norms) contributing to the determination of the periodic rate of wage inflation. This makes it clear, by the way, that conflict between normative and anomic pressures is not confined (as might be supposed from earlier examples) to cases of shortage; it can exist, that is, even when no group is paid more than its normatively prescribed wage.*

(2) *Relativities, sequence and intervals.* The other effects of a local surplus, insofar as it depresses the pay settlements of the group concerned below their normatively prescribed level, are roughly the opposite of the effects of a local shortage, and may therefore be considered briefly.

The periodic average relative pay of the group concerned will be lower than would otherwise have been the case, whether or not the periodic rate of wage inflation is reduced, although the deterioration will tend to be more pronounced in cases in which the rate of inflation is not affected or is affected (as in figure 5.16) only to a limited extent.

The timing of the group's settlements may also be affected. In particular, they may occur later than they would otherwise have done. By altering the relative intervals between settlements, this may tend further to depress the group's periodic average relative pay. By altering the sequence in which settlements occur, it may change the membership of (or the sequence in which settlements occur within) the critical subset, thus tending to alter the periodic rate of wage inflation. And by lengthening the average interval between settlements, it may reduce the calendar rate of wage inflation relative to the periodic rate.

* If, however, pay norms were such that a region of satiation existed, then to set the pay of one (or more than one) group below the normatively prescribed level could not cause enduring wage inflation – as could happen if its pay were set *above* the normatively prescribed level. The reason for this asymmetry is that paying less than the norm would not give rise to any *conflict* over relativities. Other groups would not object to being more than fairly paid relative to the group concerned, and so would not persistently seek to change their own rates of pay in response.

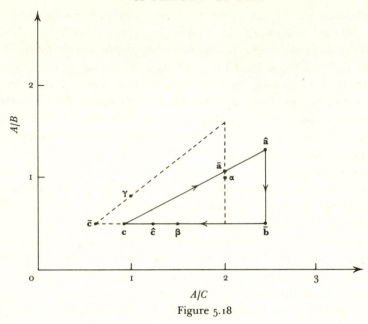

Figure 5.18

(iii) *Shortage and surpluses*

In practice, anomic pressures are likely to drive pay above the normatively prescribed level in some groups and below it in others, and to have no effect in yet other groups, with results that (on present assumptions) are a fairly straightforward mixture of those considered separately above. The precise nature of the mixture will depend on which groups are paid above the norm and which below, and to what extent, as well as on the character of their norms, the completeness of their comparisons, and the amount and type of anticipation.

Consider, for example, figure 5.18, which illustrates a case in which all comparisons are complete, settlements occur in the sequence ABC, and there is no anticipation. It is assumed that anomic pressures bid group A's pay above its normatively prescribed level to a given degree at each settlement, and hold group C's pay below its normatively prescribed level to a given degree at each settlement, while group B's pay is set strictly in accordance with normative considerations. Relativities thus oscillate around the triangular path marked with a continuous line. This may be compared with the triangle marked with broken lines, which shows what the outcome would be if, other things being equal, the pay of all three groups were set strictly in accordance with normative considerations.

It is apparent that in this instance anomic pressures decrease the periodic rate of wage inflation, the effects of 'underpayment' in group C more than offsetting the effects of 'overpayment' in group A. There are no coat-tail settlements, and the rate of inflation is determined partly by damped normative conflict between groups B and C and partly by conflict between normative and anomic pressures on group A's relative pay.

It is also apparent, since the triangular path is shifted to the right, that anomic pressures reduce group C's periodic average pay relative to both group A and group B. Group A, however, although its pay is set above the norm, tends to become worse off relative to group B (as may be seen from the reduced height of the triangle), the reason being that in the absence of anomic pressures C's settlements would have been at a lower value of B/C, which would have caused A's settlements, though at a lower value of A/C, to have been at a higher value of A/B. Group B thus tends to gain relative to both other groups.

The anomic pressures on groups A and C could also affect the timing of their settlements, hastening the former and delaying the latter. This might alter only the relative intervals between settlements, tending to improve the periodic average position of A and to worsen that of C. But it might also affect the calendar length of each period, thus changing the calendar rate of wage inflation relative to the periodic rate. In addition, it might alter the sequence of settlements, which could be a further source of change both in the periodic rate of wage inflation and in the periodic average value of relativities.

Finally, it is worth noting that the argument of the present section is not confined, as some of the examples may have suggested, to cases in which employees attempt directly to coerce employers into conforming with their norms. It applies also to the sort of case (discussed on pp. 10, 73) in which, to the same end, the supply of labour is artificially restricted. In cases of pure supply restriction, of course, the wage is always set at its anomically 'optimal' level; but if the degree of restriction is appropriate, the anomically optimal wage coincides with the normatively prescribed wage.

5.5 NORMATIVE AND ANOMIC PRESSURES: ANOMIC INTERDEPENDENCE

In discussing the impact of anomic pressures in the previous section I took the nature of the outcome in each group as given, and concentrated on the consequences of pay being set at, above or below the normatively prescribed level in particular groups. But one must also recognise that the character of the anomic pressures (and thus in many cases the nature of the outcome) in any given group is influenced by the nature of the outcomes in other groups. In other words, although most of this chapter has been devoted to analysing normative interdependence between pay settlements in different groups, nothing has yet been said about anomic interdependence (which is, of course, the basis of orthodox general equilibrium theory).

I shall approach the complicated subject of anomic interdependence in a comparatively simple way, by considering two hypothetical pay groups, I and J. I shall enquire how, through anomic channels, the absolute money level of group J's pay might be affected by group I's pay being set, for normative reasons, above the anomically optimal level. In doing this, I shall take everything else as given, including the levels of pay in all other groups. I shall proceed in three distinct steps.

(i) *Demand and supply*

The first step is to review the various ways in which conditions of demand and supply in group J might be affected by a higher level of pay in group I.

(1) *Demand.* The demand for labour in group J may be altered because the services of its members are substitutable for the services of those in group I, either directly (in the production of a given commodity) or indirectly (through changes in the commodity composition of consumption or government expenditure). Whether the effect is positive or negative will depend on the elasticity of the demand for labour in group I: if it is high, an increase in group I's pay will tend to increase demand in group J; but if it is low, an increase in group I's pay will tend to reduce demand in group J because expenditure on the services of group I will absorb a greater proportion of aggregate demand. Higher pay in group I would also tend to reduce demand

in group J if the services of the two groups were complementary in production or consumption.

A higher level of pay in group I will alter the income and hence the expenditure of its members, and this also may affect the demand for group J's services, although whether the effect is positive or negative will again depend on the elasticity of the demand for labour in group I. If, for example, this elasticity were large, higher pay in group I, other things being equal, would cause the total pay of its members to be lower, which would tend to reduce demand in group J. The size of the change in demand in group J (whatever its direction) will depend on the expenditure pattern of those in group I, and on their propensity to save, as well as on the level and progressivity of the taxes to which they are subject.

A higher level of pay in group I will tend to increase the general price level in the economy. There are several ways in which this might alter the demand for labour in group J. For example, if people wished to maintain the real value of their stocks of financial assets, it might lower expenditure on consumption goods. Or it might, by raising the transactions demand for money, increase the money rate of interest, which could reduce the level of certain sorts of investment expenditure. Alternatively, by raising the expected future rate of price inflation, it might reduce the expected real rate of interest associated with any given money rate of interest, and might thus tend to stimulate certain types of consumption and investment.

(2) *Supply.* The effect of a higher wage in group I on the supply of labour to group J depends on the potential for mobility between them, both among those currently employed in these two groups and among recruits from elsewhere. This in turn depends on the propinquity of the places of employment of the two groups, and on the availability of information. It also depends on the relationship between the skills required in the two groups – it being much harder, say, for labourers to become joiners, or for joiners to become welders, at any rate in a short time, than for joiners to become labourers, or for labourers (or joiners or welders) to switch from one firm to another. Mobility may also be affected by employment norms, especially those concerning qualifications and hiring and firing practices.

To the extent that mobility between the groups is possible (and the possibilities need not be symmetrical), setting the wage in group I above its anomically optimal level will tend to have two sorts of effect.

(a) By reducing the level of employment in group I (to an extent dependent on the elasticity of demand there), it will tend to increase the *size* of the supply of labour to group J.

(b) By making group I more attractive to employees, and by making the employer in group I more reluctant (see pp. 54, 97–9) to hire low quality workers, it will tend to reduce the *quality* (in terms of innate ability, formal training and transferable experience) of the supply of labour to group J. The strength of this tendency will depend on the degree of similarity between the skills required in the two groups – the closeness of the correlation between the relative quality of any given employee's performance in one group and the relative quality of his performance in the other group.* It will also depend, over any given period, on the rate at which (through natural wastage, dismissals or expansion) vacancies arise in group I.

The two tendencies are not independent of one another. The improvement in the quality of the labour supply to group I might affect the extent of the reduction in employment there, and might thus affect the extent of the increase in the size of group J's labour supply. Likewise, the induced reduction in the employment in group I (or the initial superiority of the quality of its labour force) might be so great that the quality of group J's labour supply, even though reduced relative to group I, would actually rise in absolute terms.

(ii) *Anomic pressures*

The second step is to examine the ways in which these changes in demand and supply conditions might alter the anomically optimal level of the wage in group J.

A change in the demand for labour in group J need not alter the anomically optimal wage – if the supply of labour is very elastic, it will merely alter the anomically optimal level of employment. But to the extent that (over any given period of time) the supply of labour to group J is inelastic, whether because of a need to make use of scarce talents or because of lags, ignorance and other types of friction, a change in the demand for labour will tend to change the anomically optimal wage in the same direction.

---

* If this correlation were zero, as it might be if the two groups contained very dissimilar occupations, there would be no tendency for the quality of group J's labour supply to decline. If the correlation were negative (although this is exceedingly unlikely), the tendency would be reversed.

Similarly, although an increase in the size of the labour supply to group J will usually tend to reduce the anomically optimal wage, it need not do so. If the demand for labour were very elastic it would affect (though perhaps not before some time had elapsed) only the anomically optimal level of employment. And if the anomically optimal wage in group J were already at a floor established by, say, the attractions of leisure, a larger supply of labour might affect neither the anomically optimal wage nor the anomically optimal level of employment.

A decrease in the (absolute) quality of group J's labour supply will usually tend to raise the anomically optimal wage, to a degree dependent on the intensity of the employer's need to maintain the quality of his labour force. But again there are exceptions. For example, the pool of surplus labour seeking work in group J might already be so large that, even if its average quality were diluted somewhat, the employer would still have plenty of applicants of adequate quality.

The effect of group I's pay being set above its anomically optimal level will therefore depend on which, if any, of the various demand and supply tendencies are relevant, on the directions in which they pull, and on their relative strengths and speeds. The anomically optimal level of group J's money wage may thus be unaffected, or it may rise or fall – or do both, over different time horizons.

(iii) *Outcomes*

The third step is to recall the effect of a change in group J's anomically optimal wage on its actual wage. This depends on the relative strength of normative and anomic pressures, and on whether the anomically optimal wage is greater or less than the normatively prescribed wage (and it should be borne in mind that changes in I may affect also the normatively prescribed level of J).

If the employees in group J are very weak, or if normative pressures hold the actual wage a given distance above the anomically optimal wage, or if the anomically optimal wage exceeds the normatively prescribed wage, then any change in the anomically optimal wage will be fully reflected in the actual wage. But if the anomically optimal wage is below the normatively prescribed wage and the employees in group J are powerful, then changes in the anomically optimal wage may have no effect, or only a limited effect, on the actual wage. For example, the employees in group J may be able strictly to enforce the normatively prescribed wage, regardless (within certain limits) of how far it lies above the anomically optimal wage; or, in the face of a decline in the anomically optimal wage, they may be able to widen the gap between it and the actual wage, even though the latter is below its normatively prescribed level.

There is also another way in which a change in the anomically optimal wage might tend to move the actual wage in the same direction, even if the employees in group J were very powerful, which is by altering the number of redundancies (if any) that would result from setting the wage at (or at any given distance below) its normatively prescribed level. For this might alter the preferences of the employees in group J concerning the relationship between the actual wage and the normatively prescribed wage. It is also possible that induced changes in demand and supply conditions of the sort discussed above might alter the amount of normative pressure that the employees in group J can exert on their employer (for example by changing the size of the costs which a strike would impose), though not necessarily by enough to affect the nature of the outcome.

In addition, it should be remembered that any tendency for the actual wage to change may be frustrated by government intervention. For example, a strictly enforced minimum wage law might prevent a decline in the anomically optimal wage in group J (induced by a rise in group I's pay) from depressing the actual wage, even in the absence of normative pressures.

(iv) *Implications*

As these three steps make clear, the anomic chain of influence from the pay of any one group to the pay of any other group is in a logical sense a long one, and one whose character can vary widely according to a large number of attendant circumstances. It may be broken completely at one point or another, it may work in a positive or a negative direction, it may produce a large or a small effect, and it may act quickly or slowly. There are, moreoever, many such anomic chains of influence in the economy (twice as many, in fact, as there are pairs of pay groups), and the character of each of them is dependent on the character of some or all of the others.

For these reasons, it is virtually impossible to introduce anomic interdependence into the present (or indeed any) theoretical model in a way which is both comprehensive and comprehensible. But it is easy enough to explain its main implications (although I shall not fully develop some of the more specifically macroeconomic implications until the last section of the chapter).

(1) *Relativities.* Anomic interdependence implies that the influence of normative pressures on a group's periodic average relative wage cannot in general be gauged simply by comparing its actual wage with its anomically optimal wage. For the anomically optimal wage itself may be indirectly affected by normative pressures on the pay of other groups.

In some cases, anomic interdependence will cause the group concerned to benefit from the normative exertions of other groups. For example, assuming the pay of private sector secretaries to be anomically determined, suppose that the pay of government secretaries were set above the anomically optimal level for normative reasons. By making it harder for employers in the private sector to attract and retain good secretaries, this might cause private sector secretarial pay to be higher relative to other jobs (though perhaps lower relative to government secretarial pay) than it would otherwise have been.

In other cases, however, anomic interdependence will have quite the opposite effect. The high pay of secretaries in general, to continue the example, might reduce the number of secretaries hired by both the government and the private sector. This in turn might cause more people to seek work as (say) shop assistants, which if shop assistants were a weak group might depress their pay below what it would otherwise have been, relative both to secretaries and to workers in other jobs.

(2) *Wage inflation.* The implications of anomic interdependence for the process of wage inflation in the present type of model may best be explained by considering three different sorts of possibility. In each case I shall assume for simplicity (a) that the pay settlements of all groups but one are strictly normatively determined and (b) that the pay of the remaining group is at each settlement fixed either at its anomically optimal level or at some constant proportional distance above it.

Consider first the case of a group whose anomically optimal wage, as a result of particular sorts of anomic interdependence, happens to *rise at exactly the same rate* as the normatively determined wages of other groups. By virtue of (b) above, its actual wage must also rise at the same rate, thus maintaining relativities unchanged from period to period. This corresponds with the assumptions made in the examples depicted in figures 5.13 to 5.18. But the interpretation of these examples is altered.

The settlements of the group concerned (as in the case of group A in figure 5.16) may lie outside the critical subset, and may thus have no influence on the periodic rate of wage inflation. Even so, anomic interdependence provides an explanation for something that was left unexplained in the previous section, namely *how*, when wage inflation is generated by normative conflict, a group whose actual wage is strictly tied to its anomically optimal wage may nonetheless be a coat-tail group. For such a group may keep up with the pack simply because the demand for its services rises as a consequence of increases in the income and expenditure of other groups and because higher wages in other groups oblige its employer to pay more in order to maintain the quality of his labour force.

Anomic interdependence has even more significant implications when the settlements of the group concerned (as in the case of group A in figure 5.17) are in the critical subset and thus influence the rate of wage inflation. For it then implies that the contribution of anomic forces, which may either dampen or exacerbate the degree of conflict within the critical subset, is endogenous in character. Not only, that is, are the effects of normative forces modified in various ways by anomic pressures, but these anomic pressures are themselves shaped by normative forces. The influence of anomic pressures should thus be regarded not as something external to the basic model, but as an integral and internally generated part of the wage–wage spiral.*

Consider, to take a very simple example, two industries, say steel manufacturing and food processing, in the former of which the work is inherently much less attractive. Suppose that for normative reasons the employees in the food industry drive their pay at each settlement up to whatever level is prevailing in the steel industry. Suppose

* For this reason, anomic interdependence may affect whether or not the settlements of a particular group are in the critical subset. For important anomic influences on the settlements of a group in the critical subset may stem from the normative settlements of another group which, but for anomic interdependence, would have been a coat-tail group.

further that, in order to maintain the quality of his labour force in the face of the unattractive nature of the work in his industry (and despite a considerable surplus of low quality labour), the employer in the steel industry wishes to fix the pay of his employees at each settlement 25 per cent above whatever level is prevailing in the food industry, which is, let us assume, more than his employees would demand on normative grounds. The obvious result of this conflict between normative and anomic pressures is an endogenously generated escalation of pay in the two industries. In each period a wage increase caused by a shortage of labour in the steel industry rekindles normative pressures for a wage increase in the food industry, which in turn recreates the shortage in the steel industry.

(3) *Wage inflation: limping and galloping.* Let us consider next the case of a group whose anomically optimal wage, as a result of particular sorts of anomic interdependence, is *pulled up* by the normatively determined wage increases of other groups, *but at a slower rate.* Since the actual wage of the group concerned is by assumption tied to its anomically optimal wage, its relative position must deteriorate over time.

In this sort of case, relativities clearly cannot tend to oscillate perpetually around one specific path – which implies, among other things, that any illustrative diagram will look rather different from those so far drawn in this chapter. Figure 5.19, for example (which assumes complete comparisons, no anticipation, and settlements in the sequence ABC), illustrates a case in which group C's pay, although it increases in absolute terms at each settlement, falls further and further behind the strictly normatively determined pay of groups A and B. The triangular path around which relativities oscillate, which starts from c^1 (superscripts refer to periods) accordingly tends to move progressively to the right.

If the group concerned is initially in the critical subset (as is the case with group C in figure 5.19), and so long as it remains there, the proportional wage increases of all the groups in the critical subset will become smaller and smaller from period to period, thus tending to decelerate the rate of wage inflation. The underlying reason, of course, is that anomic interdependence is causing the degree of conflict within the critical subset to decline over time, either by damping the conflict between different norms or by reducing the intensity of conflict

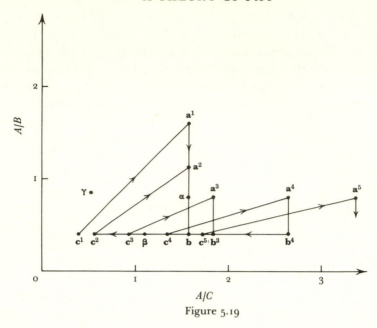

A/C

Figure 5.19

between normative and anomic pressures. Successive normatively determined wage rises in the food industry (to pursue an earlier example) might cause the demand for labour there to decline, and hence the supply of labour to the steel industry to increase, to such an extent that the anomically determined excess of the steel industry wage over the food industry wage was reduced from 25 per cent to 20 per cent, then to 15 per cent, and so on.

On present assumptions, the settlements of a group of this sort will eventually drop out of the critical subset (as is the case with group C in figure 5.19 after period two), since its relative pay will eventually decline so far that it ceases to be the most favourable comparison for any of the other groups in the subset. Beyond this point, the group concerned (which might of course have been outside the critical subset to begin with) will become a *limping coat-tail* group which, like other coat-tail groups, has no influence on the rate at which wages in the critical subset are increasing. But unlike the coat-tail groups so far considered in this chapter, its settlements will still have some influence on the rate of wage inflation. For the rate of wage inflation is an average of the rates of wage increase in all individual groups; and if the pay of one group rises more slowly than the rest, it must reduce the average.

148

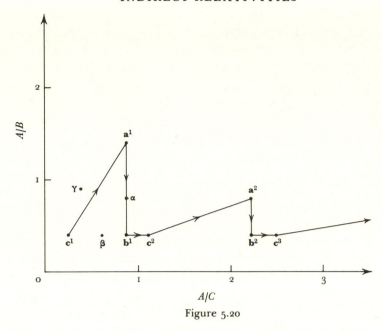

A/C

Figure 5.20

It is possible, incidentally, that anomic interdependence may have the opposite effect, causing the pay of one group to rise faster than the normatively determined pay of other groups. The implications of this possibility, which I shall call *galloping*, are roughly the reverse of those outlined in the previous two paragraphs.

(4) *Wage inflation: punch-bag groups.* Consider finally the case of a group whose anomically optimal wage, because of particular sorts of anomic interdependence, actually *declines in absolute terms* as a result of normatively determined wage increases in other groups, which by assumption depresses its actual wage to an equal degree.

In this sort of case, the appearance of any illustrative diagram will differ substantially from that of the previous diagrams in this chapter, since the group concerned will systematically move in the 'wrong' direction. Consider, for example, figure 5.20, whose assumptions are similar to those of figure 5.19 except that group C's absolute pay is assumed to decline, rather than increase, at each settlement. The result is not (as in previous examples) oscillation around a triangular path, but an irregular progress towards the right. Group C's relative pay thus persistently (and in this example rapidly) declines, unless or until it hits some floor.

A group of this sort, since it in effect always turns the other cheek, cannot be involved in sustained conflict with other groups, and hence cannot remain in the critical subset for more than one period. Nor indeed can a group of this sort sensibly be described as a coat-tail group; it is, rather, a *punch-bag* group. But it will affect the rate of wage inflation in the same way as (though, ceteris paribus, to a greater extent than) a limping coat-tail group, namely by holding down the *average* rate at which wages in the economy are increasing.

5.6 INTERNAL RELATIVITIES AND MULTIPLE NORMS

So far in this chapter I have assumed for simplicity that in each of the various pay groups in the economy there is only one wage rate and only one norm. In this section I shall consider the consequences of relaxing these two assumptions, drawing on the discussion in chapter 4 of internal relativities and multiple norms in the context of a single pay group.

(i) *Internal relativities*

Whenever a pay group contains more than one job or more than one type of employee, it must also contain a corresponding number of distinct (though not necessarily unequal) wage rates. But, bearing in mind that the essence of a pay group is that the pay of all the employees within it is settled jointly, it is in principle easy to fit internal relativities into the type of model developed in this chapter. For a single pay group containing several wage rates is formally identical to several pay groups, each containing a single wage rate, which happen (a) to make simultaneous settlements and (b) to share the same (normatively or anomically determined) objective.

It is somewhat less easy to incorporate internal relativities into the sort of diagram used in this chapter, which cannot accommodate more than three different wage rates. The best one can do is to illustrate a hypothetical economy with two pay groups, AB (which contains two wage rates) and C (which contains one).

(1) *Normative pressures.* If all pay settlements were made strictly in accordance with normative considerations (and I shall continue to assume for the time being that there is only one norm per pay group), the introduction of internal relativities would make no substantive difference to the type of model developed in this chapter. For the

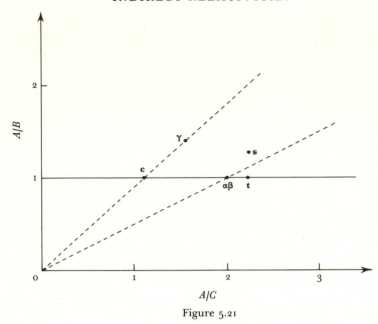

Figure 5.21

internal relativities of each pay group would be directly determined by the relevant aspects of its norm, and would be unaffected by the behaviour of pay in other groups. Since all the wage rates in each group are fixed simultaneously, internal relativities (barring changes in norms themselves) would remain constant over time, both within and between periods, while the external relativities between groups would oscillate in much the same way as if each group contained only one wage rate. The sole difference would be that each group's most favourable comparison would in general be not with the pay of some other group as a whole, but with one particular wage rate within some other group.

Consider, for example, figure 5.21, in which group C's norm is labelled γ and group AB's norm αβ. Group AB will always set the wage rates *A* and *B* at levels such that the internal relativity *A/B* conforms with its norm, and thus the outcome must at every stage lie somewhere on the horizontal line through αβ. Because there is only one other wage rate in the economy, group AB does not face the problem of inconsistent comparisons, and can therefore, whenever it makes a settlement, set the wage rates *A* and *B* so that relativities conform exactly with its norm. But group C (assuming its comparisons to be

151

complete) must decide which of the two wage rates within group AB will be the basis of its own settlements. On the most favourable comparison principle, it will evidently choose B. As a result, and provided that there is no anticipation, relativities will tend to oscillate backwards and forwards between the points $\alpha\beta$ and c (there being only one possible sequence of settlements in a two-group economy), and the general money wage level will tend to rise at a periodic rate determined by the extent of the normative conflict between groups AB and C over the external relativity B/C.

(2) *Normative and anomic pressures.* When rates of pay are influenced also by anomic forces, the introduction of internal relativities has more of an impact on the character of the model. To begin with, it makes the model more complicated, since it increases the number of types of linkage that must be considered. The anomically appropriate configuration of external relativities between certain groups may be affected by normative pressures on internal relativities, both in the groups concerned and (because of anomic interdependence) in other groups. Anomic pressures may likewise cause the internal relativities of a given group to be affected by the behaviour of pay in other groups.

Without attempting completely to disentangle this complex web of inter-relationships, it is worth recalling one or two general points from the final section of chapter 4 and considering their implications for the model developed in the present chapter.

In discussing the interplay between normative and anomic pressures in the present chapter, I have always taken it for granted that a local shortage of labour (an excess of the anomically optimal over the normatively prescribed wage) will cause the pay of the employees concerned to be bid up at each settlement to the anomically optimal level. This ceases to be invariably true when there are strong normative pressures on internal relativities. For if the shortage is confined to a few of the categories of employee within a pay group, the employer may choose to pay these scarce categories below the anomically optimal level because the gains from doing otherwise would be outweighed by the costs of having to increase the pay of all the other employees in the group, or by the costs of resisting their demands for such an increase. Thus although a general shortage of labour in a pay group is bound to raise most or all of the wage rates within it, the connection between shortages and wage increases is not quite so automatic as might be supposed from the argument of the previous two sections.

Consider, for example, figure 5.21 again, and suppose that the anomically optimal levels of the wage rates A and B, given the level of pay in group C, are represented by the point s. This implies that at the normatively prescribed levels of A and B there would be a shortage in category A (since s is at higher values of A/C and A/B than $\alpha\beta$) and a surplus in category B (since s is at lower values of B/C and B/A than $\alpha\beta$). Ideally, the employer in group AB would like to set his wage rates at the point s. But if his employees (especially those in category B) are able and willing to enforce their norm, the employer's choice is confined to outcomes which are on the horizontal line through, and to the right of, $\alpha\beta$. He must choose, in other words, between paying neither category of employee above the norm and paying both of them above the norm.

In some circumstances, the latter alternative would be preferable, and the employer would choose some point such as t (which in this example would cause a higher periodic rate of wage inflation). But if the shortage in category A were not acute, or could not be alleviated without some change in internal relativities, or if the employees in category B were relatively numerous, the employer might well adhere strictly to the norm, $\alpha\beta$, with the result that the shortage in category A would have no effect on the outcome at all.

Normative pressures on internal pay relativities may be important also in cases in which there is a surplus of labour, especially because (as explained on pp. 95–101) they may be sufficient to deter an employer from setting certain wage rates low enough to eliminate excess supply. This applies to internal relativities not only between different jobs but also between different types of labour within specific jobs.

In particular, normative pressures on this latter sort of internal relativity have an influence on one important aspect of anomic interdependence. It was mentioned in the previous section that an employer in one group might need, in response to normatively determined wage increases in other groups, to raise his wage (or to refrain from cutting it by as much as he would otherwise have done), despite an increase in the size of his labour supply, in order to maintain the quality of his labour force. If the employer were completely unconstrained by normative pressures on internal relativities, this need would be less likely to exist. For even if the employer found it necessary to raise the pay of his good quality employees, he could at the same time take advantage of any increase in the supply of low quality labour by cutting its wage, with the result that the *average* wage of his employees might fall.

If, however, the employer is obliged by normative pressure to conform with the rate for the job principle (or to adopt some less extreme but still anomically sub-optimal degree of wage differentiation according to quality), he will not have the option of simultaneously raising the pay of good quality workers and cutting the pay of low quality workers – or, more generally, of widening the pay differential between them to an anomically appropriate extent. Thus, if in order to keep a certain number of good quality employees, the employer decides to increase their pay (or not to cut it by more than a certain amount), he must do much the same for his low quality employees, even if there is a surplus of low quality labour.

In this way, normative pressures on internal relativities between different qualities of labour unobtrusively exert an important influence on external relativities and on the process of wage inflation. They help to explain why employers in some groups choose, without direct coercion from their employees, to raise pay in response to normatively determined pay increases in other groups. They also help to explain why employers in certain other groups may choose not to cut wages far enough to absorb the whole of an increased supply of labour.

(ii) *Multiple norms*

To take account of the existence of a variety of pay norms within most pay groups, it is not necessary to alter the formal model developed in this chapter. But it is necessary to alter the way in which one interprets the model. In particular (and regardless of the number of internal wage rates involved), one must interpret what I have been calling *the* norm in each group as the *dominant* norm.

The concept of the dominant norm is no more than a convenient device to avoid the complexity of separately considering all the normative pressure functions within each group (in the way that was done for a single group in chapter 4). Its meaning is straightforward in cases in which, within a group, there is only one employee bargaining unit (whose objectives are a compromise between the norms of its individual members), and in cases in which, although there are several bargaining units with different objectives, one is unambiguously the most powerful. Its meaning is more elusive when there are several bargaining units of roughly similar power, although in most such cases there will exist some compromise (or range of compromises) between their various objectives at which the amount of normative pressure that they would collectively exert on their employer is minimised.

But in all cases, the implications of multiple norms for the interpretation of the model in this chapter are much the same.

(1) As a general rule, no pay settlement will exactly satisfy all the employees in a group. Even settlements which are strictly in accordance with the dominant norm will usually strike some employees as more than fair, while failing to satisfy others. In consequence, one should not take the phrase 'region of complete satisfaction' too literally, and one should recognise that the determinants of a group's militancy may be more complex than was suggested on page 113 above.

(2) Insofar as a given settlement is not anomically optimal, it becomes harder to say *whose* norms are prevailing. For in some circumstances the actions of the individuals and bargaining units whose norms lie closest to the actual outcome are a less important influence on the nature of the settlement than the actions of those whose norms lie further away. For example, the less than completely successful efforts of a powerful bargaining unit to bring pay into line with its norm may cause the outcome to coincide with the norm of a weak bargaining unit.

(3) In addition, whose norm (or what compromise between different norms) prevails may depend to some extent on the strength and character of anomic pressures, even though the employer does not choose the anomically optimal outcome. As a result, the existence of multiple norms also makes it harder to disentangle the influence on particular settlements of normative and anomic pressures.

5.7 MACROECONOMIC PERSPECTIVE

In this final section I shall put the theoretical model developed in this chapter into a macroeconomic context, sacrificing some microeconomic detail in order to get a broad but simple view of the behaviour of pay relativities, inflation and unemployment.

In this regard, much depends on the nature of the government's demand management policy. But the most important endogenous tendencies of the model can be explored by considering two extreme cases; that in which the government holds the aggregate monetary demand for labour constant, and that in which it manipulates demand in such a way as to maintain full employment (in a sense to be defined below).

Throughout the section I shall for simplicity take as given and unvarying a large number of factors. These include the nature of pay norms, the composition of reference sets, the power of particular groups of employees over their employers (except insofar as this is influenced by the level of unemployment), the configuration of pay groups, and the underlying determinants, listed on page 3, of the structure of the demand for and the supply of labour in particular submarkets.

(i) *Constant aggregate monetary demand for labour*

To begin with, then, I shall assume that the government manipulates taxes, the availability of credit, the exchange rate and so on in such a way that the aggregate monetary demand for labour in the economy with which we are concerned – or more accurately the aggregate money wage bill – remains constant. This extreme assumption conveniently simplifies the relationship between the general money wage level and the aggregate level of employment, since it means that an x per cent increase in the former straightforwardly causes an x per cent decrease in the latter. In addition, I shall assume that the economy is initially at or near full employment, and (for simplicity) that the size and demographic composition of the population remain constant.

I shall suppose that a struggle over pay relativities between certain groups is initially in progress, this struggle being the product partly of conflict between different norms (damped to some extent by anomic pressures) and partly of conflict between normative and anomic pressures. The pay settlements of these groups, which constitute the critical subset, are thus rising in money terms over time in the manner described in earlier sections – although for the time being I shall ignore the possibility of anticipation. In addition, there are many coat-tail groups, whose money wages are also rising, carried along with the settlements in the critical subset by normative or anomic pressures or some mixture of the two.

The critical subset and the coat-tail groups together I shall call the *first sector*. Since money wages throughout the first sector are rising (not necessarily all at the same speed), and since the aggregate monetary demand for labour and the underlying determinants of its composition are given, the level of employment in the first sector is falling. There is thus a growing excess supply of labour, especially low quality labour, to the first sector, whose effects I shall consider in two stages.

(1) *The second sector.* One effect of declining employment in the first sector is to increase the supply of labour to the remaining groups in the economy, which I shall collectively label the *second sector*. The distinguishing features of these groups are (a) that anomic forces are such that an increased supply of labour tends to depress their anomically optimal wage rates and (b) that the employees within them are unable or unwilling to prevent this depressing their actual wage rates. These, then, are the punch-bag groups.

Money wages in the second sector are thus falling (though not necessarily all at the same rate), which, by stimulating the demand for labour, is causing the level of employment in the second sector to rise. This both reduces the (average) rate of wage inflation in the economy and absorbs some of the labour released or not wanted by the first sector, thereby diminishing any tendency for unemployment to increase. Indeed, if money wages in the second sector fell far and fast enough, rising wages in the first sector would cause neither wage inflation nor unemployment, but would merely continually widen the wage differential between the two sectors.

But there are certain limits on how far and how fast money wages in the second sector can fall.

(1) In some punch-bag groups there may be sufficient normative pressure to prevent the employer cutting wages to the anomically optimal extent. Such pressure may be exerted directly on external relativities; alternatively, if the employer is forced to adhere more or less closely to the rate for the job principle, he may be inhibited from cutting wages by the need to retain at least some labour of reasonable quality.

(2) In some punch-bag groups the employer may be deterred from cutting wages beyond a certain point by the existence of reasonably strictly enforced minimum wage laws.

(3) In all punch-bag groups the possibility of cutting wages and

increasing employment is restricted by the existence of other sources of income and other sorts of activity. For as wages in the second sector fall lower and lower, fewer and fewer people will *want* jobs in it. Some will choose instead to live in leisure on social security benefits, others (especially young people and married women) on intra-familial transfers. In addition, people will increasingly turn on a whole or part-time basis to a range of non-leisure activities which yield some income in cash or kind – begging, crime, gardening and other subsistence agriculture, housework, odd jobs, baby-sitting and so on.

All these non-leisure activities are in one sense forms of employment, and I shall thus refer to them collectively as the *third sector*. As in the case of the second sector, an increase in the supply of labour to the third sector raises the level of employment and depresses average earnings there: the number of beggars increases, and the pickings of each become thinner; more and more incompetent gardeners turn to cultivating less and less productive vegetable patches; and so on. But unlike the second sector, this process in the third sector reduces neither the rate of wage inflation nor the level of unemployment. This is quite simply because the earnings of those in the third sector are excluded from official statistics of pay (both wages and salaries and self-employment income), and because those in the third sector are not officially classified as employed.

This is in part a reflection of the practical difficulty of gathering information about the third sector. But it mainly reflects a very basic and important value judgement about what constitutes employment, which excludes not only leisure but also activities which are dishonest, immoral, destructive or pitifully unproductive. The dividing line is neither unambiguous nor invariable. But some such governmental value judgement is always made, in both developed and developing countries, and I shall simply accept it.

There are thus several sorts of limit on the ability of employers in the second sector to cut wages. These limits, moreover, apply in general not to money but to real or relative wages. Legally prescribed minimum wage rates and social security benefits tend to be adjusted upwards over time in line with retail prices or average earnings;* and the monetary value of leisure and of the rewards of third sector

---

* See for example *Social Trends* (1976), Figure XII and Table 5.32. These adjustments reflect governmental norms (akin to pay norms) regarding the minimum acceptable level of income in real or relative terms.

activities such as theft or subsistence agriculture also tends to rise with prices or earnings. As a result, the proportional pay differentials between the first and second sectors will widen more and more slowly, and may eventually stop widening altogether (and once the relative pay of the second sector is falling more slowly than money wages in the first sector are rising, money wages in the second sector will begin to rise). Employment in the second sector will thus rise more and more slowly, and will absorb a smaller and smaller proportion of the labour released by the first sector.

(2) *The first sector again.* But whether it is absorbed by the second sector or spills over into unemployment, the growing excess supply of labour to the first sector will tend progressively to reduce the rate at which money wages in the first sector are increasing. For it will cause anomically optimal wage rates to rise more and more slowly (and in some cases to fall or to fall faster), which will have the following effects.

(1) It will directly reduce the rate of wage increase in groups in which the anomically optimal wage exceeds the normatively prescribed wage, and in groups in which the employees are very weak.

(2) In certain groups in which the employees are moderately powerful, it will increase the anomic pressures on the employer to the point where, despite sanctions from his employees, it becomes optimal for him to set the wage below, or further below, the normatively prescribed level (though perhaps further above the anomically optimal level).

(3) In certain groups it may reduce the power of the employees to coerce their employer, for example by making it easier for him to sack and replace a large fraction of his labour force, thus intensifying the tendency for pay to fall below its normatively prescribed level. (In other groups, however, waning demand may make the employer *more* vulnerable to coercion.)

(4) In some groups in which the employees remain powerful enough to enforce the normatively prescribed wage, or to maintain the actual wage at some given distance below it, the threat of redundancies may induce them to allow the actual wage to slip below or further below its normatively prescribed level (although this effect will not be of major importance unless or until the level of employment in the first sector is declining faster than the rate of natural wastage).

For these four reasons, certain coat-tail groups will tend to fall further and further behind the critical subset, and some will be

transformed into punch-bag groups. In addition, and more importantly, the degree of conflict within the critical subset will decline;
there will be less and less opposition between normative and anomic
pressures, and the conflicts between different norms will become
increasingly damped. In consequence, the rate at which money wages
are increasing in the critical subset, and hence the rate at which money
wages are increasing in the first sector as a whole, will tend to fall over
time.

(3) *Equilibrium unemployment.* Under the present assumptions, it is
plausible to suppose that the degree of conflict (and thus the rate of
wage increase) within the critical subset eventually becomes zero. At
this point (assuming for convenience that there is no further
alteration in the relative positions of coat-tail groups), money wages
in the first sector cease to rise, employment in the first sector ceases
to fall, and (if this has not already happened) the inter-sectoral pay
differential ceases to widen and employment in the second sector
ceases to rise.

The economy thus ultimately arrives at a state which is an equilibrium in the basic sense that a stable pattern of indirectly determined
pay relativities has emerged, and with it a stable general money wage
level. Some rates of pay are at their anomically optimal levels; others
are suspended more or less far above their anomically optimal levels
by normative pressures. But no employer or employee who has the
power to change a rate of pay wishes to do so.

In this hypothetical state, there will be no wage inflation. But there
will be a certain (and quite possibly a large) amount of unemployment.
The level of this *equilibrium rate of unemployment* depends on two
things: (a) how large an excess supply of labour to the first sector is
needed to extinguish all conflict within it, which depends on, among
other things, the nature of pay norms and the power of particular
groups of employees; and (b) how much of this excess supply can be
absorbed by the second sector, which depends on the elasticity of
demand there and on the degree to which wages in the second sector
can be reduced relative to wages in the first sector.

The existence of this sort of terminal state does not depend on the
assumption that the government holds the aggregate monetary
demand for labour constant, or on the assumption that the size and
composition of the population do not change. All that is necessary is

to assume that the government responds to wage inflation by causing or allowing the proportion of the population unemployed to rise continually over time. How drastically the government responds in this regard will evidently affect the amount of time that elapses before the terminal state is attained, and the terminal general money wage level. It may also affect the equilibrium rate of unemployment, especially because the number of redundancies associated with a given reduction in employment depends on the speed with which it occurs.

Nor does the existence of this sort of terminal state depend on the assumption that there is no anticipation, although anticipation would affect the path by which the terminal state was attained and hence possibly its precise character. In particular, if employers and employees anticipated future wage increases on the basis of adaptive expectations, it is plausible to suppose that the economy would tend to approach the equilibrium rate of unemployment (whatever its level) by a series of damped oscillations.*

Finally, it may be noted that what I am calling the *equilibrium* rate of unemployment is similar in certain important respects to what others (page 6) have called the *natural* rate of unemployment. The difference between the two concepts concerns the mechanisms at work. Those who have spoken of the natural rate of unemployment have argued that when unemployment is below this rate the general money wage level is *pulled up* (in some models at an accelerating rate) *by excess demand*. But in the present model, when unemployment is below the equilibrium rate, the general money wage level is *driven up by normative conflict over pay relativities*. The distinction should not be exaggerated, since conflict between normative and anomic pressures, whereby induced shortages pull up certain wage rates in the critical subset, may contribute to wage inflation. Nonetheless, it is a fundamental distinc-

---

* Money wages in the first sector would initially be rising at an increasing rate (for the reasons explained on pp. 117, 133), and hence the level of employment in the first sector would be declining faster than would otherwise have been the case. But the amount of excess supply needed to extinguish all conflict in the first sector would not be sufficient at the first pass to stop money wages rising, since (for the reasons explained on p. 120) they would continue to be propelled upwards simply by expectations of future increases. Not until some greater level of excess supply had been attained would the rate of wage increase (actual and expected) in the first sector drop to zero. By this point, however, the economy would have overshot the equilibrium rate of unemployment, and the wage level and unemployment would tend to fall. But expectations of falling wages would then cause the economy to overshoot the equilibrium rate of unemployment in the other direction, thus causing the wage level and unemployment to rise again, and so on.

tion, as may be seen from the fact that in the present model conflict between the differing norms of powerful groups of employees could cause the general money wage level to rise persistently even if there were excess demand in no submarket in the economy.

(ii) *Full employment*

Let us now consider the implications of a different type of demand management policy. In particular, let us assume that the government manipulates aggregate monetary demand in such a way as to maintain full employment, regardless of the behaviour of the general money wage level – although the essence of the argument would be the same if the government were to maintain *any* constant rate of unemployment below the equilibrium rate (and above the full employment rate).

(1) *Full employment defined.* I shall define full employment as a state in which there is a negligible amount of sustained involuntary unemployment – in which, on average during any year, only (say) one per cent of the adult population has been involuntarily unemployed for (say) more than three months.

I shall define someone as involuntarily unemployed if (a) he is not employed (not counting third sector activities as employment) and (b) there is at least one job (or category of labour within a job) in which he would be both willing and able to work if, other things being equal, its relative wage were reduced. An involuntarily unemployed person, it should be emphasised, need not be willing to work for a reduced wage in *every* job – he may indeed be refusing employment in certain jobs at the prevailing wage. But it is not sufficient for him to be *willing* to work for a reduced wage in at least one job; it must also be that he would be *taken on* at that wage.

The willingness of employers to take workers on in particular jobs depends not only on relative wages but also on the aggregate monetary demand for labour in relation to the general money wage level. I shall therefore take it for granted that the level of involuntary unemployment in the economy can, if the government so chooses (and is permitted to do so by the governments of other countries), be reduced to and maintained at an arbitrarily low level by means of fiscal, monetary and exchange rate policy.

(2) *Shaking down: the second sector.* Since, at full employment, unemployment is below the equilibrium rate, money wages in the first sector will be continually driven up by normative conflict. This, as explained above, will tend to widen the wage differential between the first and second sectors and to increase the level of employment in the second sector.

I shall assume, however (and I believe this to be a reasonable approximation to the truth as regards modern capitalist economies), that relative pay in the second sector quite soon encounters, or is already at, some fixed floor established by legal minimum wage rates and social security benefits tied to average earnings. Once this floor is reached, there is no further transfer of employment from the first to the second sector, and the rate of wage inflation in the economy as a whole becomes equal to and determined by the rate at which money wages are increasing in the first sector.

(3) *Shaking down: the first sector.* Once the transfer of labour to the second sector has stopped, and given that the rate of unemployment is held constant, the (proportional size of the) excess supply of labour to the first sector will cease to grow, and thus there will be no further tendency from this source for the rate of wage inflation to decline.

For a certain period, however, the rate at which money wages are increasing in the first sector may tend to decline for another reason, namely the elimination of temporary shortages and surpluses. One aspect of this concerns geographical mobility by employers and employees. Of equal importance, however, is the acquisition of the sorts of skills which, although they may temporarily be scarce, can be acquired at a given cost in a fairly short time by virtually any employee.

This is of special relevance with regard to the need, discussed in earlier sections, for certain employers to 'match' normatively determined wage increases in other groups in order to maintain the quality of their own labour forces. For insofar as 'quality' is simply a matter of freely (though not necessarily costlessly) acquirable skills, this need will tend to disappear over time as low quality workers, in order to get better jobs, transform themselves into high quality workers.

What remains important even in the long term, of course, are those aspects or determinants of quality which are genuinely scarce; innate or fortuitously acquired physical and mental abilities, age, and skills acquired in institutions whose capacity is for one reason or another limited. It is ultimately the need of employers to maintain the quality of their labour forces in terms of these sorts of attributes which causes normatively determined wage increases in some groups to raise anomically optimal wage rates in others.

(4) *Steady state*. When the excess supply of labour to the first sector has stopped growing, and the various temporary shortages and surpluses have been eliminated, the membership of the critical subset and the degree of conflict within it will cease to change. Moreover, the pay of all other groups in the economy (both coat-tail groups and those in the second sector) will be rising from period to period at the same speed as the pay of the groups in the critical subset.

In this hypothetical steady state (which resembles that which was assumed to exist in most of the examples in earlier sections of this chapter), wage inflation, if there is no anticipation, will proceed at a constant periodic rate determined straightforwardly by the degree of conflict within the critical subset both between different norms (damped to some degree by anomic pressures) and between normative and anomic pressures. But if the groups in the critical subset anticipate, and in particular if they anticipate on the basis of adaptive expectations, then wage inflation will (for reasons explained earlier) continually accelerate, at a rate governed by the speed and sensitivity with which expectations are revised in response to the nonfulfilment of past expectations.

(iii) *Productivity, prices and real wages*

It remains very briefly to tie up one or two macroeconomic loose ends. The average *real* wage tends to rise over time in line with average productivity (in the broadest sense), although it is also affected by changes in the share of profits, tax rates and land and raw material prices. Clearly, the faster productivity is growing, the lower will be the rate of *price* inflation caused by any given rate of wage inflation. In addition, the faster the average real wage is rising, the less militantly, on average, will employees tend to respond to unfair relative pay, and hence the slower will be the rate of wage inflation.

The average real wage, moreover, is not in general independent of the rate of unemployment, for a number of reasons, two of which are (a) that higher unemployment tends to permit foreign trade to be in balance with a higher exchange rate and hence lower import prices, and (b) cutting the other way, that higher unemployment, by increasing the proportion of the population living on social security benefits, tends to require heavier taxation of employed workers. These sorts of linkages, in conjunction with the dependence of wage inflation on the behaviour of the average real wage, evidently complicate the relationship between wage inflation and unemployment. For example, if effect (b) were important, the depressing effect of rising unemployment on the rate of wage inflation would be less pronounced, and the equilibrium rate of unemployment would tend to be higher.

6

THEORY AND REALITY

6.1 INTRODUCTION

In this chapter I shall attempt in a limited way to test the theory of pay relativities and wage inflation developed in the previous four chapters. This is a difficult undertaking, for several reasons.

One is that the theory itself is fairly general. It asserts that both normative and anomic pressures are important, but it does not depend upon the existence of any *particular* mixture of normative and anomic ingredients. From one point of view this is a considerable advantage, since in practice the mixture varies – over time, between countries, and from sector to sector. But it evidently makes the theory much harder, in principle, to refute. It also makes it harder to draw a sharp line between the predictions of the present theory and the predictions of the alternative, more narrowly anomic or normative, theories reviewed in chapter 1.

None of this, however, precludes an attempt to test the present theory in the broad sense of assessing its usefulness and validity as a source of more specific hypotheses and as a framework on which to hang a more detailed explanation of particular facts. Thus in this chapter I shall examine a selection of evidence on pay relativities and wage inflation in industrialised capitalist economies. I shall attempt to show that in reality neither anomic nor normative pressures can be ignored, and I shall attempt to establish the extent to and the respects in which each is important.

The amount of empirical material in this area is vast, and for this reason I shall restrict most of my attention to certain countries, especially Britain. For the same reason I shall neglect certain important sorts of pay relativities, including the relative pay of women and racial minorities (although an excellent and comprehensive empirical study of all aspects of relative pay is to be found in Phelps Brown, 1977).

The chapter is arranged in the following way. There are three, quite long, sections on pay relativities, whose main conclusions are then very briefly summarised in a short section (pp. 203–4). After this there is another, quite long, section on wage inflation.

6.2 INTER-ESTABLISHMENT RELATIVITIES

In this section I shall examine the relativities between the pay of similar occupations in different establishments – different firms, plants, institutions, and so on. I shall divide the discussion into two parts, considering first relativities within, and then relativities between, broad industrial categories.

Most of the available evidence relates to male manual employees, and even these are not always stratified by skill level or detailed occupation. Moreover, in both this and the next two sections, one must reckon with two further sorts of imperfection in pay relativity statistics.

(1) The measure of pay is usually neither ideal nor consistent. Whenever possible, I shall use average hourly earnings (i.e. total earnings, inclusive of all premia and supplements, divided by the number of hours worked) as the measure of pay, although I shall be obliged for the most part to ignore both fringe benefits and the effects of taxation.

(2) Pay relativities fluctuate erratically in the short run, both because the pay settlements of different groups do not occur simultaneously, and because cycles in aggregate economic activity have different effects in different firms, industries, and occupations. In practice there is no way to correct for this, except by taking more notice of moving averages and secular trends than of observations at particular moments and short-term variations.

In what follows, incidentally, the country to which the data refer is always Britain, unless otherwise explicitly stated.

(i) Intra-industry relativities

The broad facts concerning pay relativities between different establishments in the same industry are as follows.

(1) In certain industries, which in total employ about one third of the labour force, rates of pay are fairly similar in most establishments.* The great majority of these industries are in the public sector, examples being education, national and local government service,

---

* More precisely, the basic rates settled at industry level are closely followed in almost all establishments, although there is some variation in the extent of overtime working (at premium rates): NEDO (1971), esp. sections 3 and 4; Donovan (1968), esp. pp. 20, 66, 80–1, and app. 5.

mining, electricity, and postal services. The remainder (with excep-tions such as shipping, textiles, and electrical contracting) are Wages Council* industries – notably agriculture, clothing, and road haulage – although not all Wages Council industries exhibit this characteristic.

(2) In other industries, almost all of which are in the private sector, inter-establishment pay differences are commonly large, even within particular geographical areas. For example, Mackay (1971), in a study of manual engineering workers, discovered that in Birmingham some establishments consistently paid nearly twice as much as others to employees in comparable occupations. Similar results have been ob-tained for clerical and secretarial staff in London by Hay–MSL (1976), and for a variety of occupations, industries and countries by Wilkinson (1973), Robinson (1967, 1970) and those cited in Phelps Brown (1977, p. 273).

(3) Differences in pay between establishments are positively corre-lated with differences in the size of establishments. Among those who have noted this in Britain are Crossley (1966), Ingham (1970), Mackay and Wilkinson. A similar correlation has been observed in other countries. Lester (1967), for example, discovered that within US manu-facturing industries the largest establishments typically pay 25 to 30 per cent more than the smallest, and that this pattern has existed since at least the 1920s. The correlation is even more pronounced if fringe benefits are included in pay since, as Lester notes, these tend to be markedly superior in large establishments.

(1) *Anomic pressures.* Most of those who have studied inter-establishment pay relativities have argued that orthodox competitive theory would predict equal pay in different establishments in the same industry and area, and thus cannot explain the large and persistent discrepancies observed in most private sector industries (especially since, as Ingham and Mackay discovered, workers are aware of their existence). But it seems to me that the discrepancies in question are to a considerable extent generated by one exceedingly orthodox factor, namely differences in the non-pecuniary attractiveness of work in different establishments.

The main evidence in support of this hypothesis is the correlation between pay and size of establishment, in conjunction with various

---

* A Wages Council is a tribunal which lays down legally binding minimum wage rates. For a fuller description, see Donovan (1968), pp. 57–60.

studies which show that most people prefer to work in small establishments. The most important such study is that of Ingham, who
examined a number of large and small engineering firms and discovered that in the large firms there was less social interaction between
workmates on the job, less variety of job content (because of greater
specialisation), and less contact between workers and their boss, both
at and outside the workplace. Ingham also discovered that workers
disliked these features of large establishments, that they were aware
of the more interesting and sociable nature of work in small establishments and that their knowledge in this regard actively influenced
their job choices. The workers also mentioned another disadvantage
of working in a large establishment, namely that it tends to involve
a longer journey to work (which is confirmed by the statistics in
Mackay, pp. 250–1).

Ingham's findings accord with common sense; if the pay were the
same, who would travel ten miles to work in a large impersonal firm
if he had the option of a similar job in a small firm down the road
from his home? In addition there is a substantial body of evidence that
large establishments suffer from more strikes, more absenteeism, and
more sick leave, all of which tends to support the inference that work
in large establishments is less congenial (DE, 1976, 1976a; Ingham, pp.
16–22).

Even in the private sector, however, the association between pay and
size of establishment is not particularly close. The range of pay between
establishments in a given industry is much greater than the range of
pay between large and small establishments, and the one study
(Wilkinson) which calculates correlation coefficients reveals that (for
specific occupations in the steel industry) about half the variance of
pay between establishments is unexplained by size. In addition, the
hypothesis that higher pay in large establishments simply and completely compensates for their less attractive working conditions is called
into question by the fact that some writers have reported a significant
simple correlation in certain private sector industries between establishment size and labour turnover (Ingham, pp. 22–5; Mackay, pp.
154–9).

Thus other forces must also be at work, even in the private sector,
of which I shall consider first the anomic possibilities.

(1) Size of establishment is not the sole determinant of the non-
pecuniary attractiveness of work, even within a given industry and

occupation. The precise nature of the product may make a significant difference to working conditions, as may the internal organisational structure of the establishment. One must also reckon with the effects of remoteness unrelated to size, as in the case of high-paying offshore oil rigs and back-country construction projects.

It seems to me probable that these other aspects of non-pecuniary attractiveness contribute significantly to explaining that part of the variance of pay between establishments which is unexplained by size. But it seems most improbable that they explain anything like the whole of the remaining variance, since the rate of labour turnover varies widely between establishments in the same area, even in the private sector (Mackay, chs. 6, 7).

(2) An anomic explanation of this variation in turnover rates, and indeed more generally of the variance of pay unexplained by differences in non-pecuniary attractiveness, would be differences in the *quality* of the labour needed in different establishments, according to the precise nature of their products and technologies.

This is undoubtedly true to some extent. In certain industries, such as clothing and some sorts of engineering (Crossley, Lester), the smallest and most attractive firms are not the lowest-paying, but contain highly skilled workers producing limited amounts of specialised products in response to specific orders. Conversely, there are in some industries certain very unattractive establishments, large and small, which pay low wages because it is most economical for the employer to operate with low quality labour and a high rate of turnover.

But this explanation of inter-establishment pay differences does not seem generally valid. Neither Lester nor Mackay found a strong correlation between pay and labour quality, except in a few very high-paying and very low-paying establishments. Moreover, the existence of such a correlation leaves open the question of causation, since (as was argued in earlier chapters) an employer who is forced by normative pressure to pay above the anomically optimal wage will for that very reason tend to have a high quality labour force.

(3) A final possible anomic explanation of inter-establishment pay differences in the same area is differences in the rates of growth of employment in different establishments. This hypothesis also was tested and rejected by Mackay (1971, ch. 6). However, it is surely true that some pay differences between establishments in *different areas* are

to be explained by differences in the tightness of local labour markets (Phelps Brown, 1977, pp. 280–1).

(2) *Normative pressures.* There are important normative pressures on inter-establishment relativities. In particular, employees frequently attempt by collective action to eliminate differences in pay between establishments within an industry, partly in order to safeguard employment in higher-paying establishments, but mainly on the grounds that workers in different establishments have equal needs. One form in which normative pressure of this sort is exercised, which is common in Britain and other European countries, is industry-wide wage bargaining, whereby representatives of employers and employees negotiate rates applicable to all establishments in an industry. Another form is efforts by workers in individual establishments to raise their pay into line with that in higher-paying establishments.* A third form, which is in effect a mixture of the other two, is systematic 'pattern bargaining' (Seltzer, 1951; Levinson, 1960).

Normative pressures of this kind, it seems to me, account for the smallness of inter-establishment pay differences in most public sector industries in Britain. For not only is the typical such industry strongly unionised. It is also, so far as any given occupation or set of occupations is concerned, a single pay group, for the fundamental reason that there is only one employer, or, more accurately, because the managers of individual establishments (particular schools, railway stations, and so on) are all subordinate to the same higher authority. This is clearest where the employer is the central government or a nationalised industry; but it is often also true where the employer is in fact several different local authorities, partly because these authorities are financially dependent on the central government, and partly because, being non-competing local monopolists, they have little to lose and much to gain (in terms of bargaining power) by adopting a united front on pay.

As a result, in the typical public sector industry a union of employees, by exerting pressure at the centre, can force the managers of individual establishments to adhere strictly to the rates agreed at industry level. Of course, this sort of uniformity cannot be imposed overnight, especially because of resistance from employees in higher-paying establishments. It was many years after the nationalisation of the

* For examples from the British vehicle industry, see Turner (1967), pp. 142–4.

coal-mining industry, for example, that pay differences between pits were more or less abolished, and this has not yet happened in the iron and steel industry (Pay Board, 1974a; Wilkinson, 1973).

Moreover, this sort of uniformity of pay tends to result in the coexistence of labour scarcity in large (or otherwise unattractive) establishments and excess supply in small (or otherwise attractive) establishments. The former sometimes leads to limited attempts at reintroducing inter-establishment differentials, both by special official allowances (such as the London allowance, the police undermanning allowance, and allowances to teachers in schools in deprived areas: Pay Board, 1974b; Devlin, 1976), and by unofficial juggling of such things as upgrading and points of entry on to incremental scales. And especially for manual workers, variations in overtime tend to have a similar but automatic effect; in establishments where labour is scarce there is more opportunity for extra work at premium rates and thus average hourly pay is somewhat higher than in establishments where there is no such scarcity. On the whole, though, anomic pressures seem to have a rather weak influence on inter-establishment relativities in the public sector.

In the private sector, things are different, there being evidence (discussed earlier) not only that pay varies widely between establishments within certain industries but also that this variation is to a considerable extent generated by anomic pressures. The reason for this is that the typical private sector industry, even one in which there is industry-wide wage bargaining or a Wages Council, is not in certain basic respects a single pay group, since it is composed of many, financially autonomous, employers, who are further divided by the fact of being product market competitors, and who stand to gain from joint action only to a limited extent. Thus a typical industrial employers' federation has relatively little power over its individual members, which makes it hard for a union of employees, by exerting pressure at the centre, to enforce the payment of uniform wages in all establishments.

As a result, the rates of pay negotiated (or laid down by Wages Councils) at industry level in the private sector are in practice almost invariably regarded as minima, which individual employers are free to exceed (Donovan, 1968, pp. 20, 35, 57–60). And this is something which large and otherwise unattractive establishments must ordinarily do in order to avoid labour shortages and undesirably high rates of turnover, even though small and otherwise attractive establishments may get away with paying the minimum. For labour of most types is fairly mobile between establishments, at any rate in the same industry and area, and drifts steadily away from those which offer neither good pay nor good working conditions.*

There is thus a much stronger tendency in private than in public sector industries for something like the anomically appropriate structure of inter-establishment relativities to assert and maintain itself. But the strength of this tendency varies from industry to industry according to two factors.

(1) Insofar as there is industry-wide wage negotiation, formal or informal, statutory or voluntary, much depends on the level at which the industry-wide minimum is set, and on how rigorously it is enforced, as well as on other factors affecting the balance of supply and demand in the industry and occupation in question.

If the minimum is set rather low, or if demand in the industry is expanding rapidly, or if for some other reason there is a shortage of labour in the industry concerned, then the need for large and otherwise unattractive establishments to pay in excess of the minimum will be great, and thus anomic pressures will have a rather large influence on inter-establishment relativities.† The same will be true where industry-wide minimum rates are not strictly enforced, as in such industries as catering and retailing, because of low union membership in small establishments or inadequate official policing of Wages Council orders (Wigham, 1976, 1977).

If, on the other hand, there is an excess supply of labour in the industry and occupation in question (because the minimum rate is high and strictly enforced, or because demand for labour in the industry is declining, or for some other reason), then the need for large and unattractive establishments to pay in excess of the minimum will be reduced and thus anomic pressures will have a rather small influence. This may explain, for example, why the inter-establishment pay differ-

* For evidence that the amount of inter-establishment mobility is much greater than is sometimes suggested, see OECD (1965), pp. 49–51; Mackay (1971), studies cited on pp. 28–9, and chs. 6–9; Thatcher (1976), pp. 91–3.
† Birmingham from 1959 to 1966 was one of the objects of Mackay's (1971) study. He found (pp. 71–4) that inter-establishment differences in that tight labour market were larger than in Glasgow, an area of high unemployment, and that they were larger for skilled than for unskilled labour. Moreover, the Hay–MSL (1976) survey of clerical and secretarial pay, which revealed large inter-establishment differences, was conducted in London, an area of labour scarcity.

ences in clothing, textiles and agriculture in Britain are comparatively slight.

(2) In addition, whether or not there is industry-wide wage negotiation, the influence of anomic pressures on the inter-establishment wage structure will be reduced insofar as the employees in particular establishments are powerful enough unilaterally to force their employers to pay more than either the industry minimum or the anomically optimal wage for the establishment concerned. For the drift of labour from unattractive to attractive establishments, which is what tends to enforce the anomically appropriate wage structure, cannot proceed faster than the rate at which vacancies arise in attractive establishments.

In consequence, repeated efforts by powerful groups of employees in attractive establishments to keep their wages in line with high-paying unattractive establishments (or to enforce some other sort of pay norm) can permanently offset the influence of anomic forces. In such cases, the influence of normative pressures will not necessarily be manifest in greater uniformity of pay across establishments; in some instances, and especially where there is no industry-wide wage negotiation, it will tend to *increase* the dispersion of pay between establishments in a given industry and area.

The exercise of normative pressure by employees in individual establishments has been studied by those who have investigated the effects of unionisation on wages within particular American industries (see the survey in Lewis, 1963, ch. III). Most of these studies have revealed that unionised establishments pay significantly and in some cases substantially higher wages than non-unionised establishments, although one must be wary of making too strong a causal inference inasmuch as not all of the studies controlled for size of establishment, which tends to be positively correlated with degree of unionisation.

In summary, then, it would appear on the basis of the limited evidence available that normative pressures are not only the main influence on inter-establishment relativities in public sector industries, but also have a substantial influence on inter-establishment relativities in the private sector, especially in certain occupations and industries. Anomic pressures also exert a strong influence in the private sector, but the studies discussed earlier suggest that they leave a considerable part of the variance of pay between establishments unexplained, and that this cannot be accounted for to any great extent by ignorance or inertia on the part of employees.

(ii) *Inter-industry relativities*

Let us now consider relativities between the pay of similar occupations in establishments in different industries, regarding which the broad facts are as follows.

(1) There are substantial variations in pay between industries, in all countries and time periods. For example, in Britain in 1970, the median hourly earnings of semiskilled male manual workers in three highly-paying industries (chemicals, metal manufacture, and vehicles) were 1.45 times those in three badly-paying industries (distribution, miscellaneous services, and public administration; NES, 1970, table 42). The inter-industry variation of pay tends to be somewhat larger in manual than in non-manual occupations (UN, 1967, ch. 5, tables 4–6).

(2) Inter-industry pay relativities in industrialised countries are rather stable over periods of a decade or more, especially within the manufacturing sector.* This stability is more pronounced for earnings than for basic wage rates (UN, 1967, ch. 3, p. 26).

(3) The pattern of inter-industry relativities is broadly similar in different industrialised countries, capitalist and communist (UN, 1967, ch. 5, pp. 9–11; Papola, 1970, and the studies cited therein).

(1) *Anomic pressures.* The stability of inter-industry relativities over time has suggested to many people that normative forces – custom and convention – are at work. But the similarity of inter-industry relativities in different countries tells against this interpretation, and in favour of an anomic explanation, since it is inconceivable that conventions could be so alike and so potent in all industrialised countries, regardless of differences in political and social structure, historical development and degree of unionisation.

I would suggest indeed that inter-industry relativities, like intra-industry relativities, are to a considerable extent governed by the most orthodox of anomic pressures, namely differences in the non-pecuniary attractiveness of work in different industries. Where the work is particularly arduous, boring or unpleasant (as in mining, steel manufacture and vehicle assembly), the pay tends to be high; where the work is comparatively light, varied or pleasant (as in agriculture, retailing and services), the pay tends to be low.

Such differences in the nature of the work in different industries

* OECD (1965), pp. 22–7; Crossley (1966), p. 200; UN (1967), ch. 5, pp. 2–12; Papola (1970); Godley (1977), pp. 462, 469; Turner (1969).

stem mainly from differences in the technology of production (in its broadest sense), which also cause differences between industries in the size of the typical establishment. Thus, for reasons discussed earlier, the hypothesis that inter-industry differences in pay reflect differences in non-pecuniary attractiveness is supported by the fact that they are positively correlated with inter-industry differences in establishment size (Brown, 1962; Weiss, 1966; Kleiman, 1971). It is supported also by the fact that the inter-industry variation of non-manual pay is less than that of manual pay, since working conditions in different industries are in general less different for non-manual than for manual workers. Clerks and secretaries, for example, although the size and surroundings of the establishments in which they work vary considerably, perform essentially the same tasks in all industries.

According to this hypothesis, then, the inter-industry pay structure is similar in different industrialised countries because all such countries use roughly the same technology of production; and the inter-industry pay structure changes slowly over time because the fundamental characteristics of the technology of particular industries also change slowly over time.

Much of the inter-industry pay data mentioned above, incidentally, is imperfectly standardised for differences in occupational composition. Such differences, which also stem from differences in technology, must thus be regarded as a further contributor to the statistical similarity of the inter-industry pay structure in different periods and countries.* Moreover, even within specific occupational categories, it is probable that the necessary quality of labour varies somewhat across industries, which could be an additional anomic influence on the inter-industry pay structure.

Another possible sort of anomic influence on the relative pay of particular industries is their differing rates of expansion or decline. A number of empirical studies have investigated this possibility (Reddaway, 1959; OECD, 1965, ch. VI; UN, 1967, ch. 5, p. 13). All have discovered some tendency for the relative pay of rapidly expanding industries to rise, and for the relative pay of declining industries to fall. But all these studies have also concluded that the effect of differing growth rates is very small.

* Using data from NES (1970, tables 16, 18, 34, and 158), I have estimated that in Britain differences in skill mix alone explain about 15 % of the variance of the hourly pay of male manual workers across broad industrial categories.

On the whole, then, the available evidence quite strongly suggests that inter-industry pay relativities are to a substantial extent governed by anomic pressures of one sort or another. But the evidence also suggests that other forces are at work. For a closer examination of the international comparisons mentioned earlier reveals a considerable number of differences between countries, in three respects.

(1) Even where the ranking of broad industrial categories in terms of pay is similar, the magnitudes of the pay differentials between industries vary.

(2) There are also some discrepancies between countries in the ranking of broad industrial categories. This is especially marked for industries (such as electricity, gas and water) which are in the public sector in most countries, but it is also true of certain private sector industries, such as printing (UN, 1967, ch. 5, pp. 2–12).

(3) The ranking of *narrow* industrial categories and the pay differentials between them vary widely from one country to another (Phelps Brown, 1977, pp. 61–5).

Some of these discrepancies reflect statistical problems. Others may be the product of anomic forces, including international differences in the availability and use of particular technologies. But it is hard to believe that all or even most of the discrepancies could be explained in these ways. A more plausible inference is that the observed structure of inter-industry pay relativities cannot satisfactorily be accounted for in terms of anomic pressures alone.

(2) *Normative pressures.* Inter-industry relativities are subject to normative pressures partly through the actions of employees in individual establishments or groups of establishments, but mainly (at any rate in Britain) through the mechanism of industry-wide wage bargaining and Wages Councils. To some extent, however, these normative pressures do not conflict with anomic forces, since an important secondary norm concerning relativities within broad occupational groups is sacrifice. In particular, it is widely accepted that pay in industries where the work is conspicuously exhausting or disagreeable ought on moral grounds to be relatively high. Thus workers in other industries do not in general strive for parity of pay with, say, dockers or coal miners.

But one should not underestimate the degree of conflict in this area, either between normative and anomic pressures, or between different norms, especially where less striking differences in the attractiveness of work are concerned. To begin with, differences in non-pecuniary attractiveness are not the sole source of anomic pressure on inter-industry relativities; one must also reckon with different labour quality requirements in different industries, and with differing growth rates. In addition, people are liable, partly through differing information and partly through differing tastes, to entertain differing opinions about the niceness or the nastiness of the work in particular industries.

Furthermore, the principle of payment according to sacrifice must contend with another secondary norm, namely payment according to need, which dictates that workers in different industries should all be paid the same. Most people in fact adhere to both secondary norms, but attach varying weights to them – weights, moreover, which are unlikely to correspond with the pattern of inter-industry relativities that would be generated by anomic forces alone. For example, government employees usually feel that despite their greater security of employment their pay should be equal to that of similar occupations in the private sector. Finally, employees in industries which, for what-ever reason, have been highly paid in the past tend to strive to maintain their relative position both in the face of opposition from groups in other industries with differing norms and in the face of changing anomic pressures.

But to the extent that normative pressures (and particularly press-ures to equalise pay between industries) conflict with anomic press-ures, the evidence cited above suggests that anomic pressures have quite a strong tendency to win out. This happens because there is a fair amount of labour mobility between establishments in different industries, except among workers with highly specialised skills (see the references on p. 173).

As a result, attempts at levelling up the pay in comparatively attractive industries tend to cause labour, especially good labour, to become scarcer in less attractive industries (both public and private), which causes employers in the latter to offer higher pay, either by collectively conceding a higher industry minimum wage, or (at any rate in the private sector) by individually increasing the degree to which they pay above the minimum. Furthermore, if the levelling attempts occur in the private sector, through employees forcing up an industry's minimum wage, the consequent reduction in labour scarcity in the industry concerned will tend to diminish the degree to which large and unattractive establishments pay above the minimum. (All this, incidentally, would explain why, as noted earlier, there is greater stability in inter-industry earnings relativities than in basic wage rate relativities.)

But the tendency for labour to drift from unattractive to attractive industries is neither instantaneous nor complete. It cannot occur faster than the rate at which vacancies arise in attractive industries, and it may be further impeded by artificial barriers to entry into those industries. In consequence, attempts at levelling up the pay in attractive industries (or at enforcing other sorts of pay norm) will be comparatively successful if they are renewed sufficiently frequently and if the employees concerned take good account of the gap between basic rates and earnings, both in their own and in other industries.

That normative pressures have a significant effect on inter-industry relativities is suggested by the differences between countries mentioned above. One would expect this effect to be smaller in periods, countries and occupations in which there was a general shortage of labour, since this would tend to increase the degree to which a levelling up of pay in more attractive industries would cause labour scarcity in less attractive industries. Conversely, one would expect the tendency for anomically appropriate inter-industry differentials to reappear to be less strong if there were a substantial economy-wide surplus of labour. These predictions appear to be borne out by the work of Lewis (1963, chs. IV–VI), who concluded that unions in particular American industries have had a greater effect on relative wages, the greater the aggregate level of unemployment.

6.3 INTER-OCCUPATIONAL RELATIVITIES: MANUAL AND CLERICAL

In this and the next section I shall examine inter-occupational pay relativities, using the term 'occupation' to refer both to broad groupings such as professional, managerial, and skilled manual workers, and to the narrower functional categories within these broad groupings (doctors and teachers, senior and junior executives, plumbers and carpenters, etc.).

The general hypothesis that I shall advance is that in modern industrialised economies normative forces tend to have a rather larger, and anomic forces a rather smaller, influence on inter-occupational than on inter-establishment relativities. There are, it may be suggested, two reasons for this.

(1) Mobility between occupations, broad and narrow, is much less free than mobility between similar occupations in different establishments. Not only does the need to acquire specific skills mean that the speed with which labour can switch from one occupation to another is in most cases at best rather slow; but also inter-occupational mobility is often impeded to a greater or lesser extent by artificial restrictions of one sort or another.

(2) A higher proportion of inter-occupational relativities (especially between narrow occupations) than of inter-establishment relativities are directly determined. In other words, it is much commoner, at any rate in the private sector, for a single pay group to span several occupations than several establishments. This is significant because (as explained on pp. 95–101, 152–4) normative pressures, insofar as they conflict with anomic pressures, tend to have a greater effect on relativities within than between pay groups. In particular, labour shortages tend to have less of an influence on pay when they arise only in certain jobs within a group than when they arise throughout an entire group.

In the present section I shall elaborate and test this general hypothesis in the light of the evidence concerning the pay of manual and clerical occupations. In the following section I shall look at the pay of managerial and professional occupations.

(i) *Skill differentials*

To obtain a broad perspective on the determinants of relativities between manual occupations it is appropriate to begin by examining the average pay of skilled, semiskilled and unskilled workers – although such statistics must be approached with caution since skill is not always defined or measured in the same way.

(1) *Levels.* Skilled workers on average earn more than semiskilled workers, who in turn earn more than unskilled workers, in every industry, country and period for which data are available. Indeed, in a majority of industrialised capitalist countries in the 1960s the male skilled/unskilled earnings ratio in the non-agricultural sector was apparently between 1.15 and 1.25 (UN, 1967, table 5.16, chart 5.4).

These uniformities surely reflect the influence of anomic pressures, and in particular the fact that some sacrifice of productivity and earnings is usually necessary in the course of acquiring a skilled trade.

On the other hand, the range of values taken by this aggregate skill differential in different industrialised countries is quite large. In the 1960s, it varied from about 1.14 in the Netherlands and Norway to about 1.40 in France and the United States (and among communist countries from 1.15 in Poland to 1.32 in Hungary).* And when the manual skill differential in any given industry is compared across industrialised capitalist countries in any particular period, the range of values is even larger (Phelps Brown, 1977, p. 63; UN, 1967, table 5.17). This variation in the size of skill differentials between countries whose economies are broadly similar, although it may be attributed in part to anomic factors and statistical problems, suggests quite strongly that normative pressures also are at work.

(2) *Changes.* Over the last 50 to 100 years, skill differentials have narrowed considerably in Britain, the United States and other industrialised capitalist economies.† The universality of this tendency implies that it is due at least in part to changing anomic pressures, such as a reduction in the relative skill content of skilled jobs (Braverman, 1974), or, since literacy and numeracy are needed to acquire most skilled manual trades, the spread of free and compulsory elementary education (a hypothesis supported by the work of Fisher cited on p. 36 of Phelps Brown, 1977). But there are also a number of indications that the behaviour of skill differentials over time has been significantly influenced by normative pressures.

(1) As Phelps Brown (1977, pp. 73–5) has emphasised, the movement of skill differentials in different industrialised capitalist countries has been nothing like uniform.

(2) During the last 50 years there has in most of these countries been

* *Sources:* France, Netherlands, Norway: UN (1967), table 5.16, chart 5.4. Poland: Jackson (1968), p. 187, table 2. Hungary: Lane (1971), p. 78, table 8. United States: US (1960), table 28; Miller (1966), table III-6; for the US, skilled workers were taken to be 'craftsmen, foremen and kindred workers', but excluding foremen, and unskilled workers to be 'laborers, except farm and mine'; the first source cited yields a ratio of 1.37 for 1959; the second source (using data for year-round full-time workers), when corrected to exclude foremen on the basis of the data in the first source, yields an average ratio of 1.41 for 1958–60.

† Knowles (1951), Routh (1965), Ozanne (1962), OECD (1965, pp. 33–5), UN (1967, ch. 5, pp. 27–31), Marchal (1958, p. 359), Phelps Brown (1977, pp. 68–81).

a great increase in the unionisation and hence in the power of manual workers, especially those without special skills, and it has been argued that these newly unionised workers have sought to impose a more egalitarian manual wage structure. In the case of Britain, this interpretation, which has been developed and documented by Knowles (1951, pp. 115–18) and Turner (1957, pp. 131–3), is supported by a very close negative correlation over the period 1895–1969 between a skill differential index and the percentage of the labour force unionised, a correlation whose significance is enhanced by the fact that these two annual series do not rise monotonically over the period, but fluctuate quite markedly (Wood, 1972, ch. 4, pp. 29–33). In the case of the United States, the hypothesis that unions have reduced skill differentials is supported by the findings of Goldner (cited in Lewis, 1963, ch. IV) and Stafford and Weiss (cited in Phelps Brown, 1977, p. 95).

(3) That normative pressure from less skilled workers has artificially squeezed skill differentials is suggested also by the persistent scarcity of skilled labour since the second world war in Britain and other countries (Routh, 1965, pp. 126–32, 145–7; UN, 1967, ch. 5, p. 30), which has been interpreted by many as a result of the reduced financial incentive for young people to acquire manual skills (Shakespeare, 1977).

This scarcity has not been totally without effect. During the post-war period in most countries skill differentials (measured in terms of earnings rather than basic rates) have shown some tendency to widen, at any rate for part of the time (UN, 1967, ch. 5, pp. 27–30). In Denmark, Italy and Sweden there is evidence that faster wage drift among skilled workers has to some extent cancelled out attempts by unions to further narrow the skill differential (ibid, pp. 21, 27; Phelps Brown, 1977, pp. 97–8). In Britain, the same anomic pressures may have operated by causing overtime to be more freely available to skilled than to less skilled workers (although there is in fact a negative correlation between wage level and amount of overtime worked; NBPI, 1970, p. 26), and may also have contributed to the growth of self-employment and labour-only subcontracting among craftsmen in the construction industry (Phelps Brown, 1968).

But these facts, although they imply strongly that anomic pressures continue to have an important effect, are not sufficient to refute the hypothesis that normative pressures have squeezed skill differentials. For the widening of these differentials (both between skilled and semiskilled, and between semiskilled and unskilled workers) in the post-war period has been patchy and erratic (UN, 1967, tables 5.16–17, chart 5.4). More importantly, it does not seem to have been large enough to eliminate the excess demand for skilled labour.

(ii) *Intra-establishment wage structures*

Complementary but more detailed evidence on the determinants of pay relativities between manual occupations is provided by a number of empirical studies of intra-establishment wage structures, of which two (Doeringer, 1971, and Mackay, 1971), because of the thoroughness with which they address themselves to the question of causation, are of particular importance.* Moreover, although one relates to the United States and the other to Britain, and although one deals with manufacturing in general and the other with the engineering industry alone, both arrive at similar conclusions. Specifically, both conclude that anomic pressures exert a relatively small influence on intra-establishment wage structures, and that pay norms (which they refer to as 'custom' or 'notions of equity and justice'), enforced by collective action or enshrined in job evaluation methods, are of much greater significance.

Doeringer and Mackay arrived at this conclusion for two sorts of reasons. First, this was what they were told by those whom they interviewed in the establishments concerned. Second, and more important, they observed that intra-establishment wage structures did not react in the manner predicted by anomic theory, or indeed in any clear and consistent way, to shortages and surpluses of labour in particular occupations. In Glasgow, for example, the pay of fitters increased faster than that of turners, despite a greater shortage of turners, and in Birmingham the pay of labourers increased faster than the pay of skilled workers, despite a greater scarcity of skilled labour (Mackay, pp. 122–3). Both Doeringer and Mackay note exceptions to this generalisation, the former, for example, citing instances where job evaluation studies were deliberately fudged in response to serious shortages in particular occupations, but both emphasise that such cases appear to be uncommon.†

In Britain, in the engineering industry at least, intra-establishment

---

* But see also Robertson (1960), the several studies in Meij (1963), Turner (1967, ch. 5), and Robinson (1970, esp. chs. 2 and 7).

† In this regard it may be noted that the British Institute of Management's job evaluation pamphlet (BIM, 1970) classifies 'scarcity of particular skills or categories of employees' under the heading 'special allowances'.

manual wage structures exhibit less short-term stability than in the United States. For they are prone to disruption by piecework-related earnings drift, especially in semiskilled occupations, at rates which seem unrelated to surpluses or shortages of labour in the particular jobs concerned. This tends to push relativities (both between different semiskilled jobs, and between semiskilled and skilled jobs) out of line with prevailing norms, which in turn causes a constant battle to restore the normatively prescribed relativities, with varying degrees of success. This type of conflict, whose costs testify to the importance of normative beliefs about inter-occupational relativities, is less frequent in the United States (and in American-owned firms in Britain), principally as a result of greater reliance on job evaluation, less reliance on piecework and tighter managerial control of other incentive schemes, practices which are now spreading in British industry.*

But despite the tendency for intra-establishment relativities to vary over time in this way, Mackay (pp. 123–7) found that they were significantly more stable than *inter*-establishment relativities. This he regarded as further evidence in favour of the hypothesis that intra-establishment relativities are primarily determined by internal custom and practice, rather than by external market pressures. This hypothesis would also seem to be supported by the fact that the inter-occupational manual pay structure varies between establishments (although it is difficult to ensure that like is being compared with like). For several studies have remarked that not only do the magnitudes of inter-occupational differentials vary widely between establishments, even in the same industry and area, but also that the occupational pay ranking is not always the same (Mackay, pp. 114–18; Turner, 1967, pp. 145–55; Robinson, 1970, pp. 238–45).

The information gathered in the various studies cited above also suggests that the main cause of the importance of normative pressures on intra-establishment manual pay structures is *not* restrictions on mobility between occupations. For although (as emphasised by Doeringer) mobility of this sort is tightly structured and controlled in some establishments and industries, normative pressures on pay do not seem to be of lesser importance where this is not so – as for example in Birmingham, where Mackay (chs. 10, 11) discovered a good deal of occupational mobility (especially across the skilled–semiskilled line),

* On the matters discussed in this paragraph, see Doeringer, p. 70; Mackay, pp. 101–13; Turner (1967), pp. 145–64, 336–9; NBPI (1968a) and supplement; Brown (1971); Jacobs (1975).

ports of entry into most establishments at most levels, and few formal rules governing internal mobility. Instead, the main reason for the effectiveness of normative pressures on manual pay relativities within establishments would appear to be the coexistence of different occupations within the same pay group – the ability of those in one occupation, through the actual or potential threat of collective action, to influence their employer's decisions concerning pay in other occupations in the same establishment.

(iii) *Foremen*

Another aspect of inter-occupational relativities among manual workers which merits attention is the pay of foremen. In practice, foremen are almost invariably paid more than those whom they supervise; where this is not so, usually because some of their subordinates have very high piece or overtime earnings, it is regarded as an aberration and is usually a source of friction.

The normative explanation of the higher pay of foremen is that it reflects a convention that pay relativities within an organisation should symbolise authority relationships; to ignore this convention, which is accepted by superior and subordinates alike, would undermine the authority of foremen and would thus reduce the efficiency of the organisation; the convention therefore prevails despite anomic counter-pressures. The alternative, anomic, explanation of the premium which foremen receive is that it is the result of a scarcity of workers (a) willing, or (b) with the ability, to take on this sort of responsibility.

The first of these two anomic hypotheses is comparatively easy to test, and is not supported by such evidence as is available. Goldthorpe (1968, tables 54, 58), in an interview study of manual workers in Luton, discovered that 49 per cent of them liked the idea of becoming a foreman 'very much' or 'quite a lot', and that 38 per cent of those who were so inclined gave as a reason the intrinsic, non-pecuniary, attractiveness of a supervisory post. In the firms concerned, the actual ratio of foremen to manual workers ranged from one in 20 to one in 120 (ibid, p. 130); in the UK as a whole this ratio is for males about one in 13 (NES, 1970, table 28). This implies that at prevailing rates of pay there is a very large excess supply (of the order of 7 to 10 persons per vacancy) of people willing to become foremen. It also suggests that even if foremen were not paid a premium there would still be a large (of the order of 2 to 4 persons per vacancy) excess supply.

The second anomic hypothesis, that there is a scarcity of *able* applicants, is in principle much harder to test, and there appears to be no empirical evidence that bears directly upon it. But international comparisons provide some indirect evidence. The statistics available, which are of course subject to the usual caveats concerning international comparability of occupational classifications, indicate that for males the average earnings of foremen as a ratio of the average earnings of skilled workers ranged in industrial capitalist economies in the 1960s from 1.19 in Britain and 1.23 in the United States to 1.56 in France; in communist countries the range was from 1.06 in Bulgaria and Czechoslovakia to 1.56 in East Germany.*

This apparently wide variation in the size of the foreman's pay premium suggests that, at the least, it is to some extent a matter of convention, which varies from country to country. On the other hand, foremen do seem to be paid *more* than their subordinates in all countries, which might be argued, much as with (say) inter-industry relativities, to give some support to the anomic hypothesis. But there is a difference. For although it is not plausible to suppose that one industry is paid more than another in every country as a matter of convention, it seems entirely possible that a convention of payment in accordance with authority could be common to all countries. Thus the available evidence, in my opinion, does not permit one to discriminate between the hypothesis that the relative pay of foremen is partly governed by normative pressures and the hypothesis that it is entirely governed by normative pressures.

(iv) *Clerical workers*

By clerical workers I shall mean office workers without professional or technical skills, and without managerial or administrative responsibilities. In most countries, it should be borne in mind, two thirds of this category is female, but (since most of the data on pay in other occupations refers to men) I shall concentrate exclusively on *male* clerical employees.

* *Sources:* Britain: NES (1970), table 34 (average hourly earnings incl. overtime, etc.). United States: US (1960), table 28. France: UN (1967), table 5.16 (average of 1962 and 1964). Bulgaria, Czechoslovakia, East Germany: UN (1967), table 8.6 (engineering industry only).

In Britain in 1970 the average hourly earnings of clerical workers were slightly greater than those of skilled manual workers, although their average *weekly* earnings, because of a pronounced difference in the hours of work of clerical and manual workers, were slightly less than those of semiskilled manual workers (NES, 1970, table 34). In other industrialised capitalist economies the difference in hours of work is smaller (NBPI, 1970, p. 48); but apart from this the pattern appears similar to Britain, with clerical workers earning about the same as skilled manual workers.*

(1) *Secular trend.* In all countries for which data are available, the relative pay of clerical workers has declined markedly over the last fifty years or so, and the decline would probably appear bigger if fringe benefits were included in pay.† There can be little doubt that the cause of this secular decline is an anomic one, namely the introduction of free and compulsory secondary schooling, which, by removing fees and forgone earnings as barriers, has eliminated any need for higher pay as an incentive to incur the financial costs of secondary education and has relaxed the constraint on access to secondary education imposed by imperfect capital markets. This explanation of the relative decline in clerical pay seems irresistible, for three reasons.

(1) The demand for labour with a secondary education, although it is hard to measure, and although it has increased substantially (which might have caused 'temporary' shortages), does not seem to have outstripped the increased supply. For example, the percentage of 14-year-olds at school in Britain rose from 9 in 1902 to 38 in 1938 and 100 after 1945 (Robbins, 1963, p. 11), while the percentage of the male labour force in non-manual jobs barely doubled (from 20 to 40) between 1911 and 1970 (Routh, 1965, pp. 4–5; NES, 1970, table 34).

(2) The difference between clerical and manual labour lies precisely in the application of that degree of fluency in reading, writing and arithmetic which it is the object of a secondary education to impart. Hence to give all children a secondary education removes an extremely important obstacle to mobility between manual and clerical jobs.

---

* UN (1967), table 5.16; US (1960), table 28 (but see n. * on p. 181 above). Clerks in West Germany are recorded as earning the same as *unskilled* manual workers, but there is reason to suppose that this is due to a non-comparable occupational classification (UN, 1967, ch. 5, p. 27, n. 71).

† Lockwood (1958), ch. II and app. A; Routh (1965), pp. 78–81, 106; Miller (1966), table III-6; Marchal (1958), pp. 398–419.

(3) For most of the last fifty years the structure of the market for clerical labour has been rather competitive. In 1920 only one clerk in 8 was a union member, and in 1951 only one in 4 (Lockwood, 1958, pp. 139, 195); and even now a significantly smaller proportion of clerks than of manual workers are unionised. Thus whatever pay norms clerks may have entertained (and Lockwood's study makes it clear that they have in fact aspired to be paid more than manual workers), there is no reason to suppose that for most of this period they would have had enough *power* to prevent an excess supply of educated labour from driving down their relative wage.

(2) *Current position.* Clerical unionisation and militancy have substantially increased in recent years, and have undoubtedly raised the relative pay of clerical workers in certain establishments and industries (although the four studies cited by Phelps Brown, 1977, p. 95, indicate that unionisation has a slighter effect on clerical than on manual pay). Moreover, it seems highly probable that pay relativities between different clerical occupations within particular establishments, like manual wage structures, are (and always have been) strongly influenced by normative pressures, whether or not the workers concerned are formally unionised.

But although the relative pay of particular clerical workers may be significantly influenced by normative forces, it seems unlikely that the relative pay of the *average* clerical worker is normatively determined to any great extent, for two reasons. One is the similarity of clerical pay in different industrialised capitalist countries. The other is the dissimilarity of clerical pay in different industries. In particular, the ratio of clerical pay to manual pay is lowest in the industries in which manual pay is highest, and vice versa, which was argued earlier to be the result of greater inter-industry variance of manual than of non-manual working conditions.* But this in itself implies that the relativity

* See pp. 175–6 above. Using data from NES (1970), tables 38 and 42, the following regression was estimated by OLS across the 16 industries for which the necessary figures were available:

$$\log y = 0.770 + 0.296 \log x \qquad R^2 = 0.374$$
$$(0.102)$$

where y = median hourly earnings of adult male full time office and communications workers, and x = median hourly earnings of adult male full time semiskilled manual workers.
The coefficient of $\log x$ is clearly significantly smaller than unity (the number in

between clerical and manual pay in each industry is (at least to some extent) governed by the relative non-pecuniary attractiveness of clerical and manual work in that industry, rather than by some common normative rule concerning the proper relationship between clerical and manual pay.

From this viewpoint, the one somewhat puzzling feature of clerical pay is why it is as high as it is. For the working conditions of most clerks seem superior to those of most manual workers, and thus, if it were true that almost all manual workers have enough education to become clerical workers, one would expect clerks to earn not the same as skilled manual workers but less than semiskilled manual workers – as is in fact the case in most communist countries (Phelps Brown, 1977, pp. 39–42, 46–7; UN, 1967, ch. 8, tables 6 and 18).

The solution to this puzzle seems to me to be an anomic one, namely that the universality of secondary education exaggerates the universality of educational attainment. In particular, it would appear that a substantial proportion of children (whose parents are mainly semiskilled and unskilled manual workers) leave school at the earliest permitted age in a state of literacy and numeracy so rudimentary as to make clerical employment impossible for them. As a result, clerical labour is probably more highly paid (on average) than manual labour because the required abilities are somewhat scarcer. To reconcile this hypothesis with the evidence from communist countries, in which clerical labour is usually paid less than manual labour, one must suppose (not implausibly) that educational attainment in communist countries is more even, or that the relative pay of clerical labour in most communist countries has been artificially depressed for ideo-logical (i.e. normative) reasons.

6.4   INTER-OCCUPATIONAL RELATIVITIES: MANAGERIAL AND PROFESSIONAL

(i) Managers and administrators

The base of the managerial pay structure in any given (private or public sector) organisation lies somewhat above the pay of the highest

brackets beneath it being its standard error), which implies that the ratio of clerical to manual pay diminishes as manual pay increases. The coefficient is also significantly (at the 0.01 level) greater than zero; this positive correlation across industries between clerical and manual pay was argued earlier to be caused by inter-industry variations in establishment size and general working environment.

ranking manual or clerical workers, although trainee managers may initially be paid rather less. From this base rises a pyramid, the managers in each layer of which are paid more than their subordinates in the layer below. The difference in pay between the top and the bottom of the pyramid thus depends on the average pay differential between layers, the average span of control, and the width of the base (which reflects the size of the organisation). In addition, there are usually some more specialised managers, who do not fit neatly into the hierarchy.

To compare the pay of managers with the pay of manual and clerical workers is not altogether easy. In particular, account should but usually cannot be taken of differences in hours of work, differences in career earnings profiles, and the effects of progressive taxation and fringe benefits.* But with these reservations in mind it may be recorded that the average gross weekly earnings of male managers in Britain in the early 1970s were 1.5 times those of foremen and about twice those of semiskilled manual workers (NES, 1970, table 34). Moreover, managers constituted 70 per cent of those employees whose gross pay was above £10,000 per year, this being roughly seven times the median earnings of manual men; and the top managers of the largest companies earned about fifty times as much as the average male manual worker (Diamond, 1976, pp. 35, 138 and table 25).

Such statistics as are available suggest that the relative pay of senior managerial grades has declined substantially over the last forty years – gross and net of taxes and fringe benefits, in the private and in the public sector, and in Britain and in other industrialised capitalist countries.† This decline is (in a statistical sense) the result of two things. (1) It is partly a reflection of the declines, discussed earlier, in the pay of clerical and skilled manual workers relative to less skilled workers, which (because the base of the managerial pay pyramid has not altered much in relation to the pay of skilled and clerical workers) has reduced the pay of all managerial grades relative to the pay of less

* Diamond (1976), ch. 4, esp. table 49; Lydall (1968), app. 1; Lewellen (1968), pp. 154–5, 224–5.
† Diamond, 1976, pp. 58–64; Scitovsky, 1966, p. 40; Lewellen, 1968, pp. 174–80. But the pay of the *average* manager (as recorded by Routh, 1965, p. 107, and Miller, 1966, table III-6) is also affected by the relative numbers in different managerial grades. For example, the secular concentration of employment into large organisations (private and public), which has caused managerial hierarchies to become fewer and larger, must have tended to raise 'average' managerial pay.

skilled manual workers. (2) There has also been a marked compression of differentials within managerial hierarchies.

(1) *Explanatory hypotheses.* A normative explanation of the level and structure of managerial pay would be that it is determined by a convention that pay must reflect responsibility and that pay relationships must symbolise authority relationships. This convention prevails counter to anomic pressures (a) because to pay managers less than they regard as a fair rate would (in the way described on pp. 41–2) diminish the intensity and conscientousness with which they work and (b) because to pay superiors less than their subordinates would undermine their authority and would thus reduce the efficiency and the effectiveness of managerial control.

An alternative, anomic, hypothesis concerning the determination of managerial pay can be constructed from one or more of the following elements. (a) There is a shortage of people willing to accept responsibility, the more so, the greater the level of responsibility involved. (b) There is a shortage of people with the ability and experience necessary to be an effective manager, the more so, the more important the position involved. (c) It is advantageous to pay people more than their subordinates because this gives the latter an incentive to work hard as a means of obtaining promotion.

In evaluating these competing hypotheses, I shall rely mainly on the substantial body of evidence recently assembled by the Royal Commission on Income Distribution (Diamond, 1976, 1976a, 1976b).

(2) *International comparisons.* The Commission discovered that the relative pay of managers varies widely among advanced capitalist countries, in three respects.

(1) Managerial pay in relation to the average earnings of all employees: The Commission measured this approximately by the ratio of the pay of a given private sector managerial grade to GDP per economically active person. This ratio, if managerial pay is taken gross of tax, is almost twice as large in some countries as in others; if managerial pay is taken net of tax, the range is even greater (1976, p. 194).

(2) Pay relativities within managerial hierarchies: The Commission discovered that these also vary substantially between countries (1976, p. 79). For example, in 1975 the average differential between (a

matched set of) managerial grades, gross of tax, ranged from 25 per cent in Australia to 37 per cent in France (and, net of tax, from 16 per cent in Australia to 32 per cent in France).

(3) The relationship between public and private sector managerial pay: Evidence submitted to the Commission (1976b, p. 253) compared the pay of top civil servants (and also military officers and judges) with the pay of the top manager of a firm of given (large) size, in several countries. The ratio of public to private sector managerial pay, so measured, ranged from 25 per cent in France to 62 per cent in Britain. This is consistent with other evidence that the relative pay of high ranking public servants varies widely between countries (Scitovsky, 1966, pp. 40–1; Taylor, 1975; Economist, 1976).

In earlier sections of this chapter wide variation between advanced capitalist countries in relative rates of pay was taken as evidence that normative forces were at work in at least some countries. On this basis, the Commission's international comparisons would appear to give strong support to the normative explanation of managerial pay. It is true, of course, that superiors are almost always paid *more* than their subordinates in all countries, but I argued earlier (p. 186) that this fact does not necessarily tell against the normative hypothesis.

There is, however, one important feature of the evidence that tells in favour of an anomic explanation, which is that the relative pay of managers is negatively correlated across countries with per capita real income. Managers tend to be relatively worse off, that is, in richer countries. This is true not only when one contrasts developed with developing countries, but also (as may be inferred from the statistics on p. 194 of Diamond, 1976)* when one contrasts one advanced capitalist country with another. This cross-section correlation, moreover, harmonises closely with the tendency noted earlier for the relative pay of managers in advanced capitalist countries to decline over time. These two sorts of empirical regularity, taken together,

* The table in question presents statistics from two sources (with different but overlapping samples of countries) on the relative pay, gross and net of tax, of a given senior managerial grade in different countries; it also presents an index of real GDP per economically active person in these countries. I therefore calculated four simple coefficients of correlation across countries between relative managerial pay and real GDP per economically active person, with the following results.
(1) Hay–MSL data, gross managerial pay: $R = -0.35$ (insignificant at 0.05 level).
(2) Hay–MSL data, net managerial pay: $R = -0.22$ (insignificant at 0.05 level).
(3) MCE data, gross managerial pay: $R = -0.76$ (significant at 0.05 level).
(4) MCE data, net managerial pay: $R = -0.41$ (significant at 0.05 level).

suggest that managerial pay is to a significant extent governed by anomic forces of some sort; it is of interest to enquire *what* sort.

It seems very unlikely that managers are relatively better off in poorer countries because people in them are in general less willing to accept responsibility, or require more of an incentive to strive for promotion. It seems much more likely that the explanation is that managerial *talent* is scarcer in poorer countries. This interpretation is supported by the available statistics inasmuch as the correlation across advanced capitalist countries between relative managerial pay and per capita real income is (as reported in the last footnote) stronger when managerial pay is measured gross of tax than when it is measured net of tax. For this suggests that the high pay of managers is mainly a rent to a scarce factor which can be (and to varying extents in different countries is)* taxed away, rather than necessary compensation for onerous responsibilities.

One possible reason for a greater scarcity of managerial talent in poorer countries could be that managers are more mobile internationally than other sorts of workers. But the available evidence on migration gives little support to this hypothesis (Diamond, 1976, para. 147), and it therefore seems more probable that the greater abundance of managerial talent in richer countries is the result of internal forces. One such force might be a greater amount of higher education, or more equal access to education in general (which tends to tap a larger pool of innate ability). But formal education and innate ability seem less important than practical experience as ingredients of managerial talent, at any rate above a certain level. Thus it would appear that there is something about the process of economic development and growth itself which causes the supply of suitably experienced labour to expand faster than the demand for it, and that it is this endogenous mechanism which causes the relative pay of managers to tend to decline as per capita real income increases.

In any event, the evidence implies that the relative pay of managers is to a significant extent affected by anomic pressures, and that the most important such pressure is the degree of scarcity of managerial talent. But the evidence also implies that normative forces are important. For the correlation between relative managerial pay and per capita real income, although it is consistently negative and usually statistically significant, leaves most of the variation of relative managerial pay

* Diamond, 1976, pp. 187–9.

193

between advanced capitalist countries unexplained.* This, I would suggest, is attributable mainly to the influence of normative pressures, and in particular to variation between countries in what is conventionally regarded as an appropriate reward for responsibility and as an appropriate pay differential between a superior and his subordinates.

It seems very plausible to suppose, for example, that the large difference in the relative pay of managers between France and Australia (two countries with roughly the same per capita real income) reflects authoritarian attitudes in the former and egalitarian attitudes in the latter – and indeed this interpretation is supported by the detailed studies of French and German firms made by Daubigny and Silvestre (Phelps Brown, 1977, pp. 33–5). The influence of normative forces can also be seen, I would suggest, in the wide variation between countries in the relative pay of public sector managers and administrators, which appears to stem simply from differences in what is conventionally regarded as proper pay for top government officials, elected and appointed (Scitovsky, 1966).

(3) *Other evidence.* These conclusions about the determinants of managerial pay derived from international comparisons are buttressed by various other sorts of information, and in particular by the verbal evidence submitted to the Royal Commission by companies and public sector organisations (Diamond, 1976b).

This verbal evidence, although it is hard to summarise objectively, gives little support to the hypothesis that there is a general unwillingness to accept or to strive for promotion to positions of greater responsibility and authority. Isolated instances of reluctance to accept promotion were mentioned, but these appeared mainly to be refusals to accept geographical relocation (1976, para. 325). This impression of willingness to accept responsibility and authority is reinforced by the finding of Goldthorpe (1974, pp. 134–43) that in terms of 'general desirability' people ranked all managerial jobs significantly and usually substantially higher than all manual and clerical jobs, and senior managerial jobs higher than junior managerial jobs.

As regards scarcity of talent, which I argued above to be the main source of anomic pressure on managerial pay, the verbal evidence

---

* The average proportion of the international variance of gross managerial pay explained by the two relevant correlations in n. * on p. 192 is 0.35.

submitted to the Commission is rather uninformative. It would appear, however, that there is a certain amount of direct 'price' competition between companies for top executives, for some sorts of specialised manager, and for management trainees (as is confirmed for the US by the empirical studies of Freeman, 1971). It also appears that many managers are to some extent subject to an anomic system of payment by results. In particular, it is common in the private sector to set not a single rate of pay for a managerial job but a range within which the pay of the individual is set and varied according to 'merit' – although schemes of this type apparently have a way of degenerating under normative pressure into systems of routine increments.

The verbal evidence submitted to the Commission also seems to confirm that managerial pay in general is strongly influenced by normative pressures. Almost every witness emphasised that managerial pay both within the hierarchy and relative to other workers should be 'fair' or 'reasonable' or 'equitable and defensible', and that this was the principal reason for making use of job evaluation techniques. Most witnesses also stressed that departure from 'fair' rates of pay damaged managerial morale and thus reduced efficiency – this being precisely in accordance with the normative hypothesis, which implies that although managerial pay is to some extent arbitrarily determined, it cannot necessarily be costlessly altered.

Some of the verbal evidence also suggests that the secular decline in managerial pay mentioned earlier may be due not only to a reduction in the scarcity of managerial talent but also at least in part to normative pressures (Diamond, 1976, p. 147; 1976b, pp. 142, 217, 314, 340). In particular, it may be argued that over the last half-century the spread of egalitarian ideas has undermined the legitimacy of traditional inequalities of income, status and power, and has inhibited employers from increasing (especially top) managerial pay in line with the general rate of wage inflation. Whether or not this has occurred in the private sector, the extraordinarily steep decline in the relative pay of top government officials (Scitovsky, 1966; Diamond, 1976, p. 59) suggests strongly that it has happened in the public sector, presumably because the pay of top public servants is both particularly visible and peculiarly subject to social and political pressures.

(ii) *Professional occupations*

The 'professional and technical' category in most broad occupational classifications is internally so heterogeneous that it is appropriate to subdivide it. Technical workers (draughtsmen, programmers, etc.) constitute about one third of the category; there have been few systematic studies of their pay, and for this reason I shall neglect them. It is also convenient to separate off those members of this category, including many accountants and engineers, who are in effect professionally qualified managers and administrators.

Another subset of professional occupations contains artists, writers, musicians, actors, sportsmen, and so on, among whom are to be found some of the richest and the poorest people in society. Some musicians and actors are powerfully unionised. But in general it would appear that pay in this subset of occupations is governed almost entirely by anomic forces.

It remains to consider the professions proper. These themselves are by no means homogeneous. They include some relatively poorly paid occupations, such as librarianship, social work and the church – the clergy in Britain, for example, earning on average about three quarters as much as manual workers (LPU, 1977). But they also include some very well paid occupations, such as law, dentistry and medicine – the average net of tax annual earnings of general medical practitioners in Britain, for instance, being about two and a half times those of manual workers.* More generally, the 'higher professions' are, with managers, the best paid group in society.

(1) *Explanatory hypotheses.* Professional pay, and in particular the relatively high pay of certain professions, can in principle be explained in anomic terms as a result of (a) the expense of, including the earnings forgone during, professional training or (b) a scarcity of innate or fortuitously acquired talent.

Alternatively, professional pay could be explained in normative terms. Most professional workers seem to entertain rather well-developed pay norms, based partly on responsibility, partly on sacrifice and partly on social position (Houghton, 1974, pp. 36, 70; Woodroofe, 1975, p. 5; Williams, 1974, pp. 202–3). In addition, there

---

* Diamond (1976b), p. 91, corrected (on the basis of the New Earnings Survey) to allow for the fact that the manual workers in table 3 are paid more than manual workers in general.

are in many professions mechanisms capable of enforcing these norms to a greater or lesser degree in one or both of two ways.

(1) Direct pressure on employers may be exerted by collective action, as practised by teachers, airline pilots and doctors in countries with nationalised health services, and by professional associations which prescribe minimum fees and prohibit advertising (Mintz, 1977, Groser, 1976). Individual normative pressure may also be important, since professional employees are often in positions of considerable responsibility and thus their employers may fear that paying less than the 'proper' rate would cause a costly reduction in conscientousness and commitment (Houghton, p. 73; Woodroofe, p. 35).

(2) Freedom of entry into a profession may be artificially impeded by requirements imposed by professional bodies or the government concerning registration, qualifications and training, or by restrictions on the capacity of institutions which provide essential training (Friedman, 1945; Monopolies Commission, 1970).

A priori, there would seem to be certain professions in which normative pressures (although they undoubtedly influence the pay of certain subgroups) have little or no effect on the pay of the average employee, since their pay is low, they are weakly unionised, and entry is subject to few restrictions. Examples of such professions are librarianship and social work. Conversely, insofar as normative pressures on professional pay are important at all, their influence would seem likely to be most pronounced in the better paid professions (university teaching, law, architecture, medicine, stockbroking, etc.), and it is on these that I shall concentrate.

(2) *Direct evidence.* If the anomic hypothesis that high professional pay is caused simply by the high cost of training were correct, one might expect to find that the discounted lifetime earnings of professional employees, net of outlays on training, were rather similar to those of clerical and manual workers. Some studies (Diamond, 1976b, p. 42; Newbould, 1976) have concluded that this is so, but only, it seems to me, because they have used unreasonably high discount rates. For most calculations of this sort are based on cross-section age–earnings profiles, and thus (since the earnings are all at the prices of one period) the appropriate discount rate to use would seem to be the *real* rate of interest, which is typically not more than 2 or 3 per cent. At this sort of level of the discount rate, the financial advantage of the higher

professions over manual and clerical occupations, although less marked than a comparison of peak earnings would suggest, remains substantial (Diamond, 1976, p. 229).

It could be argued that this discount rate, since it takes no account of risk, is too low. On the other hand, however, this sort of calculation takes no account of the much more attractive nature of professional than of manual and clerical work. And indeed there is a great deal of direct evidence that despite the length and cost of the training there is no general shortage of people willing to enter the higher professions. In British universities in 1975, for example, there were three applicants for every place in medicine and dentistry, and more than two applicants for every place in law (UCCA, 1974–5, tables 3 and 4). In 1976, firms of accountants and solicitors were described as 'besieged' by university graduates seeking traineeships (APL, 1976, pp. 2, 12). In the United States in 1973 more than three times as many people took the law school aptitude test as there were places at law schools (Ruud, 1974). More generally, Goldthorpe (1974, table 6.6) has established that the higher professions are commonly regarded as far more desirable than clerical or manual jobs.

This body of evidence very strongly suggests that in order to explain the high pay of certain professions in anomic terms it is necessary to suppose that there is a shortage of talent. To evaluate this latter anomic hypothesis is more difficult.

It seems indisputable that the wide dispersion of pay within professions dominated by self-employment is to a substantial extent generated by anomic forces, and in particular that the extremely high pay of certain individual professional employees (top surgeons, top lawyers, top architects) is governed by natural scarcity of talent. But it also seems very probable that the relative pay of different categories and grades of professional employee within particular organisations is heavily conditioned by normative pressures (Williams, 1974, pp. 230–1; Freeman, 1971, pp. 165–6). In addition, a number of pieces of evidence suggest that the *average* employee in at any rate some professions is paid more than can be accounted for in terms of natural scarcity alone.

In Britain, about half the rejected applicants for university places in medicine, dentistry and law appear to possess the required qualifications (UCCA, 1974–5, p. 14; 1974–5a, pp. 8, 22–3). The number of solicitors was deliberately and without apparent difficulty or a rise in relative pay increased by 20 per cent in a decade (NBPI, 1968, p. 5; 1969, p. 6). Similarly, the number of university teachers was greatly increased in a decade without any appreciable decline in the quality of teaching (NBPI, 1968b, p. 9). And a Royal Commission which proposed a doubling of the number of medical school places antici- pated no difficulty in filling them with suitable recruits (Todd, 1968, pp. 24–6; see also BMA, 1962, p. 30). In the United States, Friedman (1945) concluded that the pay of physicians was inflated by artificial barriers to entry;* and Sobotka (cited in Lewis, 1963) discovered that unionisation had substantially raised the pay of airline pilots.

This type of direct evidence, although it implies that normative pressures have some influence on the average level of pay in certain professions, does not enable one to say how much of an influence. It is thus desirable to look also at two broader types of indirect evidence on the determinants of professional pay.

(3) *International comparisons.* It is far from easy to compare the relative pay of particular professions in different countries, partly because incomes vary widely within many professions and partly because the structure of certain professions (law and university teaching being prime examples) varies between countries. But with these reservations in mind it may be noted that the relative pay of most professional occupations appears to differ substantially between advanced capitalist countries.

Scitovsky (1966) estimated the pay of certain professions as a ratio of the per capita income of the occupied population in eight countries. In the 1950s, the pay of doctors, normalised in this way, varied from 4.8 in France to 2.6 in West Germany (although a narrower range is reported in an ILO study cited by Phelps Brown, 1977, p. 38); the pay of dentists varied from 5.5 in France to 1.9 in West Germany; for lawyers the range was from 3.2 to 2.3, and for professors from 4.1 to 1.9. That inter-professional pay relativities vary significantly between countries is suggested also by statistics collected by Pilkington (1960, app. F).

A more recent study of the Common Market countries indicates that in 1973 the gross of tax pay of general medical practitioners, relative to GDP per occupied person, was about twice as high in Denmark and

---

* Lewis (1963, pp. 114–35) questions Friedman's conclusion on the grounds that he used too low a discount rate. For reasons given on p. 197 above I believe this criticism to be incorrect.

the Netherlands as in Britain.* Another study, covering nine advanced capitalist countries, indicates that in 1975 the net of tax pay of a given category of male primary school teacher, relative to GDP per occupied person, was about 1.6 times as great in Switzerland and Luxembourg as in France and Finland.† A third study, also covering nine advanced capitalist countries, indicates that in 1976 the gross starting salary of the lowest category of university teacher, relative to GDP per occupied person, was about 1.8 times as great in Australia and Canada as in France, while the average gross pay of the highest category of university teacher was on the same basis about 1.8 times as great in Australia as in the United States.‡

Some of these disparities between countries undoubtedly arise from inconsistencies of classification and measurement. Others may be generated by anomic forces such as differences in the availability of higher education, in the degree to which professional training is subsidised by the state, and in tastes regarding the quality of professional services. There is, moreover, an embryonic international market in certain professional skills (Diamond, 1976, pp. 201–7; Economist, 1976a). Nevertheless, the amount of variation between advanced capitalist countries in the pay of particular professional occupations, relative both to other professions and to other occupations, seems so great as to lend considerable support to the hypothesis that normative pressures exert an important influence in at least some professions and countries. This interpretation is reinforced by the fact that, unlike the relative pay of managers, the relative pay of professional occupations is not negatively correlated (or indeed correlated in any significant way) across advanced capitalist countries with the level of per capita real income.§

* *Sources:* Doctors' pay: Diamond (1976b), pp. 39–40. GDP and population: OECD, *Main Economic Indicators,* Feb. 1977, pp. 156–7. Proportion of population economically active: OECD, *Labour Force Statistics 1962–1973,* p. 25.
† *Sources:* Teachers' pay: Pommatau (1976), pp. 2–3. GDP per occupied person: see previous footnote.
‡ *Sources:* University teachers' pay: AUT (1977). GDP per occupied person (for 1975): see penultimate footnote.
§ Using the data referred to in the previous paragraph, I calculated simple coefficients of the correlation across countries of relative professional pay with real GDP per occupied person, with the following results.
  (1) General medical practitioners: $R = 0.43$ (insignificant at 0.05 level).
  (2) Primary teachers: $R = 0.19$ (insignificant at 0.05 level).
  (3) Junior university teachers: $R = 0.29$ (insignificant at 0.05 level).
  (4) Senior university teachers: $R = 0.06$ (insignificant at 0.05 level).

At the same time, there are certain features of the international comparisons which suggest that anomic forces are also at work. One is that doctors are in most, though not all, countries the best paid profession (Scitovsky, 1966; Pilkington, 1960, app. F). This, in conjunction with the fact that doctors in general undergo the longest training, suggests not only that the relative length of training has some influence on the relative pay of different professions,* but also (since there is no shortage in the population at large of people willing to undergo professional training) that the various professions are to some extent competing among themselves and with managerial occupations for a limited pool of talent.

A second feature of the international comparisons which gives some support to the hypothesis that the relative pay of professional occupations is to some extent governed by scarcity of talent is that it tends to be higher in developing than in developed countries (Phelps Brown, 1977, pp. 36–8). A third feature which reinforces the same hypothesis is that the higher professions are in all advanced capitalist countries *better* paid (albeit to widely varying degrees) than manual and clerical occupations. This is not true, however, of some communist countries, in which professional workers are no better off, or are worse off, than skilled manual workers (Phelps Brown, 1977, pp. 38–49).

There are two possible explanations for the difference in relative professional pay between these communist countries and capitalist countries. One is that professional pay in capitalist countries is artificially inflated by normative pressures. The other is that professional pay in the communist countries concerned is artificially depressed by normative pressures (with the result that professional employees, though not necessarily in short supply, are on average less talented than in capitalist countries). The truth seems to me, on the basis of the evidence discussed above, to be a mixture of the two.

(4) *Secular trend.* It is also worth considering the limited amount of information available concerning changes over long periods of time in the relative pay of particular professions. The statistics assembled by Scitovsky (1966) and Routh (1965, pp. 62–71, 104) indicate that in most countries the pay of most professions, relative to manual and clerical occupations, has declined significantly over the last sixty or

---

* An inference supported by the findings of Psacharopoulos cited on p. 84 of Phelps Brown (1977).

seventy years – and the decline would probably appear more marked if taxation and hours of work were taken into account. The decline seems to have been comparatively great for university and school teachers (see also OECD, 1965, p. 35), and comparatively small for doctors and dentists – indeed the relative pay of doctors appears to have increased in France and the United States. Over the last twenty or thirty years the picture is much less clear cut: in some countries and professions relative pay has continued to decline; in others the decline appears to have been arrested or reversed (see also Taylor, 1975; APL, 1976, p. 17; Lewellen, 1968, p. 175).

These facts seem to me to be broadly consistent with the other evidence on the determinants of professional pay. The general secular decline would appear to reflect the underlying influence of anomic pressures, and in particular to have been caused mainly by a great increase in the supply of people with a secondary or higher education. That this is the case is suggested by the comparatively large decline in the pay of school and university teachers, whose training consists mainly of standard education (and by the comparatively high proportion of people of working class origins in these professions – Leggatt, 1970, pp. 166–7; Williams, 1974, p. 28).

Doctors, dentists, lawyers and other professions whose training is more specialised and less a part of the general educational system have been better insulated from the effects of its expansion. Nonetheless, it seems probable that the enlargement of the educational system has indirectly exerted a depressing influence on the relative pay even of these professions, both by tapping a larger pool of innate ability and by making artificial barriers to entry based on required educational qualifications harder to maintain. In addition, the relative pay of all professions must have been subject to downward anomic pressure arising from the secular decline of relative managerial pay.

The influence of normative pressures, on the other hand, may be discerned in the different patterns of movement in different countries and professions, especially over the last twenty or thirty years. For, partly as a result of increased governmental regulation of training and practice and partly in response to the erosion of their accustomed relative pay, the professions have become increasingly well organised and have increasingly resorted to direct collective action. Thus despite further expansion of the higher education system some professions in some countries have managed to check or reverse the decline in their relative pay. These efforts, however, have to some extent been offset, I would suggest, by the spread of egalitarian ideas, which have both altered the pay norms of professional workers themselves and made it harder for them to preserve their traditional privileges, especially in professions and countries in which the state is the major employer.

6.5 PAY RELATIVITIES: A SUMMARY

In the past three sections I have considered pay relativities between similar occupations in different establishments and industries, and between different occupations – manual, clerical, managerial and professional. I have looked at various sorts of direct and indirect evidence regarding the determinants of these various sorts of relativities in advanced capitalist countries. But despite the variety of subject matter, and indeed despite the shakiness (or non-existence) of the evidence on many specific points, a moderately consistent picture has emerged, whose main features may be summarised as follows.

(1) Anomic forces exert an extremely powerful influence, especially in shaping, preserving and changing the broad framework of pay relativities. As far as inter-establishment and inter-industry relativities are concerned, the most important source of anomic pressure appears to be the non-pecuniary advantages and disadvantages of different sorts of work. As regards inter-occupational relativities, especially those involving substantial disparities of pay, non-pecuniary factors (including training costs) appear to be of lesser significance, the most important source of anomic pressure being the scarcity of certain sorts of innate and fortuitously acquired talent.

(2) The pattern of pay relativities is powerfully influenced also by normative forces. Of particular importance are pressures to eliminate or reduce various kinds of inequality of pay, pressures by certain comparatively highly paid groups to maintain their relative position, and pressures to ensure that pay relationships reflect authority relationships. Normative pressures of these and other sorts significantly modify the broad framework of relativities between different industrial and occupational categories; they have a very large effect on relativities between particular establishments and between particular narrowly defined industries and occupations; and their influence is at its greatest as regards the various types of relativities within particular establishments and industries. Both the extent and the character of

normative pressures on pay relativities differ from one advanced capitalist country to another. In all countries, however, normative forces appear to have more of an effect on inter-occupational than on inter-establishment relativities, and more of an effect on public sector than on private sector pay.

6.6 WAGE INFLATION
(i) *The theory*

The model developed in chapter 5 implies that the general money wage level in advanced capitalist countries has a chronic tendency to rise as a result of two entangled sorts of conflict over indirectly determined relativities. The first is between different pay norms, as manifested in the efforts of groups of employees, by driving up their own rates of pay, to attain relative positions which are inconsistent with one another. The second is between pay norms and anomic pressures, and in particular the tendency for attempts at enforcing 'fair' relativities to cause employers in certain pay groups to become short of labour and to bid up pay, thus provoking employees in other groups to seek further pay increases designed to restore fair relativities.

Not all pay groups, but only those whose settlements are in the critical subset, play an active part in this process, the pay of other groups being pushed and pulled along in a more passive manner by normative and anomic pressures of various sorts. Thus the pace of wage inflation depends heavily on the membership of and the degree of conflict within the critical subset, which in turn is determined by, among other things, the following: the nature of pay norms; the degree to which people care about unfair relative pay (which is affected by what is happening to the average real wage); the power of particular groups of employees over their employers; the extent to and the way in which people anticipate the future; the underlying determinants of demand and supply in particular labour submarkets; and the aggregate demand management policies of the government. The specific character of most of these influences is obviously likely to vary both over time and from one advanced capitalist country to another.

This theory of wage inflation is difficult to test, given the evidence currently available, for three main reasons.

(1) Most econometric studies of the causes of wage inflation are macroeconomic in nature, while the present theory, in which the

driving force is conflict over certain relativities, is peculiarly micro-economic. In other words, although the determinants of wage inflation in the present model have some macroeconomic correlates, no purely macroeconomic analysis can penetrate to the heart of the process.

(2) Yet neither are most microeconomic cross-section studies of the determinants of relativities (such as those discussed in the four preceding sections) of much direct use in testing the present theory of wage inflation, although they provide valuable background information on the working of the labour market. For there is no simple or necessary connection between the intensity of conflict over relativities and its outcome; relativities, for example, might on average over time be determined principally by anomic pressures even though vigorous opposition by normative forces was causing rapid wage inflation. To investigate this one would need to examine the pattern of pay settlements in some detail, looking at short-term movements in the rates of pay of the various groups in the economy and at the interrelationships between them. Microeconometric studies of this kind, however, are extremely scarce.

(3) The present theory overlaps in important respects with the other theories of wage inflation reviewed in chapter 1. It is therefore in principle not easy, without caricaturing either the present theory or its rivals, to devise tests with a reasonable measure of discriminatory power. This problem is compounded by the fact that both the orthodox theory of wage inflation under conditions of monopoly and most of the various unorthodox theories of wage inflation are exceedingly underdeveloped.

But with these reservations in mind I shall attempt to test the present theory of wage inflation against what seem to me to be its two principal rivals. In doing this I shall refer frequently to two valuable surveys (Laidler, 1975; Trevithick, 1975) of the theoretical and empirical literature on inflation, neither of whose authors, it should be added, subscribe to anything like the present theory.

(ii) *An alternative theory*

Let us first consider the *competitive* theory. This is a purely anomic theory which contends that the behaviour of the general money wage level is governed by orthodox supply and demand forces, and that pay norms, collective bargaining and so on, although they may exist, contribute nothing of fundamental significance to the process of wage inflation. In other words, the proponents of the competitive theory, while admitting that there are monopolies in certain labour sub-markets, maintain that the behaviour of the general money wage level is best explained by supposing that the labour market as a whole is *fundamentally* similar to such markets as those in which securities and primary commodities are traded.

(1) *Evidence.* There are several well-known features of the process of wage inflation in advanced capitalist countries which suggest that the competitive theory is a much less accurate description of reality than the present theory. I shall first review these and then turn to the various defences which have been put forward by proponents of the competitive theory.

(1) The labour market appears, as the present theory would predict, to respond asymmetrically to excess demand and excess supply, rather than, as the competitive theory would predict, symmetrically. For example, in all advanced capitalist countries over the last thirty years the money wage level has persistently risen. Although its rate of increase has varied, its level has never fallen, despite the existence in certain years of a substantial aggregate surplus of labour as measured by the excess of the number unemployed over the number of unfilled vacancies. In this respect the labour market appears quite unlike, say, primary commodity markets, in which absolute falls as well as absolute increases in prices are common, even around a rising trend.

(2) Changes in the rate of wage inflation, moreover, appear to be very poorly correlated with changes in the balance of demand and supply in the labour market. The proportion of the variance over time of the rate of wage inflation in advanced capitalist countries during the last thirty years that can be explained by variations in the level and rate of change of unemployment and other indicators of the aggregate demand–supply balance is typically very low; and the simple correlation between wage inflation and unemployment over the whole period has the wrong sign (Laidler, p. 754; Trevithick, pp. 53–6, 65–78; Henry, 1976).

(3) The poorness of this correlation is especially damaging to the competitive theory because it is in a historical sense both new and associated with the rise of collective bargaining and union power. In Britain in the half-century before the first world war, when less than

a tenth of the labour force was unionised, unemployment and variations in unemployment explained about 80 per cent of the inter-temporal variance of wage inflation; between the wars, when about a quarter of the labour force was unionised, the correlation between wage inflation and unemployment was barely discernible; and since the second world war, with 40 to 50 per cent of the labour force unionised and a much larger proportion covered by collective pay agreements, the simple correlation between wage inflation and unemployment has more or less completely disappeared (Laidler, p. 754; Trevithick, pp. 53–6, 65–78; Hines, 1964).

(4) That the existence of unions contributes to the process of wage inflation is suggested also by a variety of other evidence. In Britain, Hines discovered a year-to-year correlation between wage inflation and changes in the proportion of the labour force unionised, inde-pendent of unemployment and other variables, which despite a good deal of criticism has remained (in Trevithick's words) 'virtually immune to statistical attack'; a similar correlation has been found in the United States, but not in the Netherlands or Germany (Trevithick, pp. 102–3; Dogas, 1975). Other econometric studies in various coun-tries have established that the forces which govern wage increases in highly unionised industries are different from those in less unionised industries, and that in many but not all cases there is some correlation between wage inflation and strike activity (Laidler, pp. 762–3; Trevi-thick, pp. 98–100; Silvestre, 1971).

(2) *A defence.* These several pieces of evidence, taken together, con-stitute a very strong prima facie case against the competitive theory. Its proponents, however, have maintained that much of this evidence can be reconciled with the competitive theory in one or more of four ways.

One line of defence has been to argue that official unemployment and vacancy statistics are misleading as indicators of the aggregate demand–supply balance in the labour market (Trevithick, pp. 65–7; Brittan, 1975; Parkin, 1977). On this basis, some have suggested that most unemployment in advanced capitalist countries during the last thirty years has been voluntary, and hence that the asymmetrical behaviour of the general money wage level has been the result of an almost complete absence of aggregate excess supply. Alternatively or in addition, some have suggested that the poorness of the correlation between wage inflation and measured unemployment can be accounted for by erratic changes in the relationship between true and measured unemployment caused by such things as changes in the generosity of unemployment benefits.

There is an element of truth in these suggestions. The extent of involuntary unemployment as defined on p. 162 above is extremely hard to measure accurately (Worswick, 1976). And some of those who are officially recorded as unemployed are undoubtedly voluntarily unemployed. Moreover, the availability of social security benefits surely deters some (voluntarily *and* involuntarily) unemployed people from accepting certain low-paid jobs, and thus influences the working of the labour market in the manner discussed on pp. 158–63 above. Furthermore, the relative level of unemployment benefits *has* changed on occasion, and this must have had some effect on the average duration of voluntary job search and on the ratio of voluntary to involuntary unemployment.

Even so, this type of attempt to reconcile the competitive theory of wage inflation with the evidence strikes me as broadly unconvincing, especially since it is for the most part empirically unsupported (Tobin, 1972, p. 8; Thurow, 1976, p. 57; Cripps, 1977, p. 107). It seems most implausible to suppose that the relationship between true and measured unemployment can have fluctuated in a manner sufficiently erratic to explain the poorness of the correlation between wage inflation and unemployment. It seems even less plausible to suppose that in advanced capitalist countries during the past thirty years there has never been an appreciable aggregate excess supply of labour. The number of unemployed persons (registered and unregistered) has often substantially exceeded, and has in recent years vastly exceeded, the number of unfilled vacancies; and it is extremely difficult to believe that more than a small minority of the unemployed (almost all of whom claim to want jobs) have been voluntarily so. Even those who refuse low-paying jobs usually form part of an excess supply of labour to better-paid jobs; and if the labour market were indeed fundamentally competitive this sort of aggregate excess supply, like any other sort of aggregate excess supply, would surely have a strong tendency to depress the general money wage level.

(3) *A second defence.* Another line of defence of the competitive theory involves expectations (Trevithick, ch. 7). It is argued that the presence

of inflationary expectations can explain why the correlation between wage inflation and unemployment has been so poor in advanced capitalist countries since the second world war, and why the general money wage level has not fallen absolutely in the face of aggregate excess supply.

Expectations are a part of the present theory of wage inflation. Moreover, although it is difficult independently to measure inflationary expectations, there is a considerable body of econometric evidence which is at any rate consistent with the hypothesis that expectations do in practice play an important role in the process of inflation (Laidler, pp. 759, 770–3; Trevithick, pp. 74–8, 113–16; Parkin, 1977). Furthermore, the presence of inflationary expectations in a competitive labour market would surely worsen the correlation between wage inflation and the aggregate demand–supply balance, and might temporarily prevent the general money wage level from falling absolutely in response to aggregate excess supply.

But to me the mere introduction of expectations does not seem sufficient to reconcile the competitive theory of wage inflation with the evidence. Consider, for example, the markets for primary commodities. In these demonstrably competitive markets, no-one would dispute that expectations are exceedingly important; yet prices respond in a sensitive way to excess demand and excess supply, both rising and falling in absolute terms in a manner quite unlike that of the general money wage level.

(4) *A third defence.* To this last observation a defender of the competitive theory of wage inflation might reply that the reason why the behaviour of the labour market appears so different from that of primary commodity markets has nothing to do with normative pressures or monopoly, but is a result of other sorts of labour market imperfection, especially immobility and poor information. This is undoubtedly correct in part. Nonetheless, imperfect mobility and information seem inadequate to reconcile the competitive theory with the evidence. It is hard to believe, especially in view of the empirical studies discussed in earlier sections of this chapter, that these factors are sufficient at the present time to account for much of the disparity in behaviour between the labour market and primary commodity markets. And it is absolutely impossible to believe, since transport and communications of every kind have enormously improved, that

immobility and imperfect information can explain why the correlation between wage inflation and unemployment has deteriorated so greatly over the last century.

(5) *A fourth defence.* A final defence of the competitive theory of wage inflation is that in a world of fixed or managed exchange rates its validity is more apparent at an international than at a national level (Laidler, pp. 781–6; Trevithick, pp. 6, 141–6). The argument contains two related propositions.

(1) If exchange rates are not freely floating, there will be a closer association between wage inflation and the aggregate demand–supply balance for the world as a whole than for individual countries. This proposition contains an important truth; specifically, it is essential to recognise that with fixed or managed exchange rates an increase in demand originating in country X is bound to increase demand also in its trading partner Y. But this is not inconsistent with the present theory. Nor can it save the competitive theory from the criticisms levelled at it above; in particular, such an increase in demand in country X would not, if labour markets were competitive, increase the general money wage level in Y if there were a substantial aggregate excess supply of labour.

(2) The other proposition is that inflation rates in different countries are correlated with one another, which suggests a common cause; this common cause, it is argued, is unlikely to be normative forces of the sort emphasised by the present theory, which one would expect to act differently in different countries. The empirical premise of this proposition is certainly correct in part: for although in cross-section both wage and price inflation proceed at persistently different rates in different advanced capitalist countries, there is some evidence of convergence in periods of fixed exchange rates;* and in the 1960s and 1970s inflation speeded up, albeit not exactly simultaneously nor to the same extent, in *all* these countries.

But these facts are not inconsistent with the present theory. To begin with, the theory does not preclude the possibility that wage inflation in several countries might be simultaneously accelerated by world excess demand or decelerated by a world slump. Moreover, inflation

---

* In particular, the data in Perry (1975, p. 404) and Trevithick (p. 8) suggest that the international variance (and coefficient of variation) of both wage and price inflation rates declined between 1961–5 and 1966–70.

might speed up in several countries at once as the result of a common external shock, such as the rise in the price of oil in 1973 (which, I would argue, stimulated the pace of wage inflation in advanced capitalist countries by reducing real wages). Finally, there are at least two ways in which, with fixed or managed exchange rates, the speed of normatively generated wage inflation in one country may both affect and be affected by the speed of normatively generated wage inflation in other countries.

(a) An autonomous increase (say) in the pace of wage inflation in country X, unmatched by an increase in productivity growth, will tend to cause unemployment and a balance of trade deficit in X, and excess demand and a trade surplus in its trading partner Y. In consequence, insofar as the pace of the wage–wage spiral in each country is sensitive (in the manner discussed in section 5.7) to variations in the aggregate demand–supply balance, wage inflation will tend to slow down in country X and to speed up in country Y. This process may be reinforced by government intervention; not least, the government of X may introduce wage controls or implement deflationary measures to eliminate the trade deficit.

(b) The autonomous increase in wage inflation in country X will also tend with fixed or managed exchange rates to raise the average real wage (of those workers who remain employed) in country X, and to depress the average real wage in country Y. This will tend to decrease militancy and damp down the wage–wage spiral in X and to increase militancy and speed up the wage–wage spiral in Y.

These two mechanisms would tend in a world of fixed or managed exchange rates to cause changes in inflation rates in different countries to be correlated with one another, and to reduce the variance of inflation rates across countries. But they may not act very powerfully. In particular, the collapse of the 'fixed' exchange rate system in 1971, after several years of increasing strain, suggests that inflation rates in individual countries have a rather strong tendency to lead lives of their own, which in turn is consistent with the present hypothesis that internal normative influences on the pace of wage inflation are important.

(6) *Conclusion.* For the various reasons outlined above, the available evidence seems to me to lead ineluctably to the conclusion that the competitive theory is a less accurate description of the process of wage

inflation in advanced capitalist countries than the present theory. There are, that is to say, a number of features of reality that appear very puzzling if the labour market is viewed as being fundamentally competitive, which make perfectly good sense if the labour market works in the way that I am suggesting. And there are as far as I can see no features of reality of which the opposite could be said.

I should immediately and most emphatically add that I am not denying the importance of anomic, competitive pressures in the process of wage inflation. On the contrary, both normative and anomic pressures play a vital part in my theory. What I am denying is that any *purely* anomic theory (or for that matter any purely normative theory) can provide a satisfactory description of reality.

(iii) *Another alternative theory*

There is, as I have already remarked, no well-developed orthodox theory of wage inflation under conditions of monopoly; and most unorthodox theories are in an analytical sense underdeveloped. But one unorthodox and reasonably coherent rival to the present theory is the *pure wage–price spiral* theory described on page 19 above. Like the present theory, it postulates that collective bargaining is important in the process of wage inflation (and thus in comparing it with the present theory I shall for convenience neglect anomic pressures). But unlike the present theory it maintains that union wage targets are cast in real, not relative, terms.

It is in principle difficult to assess empirically whether or not the pure wage–price spiral theory is a better description of reality than the present theory, for two reasons. The first is that the real wage of each individual group of employees depends to a very large extent on its relative wage, which makes it hard in practice to distinguish efforts to attain real wage targets from efforts to attain relative wage targets. The second is that the present theory is not a pure wage–wage spiral model, but attaches considerable significance to the effects which changes in the average real wage can have on militancy and hence on the pace of wage inflation. For example, if the average real wage falls, most people will find it harder to make ends meet, which will increase their resentment of unfair relative pay and the vigour and frequency of their efforts to eliminate it.

The problems created by this conceptual blurring of the distinction between the two theories are compounded by a shortage of suitable evidence. Macroeconometric wage equations in particular are of little use. It is true, for instance, that many such equations indicate that there is a significant correlation between the current rate of wage inflation and past price increases (which in some wage–price spiral models are regarded as affecting wages via their influence on expectations of *future* price increases). But this correlation is consistent with both theories; even in a pure wage–wage spiral one would expect substantial serial correlation of wage increases, and past wage increases are the main determinant of past price increases.* Nor can one infer very much from the estimated *size* of the coefficients on past price changes, especially since these vary widely according to the place and period under consideration, the specification of the wage equation, and the method of estimation (although this in itself makes one doubt that wage increases depend on price increases in the straightforward manner suggested by the pure wage–price spiral theory).†

Of more use in discriminating between the two theories is microeconomic information on employee wage targets and the process of wage inflation. There is, to begin with, plenty of casual and systematic evidence that people care about real wages: not only are price increases very frequently adduced as arguments for wage increases in the course of particular negotiations (Daniel, 1976); but also in some countries escalator clauses, whereby wages are linked in some formal way to prices, are commonly included in wage contracts. This does not prove that people are indifferent about relative pay – the invocation of price increases may be largely a bargaining tactic, and escalator clauses a convenient if rough method of preserving a particular relative position. But it would make a *pure* wage–wage spiral theory hard to defend.

There is, equally, a great deal of casual and systematic evidence that

* Perry (1975), estimating wage equations for eight advanced capitalist countries over the period 1960–72, tried inserting among his independent variables lagged wage increases as an alternative to lagged consumer price increases. In only three countries did this appreciably worsen the fit of the wage equation, and even this deterioration can be explained in terms of the present theory on the grounds that completely to omit consumer prices ignores the average-real-wage-militancy effect.
† For some estimates of the size of these coefficients, see Perry (1975), Parkin (1977), Henry (1976) and the works cited in Laidler (p. 759) and Trevithick (pp. 72–3, 114–16). It may be argued, although it remains to be demonstrated, that the variability of these estimates is not inconsistent with 'disposable real wage' versions of the pure wage–price spiral theory, but is attributable instead to failure in most cases to take account of the effects of direct taxation.

sentiments about relativities play an extremely important part in wage determination. One is forever reading in the newspapers of imitative pay settlements, of demands for parity, and of strikes and other efforts to restore differentials. These impressions are reinforced by the experiences of those who have attempted to administer wages policies (Clegg, 1971, ch. IV; Fels, 1972, pp. 103–23; Pay Board, 1973; 1974); by the results of more formal studies in a number of countries of wage contours, pattern bargaining and wage leadership (Laidler, p. 760; Trevithick, pp. 95–6, 103–4); and by the results of more general surveys which have shown that people tend to evaluate their own financial well-being, and that of others, in relative terms (Thurow, 1976, pp. 46–7, 105; Hirsch, 1977, p. 111).

On the basis of this evidence, the pure wage–price spiral theory must be regarded as less accurate than the present theory. This conclusion, however, requires qualification in two respects.

(1) Inflation could be generated by a wage leadership process in which all groups but one, animated by a concern to preserve fair relativities, passively aped the settlements of a leader *whose wage target was real*. If this were so, the substance of the pure wage–price spiral theory would be correct even though most groups were exclusively preoccupied with relativities. But the available evidence does not bear out this hypothesis. Empirical studies of wage leadership have established the importance of imitative wage settlements, but they have not produced any consistently successful explanation of the behaviour of the wage leader (Laidler, pp. 760, 765; Trevithick, pp. 103–4). Nor, more fundamentally, have they succeeded in establishing that a particular group does consistently act as the wage leader – this negative finding being what one would expect if (as the present theory contends) the process of inflation is fundamentally a wage–wage spiral.*

(2) Because it can be demonstrated that people care about relativities, one can reject the pure wage–price spiral theory. But one cannot, on the basis of the evidence mentioned above, reject the weaker hypothesis that employees are *principally* concerned with real wages (which, if true, would diminish the usefulness, though not necessarily the formal correctness, of the present theory). For this would require a much greater quantity of detailed information on the

* Although in the present theory the groups whose settlements compose the critical subset could very aptly be described as the *leading sector*.

behaviour of individual pay groups than is at present available. Specifically, one would need to examine whether, controlling for other influences, the successive pay settlements of most groups are better explained by the hypothesis that their targets are real or by the hypothesis that their targets are relative, with particular reference to circumstances in which the two hypotheses predict markedly different outcomes.

But even in the absence of detailed evidence of this sort there is, I would suggest, one basic reason for believing that relative wage goals are more fundamental, which concerns the *determinants* of wage targets. Without an explanation of what governs real wage targets, wage–price spiral theories are quite hollow (there being always *some* assumption about real wage targets which, given what has actually happened to real wages, is consistent with the observed behaviour of money wages). Yet it is hard to see what, in the long run, the explanation could be, especially since actual real wages tend to increase over time, which makes it necessary to explain how real wage targets change.*

One can make some progress in this regard by supposing that current real wage aspirations are some sort of extrapolation of past experience (and indeed the present theory assumes that people are sensitive to short-term changes in real wages). But in principle this seems a precarious and unsatisfactory foundation on which to build a general theory. By contrast, relative wage targets seem inherently less transient – especially since some of their roots lie in basic moral ideas such as equality and hierarchy. It thus seems much easier to explain what governs them and why they should exert an enduring influence on the process of wage determination.

(iv) *Further comments*

The present theory of wage inflation appears to me to fit the facts better than what I would regard as its two main competitors. But it is also worth asking how well, in two respects, it fits the facts in an absolute sense.

(1) One characteristic of econometric attempts to explain variations in the pace of wage inflation in advanced capitalist countries over the

---

* This criticism applies with less force to those wage–price spiral theories which emphasise the desire of workers to squeeze the share of profits.

past thirty years, regardless of their theoretical basis, is that they have been rather unsuccessful (Trevithick, pp. 74–8; Perry, 1975; Godley, 1977, pp. 473–4, 486–8; Parkin, 1977, pp. 479–81). With sufficient ingenuity in the choice of variables and lag structures, and with the aid of dummy variables of one sort or another, macroeconometric wage equations have usually though not always been made to fit pretty closely to the data from which they were estimated. But in general they have proved poor predictors when applied to data for later years, requiring re-estimation (and often the addition or replacement of variables) to maintain their fit.

Part of the problem has been the imposition and relaxation of governmental wage controls, which have made it harder to follow the 'natural' course of events. But it is difficult to believe that this alone can explain the poor quality of the results. One is therefore led to the conclusion that wage inflation is resistant to this sort of macro-econometric modelling.

But this should not be surprising if the present theory is correct, partly because the underlying process is essentially microeconomic, and partly because, as the analysis in chapter 5 suggests, it is complex and sensitive. Quite small changes in supply and demand conditions in particular sectors, or in the power or militancy of particular groups of employees, or in the availability of information, can in the present model cause changes in the pace of wage inflation which are both quite large and from a purely macroeconomic viewpoint incomprehensible.

(2) The most notable feature of wage inflation in advanced capitalist countries over the past thirty years, apart from its persistence, is that is has speeded up, despite a great increase in unemployment. Thus one 'absolute' test to which any theory of wage inflation must be put is whether or not it can provide a plausible explanation of why this has happened.

My explanation of the speeding up of wage inflation (which is consistent with the empirical studies mentioned on p. 209) is that it has been fundamentally caused by an increase in the importance of *anticipation* in the process of wage determination, and in particular of anticipation based on adaptive expectations. For, as was explained in chapter 5, the introduction of this type of anticipation into the present theory causes normative conflict over relativities to tend to generate not steady but accelerating wage inflation.

The reason why anticipation became more important, I would

suggest, was the prior *persistence* of wage inflation, and this in turn I would attribute to (a) the spread of collective bargaining and the growth of trade union power – partly as a result of greater economic concentration and specialisation, (b) the spread of minimum wage legislation and governmental income support schemes, and (c) the maintenance of moderately low levels of unemployment for twenty years after the second world war.

Persistent wage inflation, I would argue, gradually caused people to recognise that it is not enough for a wage settlement to be fair (or otherwise appropriate) on the day that it is made, and that a margin over and above this is necessary to protect the position until the next settlement. This realisation spread contagiously, since if others start anticipating in making their wage settlements it becomes foolish not to do so oneself. There may indeed even have been some international demonstration effects, with people taking the speeding up of inflation in other countries as an indication of what was likely to happen in their own.

The process of speeding up did not proceed smoothly, or at the same pace in all countries. To explain these irregularities it would be necessary to take account also of the aggregate demand–supply balance at different times and in different countries, of movements in real wages, and of other factors peculiar to individual countries, including the timing and character of wage controls; and to look more closely at the transmission of inflation between particular countries. A detailed undertaking of this sort, however, is beyond the scope of the present book.

7
SOME IMPLICATIONS FOR POLICY

The system of pay determination in advanced capitalist countries, as portrayed in this book, may be criticised from several points of view. Many regard it as an unfair system. Some regard it as an inefficient system, both in an allocative sense and because of the cost of strikes and similar activities. But what seem to me to be the most serious disadvantages of the present system of pay determination stem from its propensity to generate inflation, and it is on this aspect of the system that I shall concentrate.

I am of course not suggesting that the general money wage level is the sole influence on the general price level, but merely that it is the most important, both because it has a strong and persistent tendency to rise spontaneously and because pay is such a large proportion of total costs. To put it another way, I believe that movements in raw material prices, profits, taxes and (in individual countries) import prices have not in themselves been the main engine of price inflation in advanced capitalist countries over the last thirty years.

Nor am I suggesting that the direct costs of inflation are necessarily very large. Hyperinflation indisputably causes catastrophic dislocation, and there is always some danger that moderate inflation will ultimately lead to this. But the direct costs of moderate inflation (whether or not it is accurately anticipated) are nothing like so serious. There is the administrative expense of continually altering prices and wages, and of economising on money. The real rate of interest may decline, and in this and in other ways wealth may arbitrarily be redistributed, often to the detriment of the old. Inflation also gives rise to widespread feelings of insecurity, which cause unhappiness and (by undermining tolerance) exacerbate social and political conflict.

But in my opinion the greatest cost of moderate inflation is an indirect one, namely that governments tend to create or welcome large amounts of sustained involuntary unemployment as a way of reducing it. Such unemployment is an appalling evil. It involves a loss of output and a lowering of the average standard of living. By increasing the number of people with very low incomes, it has an extremely undesirable effect on distribution. The unemployed also suffer the frustration and humiliation of rejection, and the demoralisation of enforced idleness; some turn to crime, others to extremist politics; others go insane. Those who remain employed, fearful of losing their jobs, are individually more vulnerable to oppression by their employers or their unions, and are collectively less willing to permit innovations designed to improve productivity and efficiency.

To increase the level of unemployment, I argued on pages 155–65, is not a completely ineffective method of controlling inflation – and efforts to expand an economy very fast, or to a point beyond full employment (as defined on p. 162), are bound to make inflation worse. But it is an intolerably costly method. The amount of unemployment necessary to keep inflation in advanced capitalist countries down even to moderate levels is large, and the amount that would be necessary to eliminate inflation altogether would be very great.

It is thus of the utmost importance to seek some less expensive way of controlling inflation. In the next section I shall put forward my own suggestion. But first I shall very briefly consider five other suggested solutions.

(i) *Indexation*

Certain sorts of indexation are a good way of mitigating some of the adverse effects of inflation; this is especially true of the indexation of social security benefits and occupational pensions. But in my opinion there is little reason to believe that widespread indexation would slow down inflation.

Suppose, for example, that all wage bargains were by law linked to a general price index (but not otherwise constrained). It was argued in earlier chapters that the fundamental cause of inflation is conflict over *relative* pay. If this is so, striking wage bargains in real rather than money terms (which is what indexation involves) would make no difference to the speed of inflation.* It was also argued, however, that militancy and thus the speed of the wage–wage spiral are affected by what is happening, and perhaps also what is *expected* to happen, to real wages. Insofar as this is the case, indexation of wage bargains would

---

* Nor would linking wage bargains to a general *wage* index solve the basic problem, although this could have a beneficial effect if expectations of future wage increases were inaccurately high.

reduce the pace of inflation if expectations of future price increases were inaccurately high. But if expectations of future price increases were accurate, indexation would make no difference; and if expectations were inaccurately low, indexation of wage bargains would cause inflation to speed up.

(ii) *Wage restraint*

By wage restraint I shall mean a government-imposed upper limit on the size of pay increases, possibly as part of a wider incomes policy. This approach has been advocated by many of those who have argued, as I have argued, that inflation is largely generated by non-competitive forces in the labour market. But for my own part I doubt that it can provide an enduring solution.

The historical record is not encouraging. Each attempt at wage restraint has usually initially reduced the pace of inflation. But after a fairly short time, usually two or three years, each attempt has broken down and has been followed by an acceleration of inflation.* Some of these failures may be attributable to remediable incompetence or bad luck. But the consistency with which wage restraint has broken down suggests a more basic weakness; and the argument of earlier chapters suggests what this weakness is.

It manifests itself most immediately in the problem of 'anomalies', a term (Pay Board, 1973) which refers to the fact that the imposition of wage restraint at any particular moment favours those who have recently obtained a pay increase and penalises those whose last settlement was some time ago. But this specific difficulty is the tip of a more fundamental iceberg, namely the existence of pay norms which conflict both one with another and with anomic pressures. Indeed what causes inflation, I have argued, is precisely that at every moment there is at least one rate of pay which is anomalous in the sense that the employees or the employer concerned would like to increase it. As a result, of course, there is no solution to the problem of anomalies; to make allowances for those 'caught' by the imposition of wage restraint will in most cases simply create fresh anomalies.

This same problem bedevils wage restraint at every turn. Except at very high levels of unemployment (p. 160), there is no equilibrium pattern of indirectly determined relativities, and hence there are

---

* The Dutch wages policy of 1948–66 was exceptionally long-lived; but eventually even it collapsed (see, for example, De Jong, 1972).

always groups with at any rate in their own eyes a strong moral or economic case for a pay increase above the generally prescribed limit. The longer such increases are denied, the greater becomes the pressure to obtain them; and there has eventually always been some group or groups of employees, or some employer or employers, who by moral suasion, economic argument or sheer power have extracted more or less open concessions from the government or its pay board. But such tactical retreats solve nothing. To make one concession not only creates further demands for concessions; it also makes them much harder to resist. Thus the retreat becomes a rout, and the whole sandcastle of wage restraint rapidly crumbles away.

(iii) *Central direction*

One possible solution to the problems of wage restraint is that of the centrally planned economies of Russia and Eastern Europe, namely for the government to prescribe most or all rates of pay and to enforce them by whatever means prove necessary. This system can and has prevented inflation and permitted full employment in the countries which have adopted it. Nonetheless, it is to me a solution whose costs exceed its benefits.

To begin with, such a method of wage determination would probably be unworkable unless the state were the main employer, owning and controlling the great majority of enterprises. It would thus involve forsaking market capitalism for a form of economic organisation which I believe to be less efficient, less adaptable and less innovative.

Potentially more important, though, are the non-economic costs of this solution. The particular type of political system found in Russia and Eastern Europe may not be a necessary concomitant of a planned economy; and indeed this type of political system may not be so undemocratic as is sometimes suggested. Nevertheless, this method of wage determination would necessarily suppress the freedom of individuals and groups of employees to bargain over their own pay; and the amount of force that would be needed to make this suppression effective could well involve the abridgement of other highly desirable types of individual freedom.

(iv) *Competition*

There are also those who see the solution to the problems of the present system of pay determination as being the abolition of trade unions and the establishment of free competition in all labour markets. In principle, this would have much to commend it, provided that it were accompanied by full employment, progressive taxation, redistributive public expenditure and every effort to promote mobility and equality of opportunity. For the result would be that inequalities of pay would tend either to compensate for inequalities of non-pecuniary advantage or to reflect rents to innate talents which could largely be taxed away. The system would tend to be allocatively efficient. And controlling inflation would involve no more than keeping the aggregate monetary demand for labour at the level appropriate to maintain full employment.

But whatever its hypothetical attractions, this is not a feasible solution. Only an intolerably authoritarian government could effectively abolish trade unions, especially because it would be necessary not only to dismantle their formal framework but also to suppress informal group action at the level of the individual plant or firm. Furthermore, to abolish trade unions and similar bodies would not be sufficient to establish free competition in all labour markets, since such a high proportion of employment in advanced capitalist economies is provided by very large organisations, private and public. Many such organisations possess substantial monopsony power, which could lead to a pattern of pay relativities that was neither equitable nor efficient. It would also be difficult to make their internal labour markets freely competitive.

(v) *Workers' control*

Another response to the problems of the present system of pay determination has been the advocacy of various forms of worker participation, of which the most extreme would involve all enterprises (at any rate in the private sector) being owned and controlled by their employees. Employee participation is an attractive idea, both in itself and as a means of increasing efficiency by improving industrial relations. But even wholesale workers' control would not, in my view, solve the most serious problems of the present system.

In particular, it would not eliminate the two types of conflict over indirectly determined relativities that I have argued to be the fundamental cause of inflation. Workers in specific enterprises would still have ideas about fair relativities inconsistent both with other such ideas and with anomic forces. Some enterprises would periodically push up their prices in an effort to obtain fair relative pay for their employees; prices and pay in other enterprises would be bid up by specific excess demand; and there would thus still be a strong tendency to inflation (as the experience of Yugoslavia, the one country in which workers' control has been implemented on a large scale, might be held to confirm). From the point of view of the present theory of inflation, in short, it makes comparatively little difference whether there is wage–capitalism or workers' control.

7.2 DIRECT RELATIVITY BARGAINING

There is in my opinion no ideal solution to the problems of the present system of pay determination. It is therefore with some consciousness of its limitations that I advance the following proposal, which I believe could in the long term provide a reasonably equitable and efficient way of reconciling full employment, collective bargaining and price stability in a capitalist market economy. I shall call it *direct relativity bargaining*.* In this section I shall outline the proposal. In the following section I shall consider some objections.

(i) *Principles*

The basic idea, which stems straightforwardly from the present theory of inflation, is to retain most of the existing apparatus of pay determination, but to alter the unit of account; to do away with pay bargaining in money terms, and to make it obligatory for all pay bargains to be struck directly in relative terms. Given the pattern of relative pay, the government would periodically prescribe the money equivalent of one (and thus of every) rate of pay – at such a level, say, that the general price level remained approximately constant. The pattern of relative pay itself, however, would not be prescribed by the government, but would be negotiated by employers and employees.

* It is, I think, a novel proposal. But it has a good deal in common with the important proposals of Brown (1973, ch. 8; 1975) and Phelps Brown (1972). I have also profited considerably from studying the proposals of Clegg (1971), Wootton (1974) and Pemberton (1976).

The object of direct relativity bargaining would be to force employers and employees to grasp the nettle of conflict over relativities, by abolishing what I have labelled indirectly determined relativities and effectively welding the economy into one giant pay group. For it is the existence of many separate and uncoordinated pay groups, in conjunction with conflict between powerful forces over relativities, which lies at the heart of the problems of the present system of pay determination. One cannot eliminate the conflict without massive unemployment or dictatorship. But one could, I shall argue, direct the conflicting pressures into a common arena in such a way as to result in some definite stable outcome, as happens at present in the case of conflicting pressures within particular pay groups, rather than in an inflationary wage–wage spiral.

What I am proposing, it should be emphasised, is not a specific pattern of relativities but a new process for determining relativities. For it seems to me that a limited amount of deliberate institutional change could solve the most basic problems of the present system, which are themselves largely the product of a spontaneous type of institutional change, namely the spread of collective bargaining.

(ii) *Organisation*

Direct relativity bargaining would be a decentralised (or more accurately a multi-tier) process, based on the existing institutional framework. Let us suppose that the lowest tier would be the establishment. The first stage of the process would thus be to settle relativities within individual establishments. At the second stage, representatives from the various establishments within, say, each industry would meet to settle relativities between establishments in terms of one (it does not in principle matter which) rate of pay in each establishment. At the third and final stage, representatives from the various industries would meet together to settle relativities between industries in terms of one rate of pay in each industry, thus fixing all the pay relativities in the economy.

The process of direct relativity bargaining could be organised in many different ways. The preceding example assumed an establishment–industry–national hierarchy; but the arrangements could be based on occupational or geographical categories, or on some mixture of categories, which would not need to be the same in every sector of the economy, let alone in every country. All that is essential is that the number and pattern of linkages should be just sufficient to connect (directly or indirectly) each rate of pay in the economy with every other rate; any strictly hierarchical framework would have this property.

The choice of a specific framework, however, is not a trivial issue, since it would in all probability affect both the administrative efficiency of the process of bargaining and the resultant pattern of pay relativities. It would also be highly desirable for employers and employees to be able to influence the broad structure of the framework and their specific positions within it. Yet too much freedom in this regard could make the structure undesirably volatile. I shall therefore assume that the framework would initially be prescribed by the government, on the basis of existing institutional arrangements, economic principles and considerations of administrative workability; but that there would be some democratic machinery for changing the framework in an orderly way.

The process of direct relativity bargaining would be repeated at, say, annual intervals. This would serve three important purposes. (1) It would permit feedback. For the full consequences of low level decisions (about, for example, relativities within establishments) cannot be known until higher level decisions (about, for example, relativities between industries) have been made, by which time the low level decisions are irrevocable. There should thus be an opportunity for subsequent revision of low level decisions.* (2) Annual repetition of the process, by providing a series of 'second chances', would make the bargaining itself much easier, and the likelihood of irretrievable deadlock or breakdown much smaller, than if relativities were to be settled once and for all. (3) Annual repetition would also enable the pattern of relativities to be altered in response to changes in market pressures, pay norms and the power of particular groups.

The government would provide an annual timetable for the process of direct relativity bargaining – a series of deadlines by which the various sets of relativities at each level would have to be settled in order that negotiations at the next level up could begin. The government would also provide an independent chairman (with a supporting secretariat) for each bargaining body at each level, who would convene and chair the bargaining sessions, and would record their outcome.

* Although one must recognise that such an iterative process of revision of relativities might not converge towards a unique solution. It might even cause relativities to oscillate substantially from year to year, in which case it would be necessary to damp the process by imposing an upper limit on the permissible size of changes in relativities from one year to the next.

(iii) *Bargaining*

Direct relativity bargaining would resemble the current system inasmuch as employers would remain formally responsible for making and implementing decisions concerning the pay of their employees. Moreover, their decisions would continue to be influenced by the sorts of pressures described in chapters 3 and 4. They would, as now, want to avoid both shortages of labour and paying unnecessarily much for labour, and to provide economic incentives for their employees. They would also, as at present, be subject to normative pressures of varying types and strengths from their employees.

Direct relativity bargaining would differ from the current system inasmuch as the object of employers' decisions would always be relative and never money rates of pay. In addition, they would have to make their decisions according to an externally imposed timetable, and they would have to abide by their decisions for an externally imposed length of time. Furthermore, in making their decisions employers would be more subject than at present to direct pressures from other employers and from the employees of other employers.

At the lowest level, matters would in many cases proceed much as at present. The employer in (say) each establishment, subject to an assortment of anomic and normative pressures and constraints, would decide on a specific pattern of internal relativities in the sort of way described in the latter part of chapter 4. This decision would be recorded by the relevant government-appointed chairman, who would also chair any formal negotiations that took place between the employer and his various groups of employees concerning both internal and external relativities.

At the next stage, there would be a meeting to determine relativities between the several establishments in (say) the same industry or locality. Although the employees in each establishment would have the right to send representatives to participate in the meeting, it would formally be a meeting of employers, and the formal intention would be that the employers should unanimously* agree on a specific pattern

---

* The unanimity requirement is important. To begin with, it is simple. It also avoids a major problem of alternative possible voting systems, namely the allocation of votes among employers. Moreover, to give each employer the right of veto eliminates the danger of a majority of employers imposing, perhaps deliberately, a pattern of relativities that would in one way or another ruin a minority of employers.

of relativities and on the appointment of representatives from among their number to participate in the next level of negotiations.

With the obvious exception of criminal acts (such as physical violence, fraud and breaches of anti-monopoly laws), no restrictions would be placed on the manner of reaching agreement. In particular, it would be entirely legitimate for an employer or a coalition of employers overtly and enforcibly to compensate another employer or employers for accepting an outcome that they would not otherwise be willing to accept.* A side-payment of this sort could for example induce an employer to accept a high relative wage that, without compensation, would make him unable to compete effectively in his product market; or to accept a low relative wage that would make it hard for him to attract sufficient labour, or would involve him in the costs of a strike or a go-slow by his employees.

In the event of failure to reach unanimous agreement, either on relativities or on the appointment of representatives, the chairman would unilaterally prescribe the outcome (although his first duty would be to attempt to secure agreement).† In doing so, he would be bound by some general formula which required him to take due account of considerations of equity, both as between different employers and as between different groups of employees, and to have regard to the national interest in promoting efficiency and minimising the costs of strikes and other forms of industrial conflict. In translating these general requirements into specific terms, however, the chairman would of course be very greatly influenced by the particular facts and arguments that had emerged in the course of the preceding negotiations. He would announce his decision (which could include compulsory compensation of some employers by others), but would then give the employers a second chance, within a limited time, to arrive at an alternative unanimous agreement; if they failed to do so, his decision would stand.

Although employers would in a formal sense be the decision making agents in the bargaining process outlined above, and although anomic pressures would thus usually have a considerable influence, the outcome (whether unanimously agreed or imposed by the chairman)

---

* The compensation could be either a specified sum or an amount contingent on some future event, such as the level of profits or the duration of a strike.
† In this respect, direct relativity bargaining would resemble the Australian system of compulsory arbitration – see, for example, Whitehead (1973, app. B) and Isaac (1972).

would in practice also often be heavily influenced, and in some cases completely determined, by the collective normative preferences of employees – as well as, of course, by the willingness of individual employees to join or to remain with particular employers, or to respond to particular incentives. Employees collectively would influence the proceedings in three different ways.

(1) The employees of each employer would bring pressure to bear on him in the various ways described in chapter 3 in order to influence his attitude in bargaining over relativities with other employers. For example, the employees in one establishment might threaten, in the course of a round of bargaining, to strike unless they were given parity of pay with some other establishment; if their demand were not met, and especially if they felt that this was because their threat had not been taken seriously, they would strike with a view to influencing the outcome of the next round of bargaining. Similarly, even without overt threats, but perhaps as the result of prior experience, an employer might press for a particular pattern of relativities in order to avoid the costs of an informal reduction of work intensity by his employees.

(2) The employees of a number of different employers might form a coalition to bring joint pressure to bear on their several employers to implement some particular pattern of inter-establishment relativities.

(3) Representatives of the employees in each establishment would participate in the formal meeting of employers, expressing the collective preferences and intentions of their colleagues. As a result, much of the bargaining at the meeting would in fact not be between different employers but between employers and employees and between different groups of employees. In some cases, indeed, the chairman's main efforts would be devoted to obtaining an agreement among the employee representatives, which the employers would then formally endorse or which (in the event of disagreement among the employers) would serve as the basis of his unilateral prescription.

In addition, the employee representatives, like the employers, would elect representatives to participate in the next level of negotiations. At this next level, and at higher levels, the bargaining process would be repeated in much the same way as described above, except that the employers involved (who would be accompanied by the lower level chairmen) would be participating not on their own behalf but as representatives of larger groups of which they were members. Likewise, the employees involved would represent the workers not only in their own establishments but also in the other establishments whose relative pay had been settled jointly with their own at earlier stages.

When the final stage of bargaining was concluded, and thus all relativities were determined, the government would as explained earlier prescribe the money level of one (and thus of every) rate of pay. This structure of rates of pay would come into effect on a specified date, and would apply until the completion of the next round of direct relativity bargaining.

(iv) *Enforcement*

Employers would be under a legal obligation to pay the rates determined in the manner described above – this being the reason why I am proposing that they, and not employees, should be formally responsible for determining the structure of relativities. Their compliance would be monitored by a government agency which had no direct connection with the process of bargaining. To pay either more or less than the prescribed rate would be a criminal offence punishable by a fine whose magnitude in each instance would be so calculated by the judge concerned as to much more than offset any financial (or non-financial) advantage that the employer would otherwise obtain by deviating from the prescribed rate. The courts would also be empowered to prohibit an employer from continuing to deviate, subject to fines of comparable but increasing severity enforced ultimately by the threat of imprisonment.

The rationale of this enforcement procedure derives from the argument of pages 78–9 and 82–3 above. For example, in the case of an employer tempted by an excess supply of labour to pay less than the directly bargained rate, or in the case of an employer tempted by a scarcity of labour to pay more than the directly bargained rate, the object would be to deter him from doing so by the threat of a fine so large as to make deviance (given the probability of it being detected) an uneconomic proposition. The same principle would apply in the case of an employer whose employees refused to accept the results of the direct relativity bargaining process and attempted by striking to coerce him into paying above the prescribed rate. Costly as the strike might be to him, the employer would be deterred from giving in to his employees by the knowledge that to do so would automatically cost him substantially more.

The fact that the outcome would be strictly enforced in this way would of course make employers think very hard before committing themselves in the course of the bargaining process to accepting any particular set of relativities or pattern of compensation. It would likewise influence the attitude of employee representatives at every stage of the bargaining; and it would naturally weigh very heavily with the chairman in circumstances in which he was obliged unilaterally to prescribe the outcome.

In the course of implementing the rates of pay determined by direct relativity bargaining, incidentally, ambiguities and obscurities concerning what actually had been decided would inevitably come to light. In such instances the chairman of the relevant bargaining body would have the authority to provide a definitive interpretation – although the issues involved might well be reopened in the next round of bargaining.

(v) *Coverage*

The discussion so far has proceeded as if direct relativity bargaining would apply to all employees. In practice, however, it would be desirable on grounds of administrative cost to exclude employers with less than, say, fifty employees, as well as certain types of casual labour; the pay of the employees concerned would, as now, be settled in money terms. But it would be undesirable to restrict the application of the system to employees covered by formal collective bargaining arrangements; in particular, if direct relativity bargaining were to be acceptable to manual workers, it would have to apply also to clerical, technical, professional and managerial employees.

The pay of employees outside the direct relativity bargaining system would in some cases become informally linked to the pay of employees within it. In addition, it might be thought desirable to retain some form of minimum wage legislation applicable to employees outside the direct relativity bargaining system; if so, it would be essential for the minimum to be specified in relative terms and for the determination of its level to be an integral part of the direct relativity bargaining process. (It might also be advantageous for the level of unemployment and other social security benefits to be tied in some way to the outcome of the direct relativity bargaining process.)

Direct relativity bargaining would not cover the self-employed, a diffuse category of people with activities and incomes so heterogeneous as to defy any sort of administrative regulation. But it would be necessary to make and enforce a definition of self-employment strict enough to prevent more than a small number of employees from evading the process of direct relativity bargaining by turning themselves into self-employed labour-only subcontractors. Moreover, although most of the self-employed operate in rather competitive markets, the government should make every effort to eliminate restrictive practices (including artificial entry barriers) in the professions.

7.3 OBJECTIONS TO DIRECT RELATIVITY BARGAINING

Many objections may be raised to the scheme outlined above. Some concern the particulars of the proposed administrative arrangements and legal issues such as the contractual status of directly bargained pay settlements (Adell, 1970). These and other practical details are of considerable importance, but it would be inappropriate to explore them here. Instead, I shall focus on six possible objections of principle to direct relativity bargaining.

(i) *Real wages*

Wage and salary earners in general, and the union movement in particular, might object to direct relativity bargaining on the grounds that to give up the freedom to bargain over money wages would be to lose control of the average real wage. But such fears in my opinion would be unfounded. For at any given level of aggregate employment, and in particular at full employment (to permit which would be the main object of direct relativity bargaining), with a given foreign trade balance and a given structure of relative wages, the average real wage is not significantly or fundamentally affected by the behaviour of the general money wage level, but is determined by a number of other factors.

The most important is the average degree of productivity, efficiency and competitiveness in employing organisations, private and public. Another is the prices (relative to the prices of other goods and services) of scarce commodities such as agricultural and mined products and land. A third is the level of government expenditure and the structure of the tax system, which determine the degree of direct and indirect taxation of pay (although some part of government expenditure may be regarded as an addition to the disposable real wage). And a fourth

is the share of profits in national income, which I have argued elsewhere to be, except in the very short run, for all practical purposes
independent of the behaviour of the general money wage level.*

At the same time, I recognise that these views concerning the
fundamental independence of the average real wage and the average
money wage, although they are held by a great majority of economists,
would not at present be accepted by some trade unionists, and that
an extensive debate on this issue would be necessary to persuade
employees to relinquish the freedom to bargain over money wages.
Furthermore, it cannot be too strongly emphasised that the above
comments relate to the *average* real wage and to the share of profits
in *national income*; direct (or any other type of) bargaining over
relative wages is bound to affect the real wages of individual groups
of workers and the relative profitability of individual companies.

(ii) *Efficiency*

Some may object to direct relativity bargaining on grounds of efficiency. It would be quite wrong, of course, to suggest that direct
relativity bargaining would cause misallocation because it would involve the government fixing the average price of labour, since what
the government would in effect fix is the average *money* wage, while
the average price of labour in the sense relevant to allocative efficiency
is the average *real* wage. But it is true that the structure of relativities
established by direct relativity bargaining would in all probability be
inefficient and misallocative, especially insofar as it was governed by
normative, as against anomic, pressures.

The relevant question, however, is whether and to what degree the
resultant misallocation would be worse than under the present system,
in which normative pressures already play a substantial part. To
provide a satisfactory answer to this question would require a great
deal of further theoretical and empirical work, not least on the implications of the system of side-payments between employers proposed
earlier. And this work might lead one to the conclusion that direct
relativity bargaining would be so much less efficient than the present
system as to make it an unattractive alternative. But my instinct is that

* Wood (1975), esp. pp. 168–9. I also argue in chapter 5 of that book that the personal
tax system provides an efficient and effective means of redistributing income away
from the owners of company securities.

there would probably not be very much difference, especially since employers would continue to be the principal decision making agents. Moreover, any loss of allocative efficiency would be offset (and perhaps much more than offset) by the fact that direct relativity bargaining would permit a reduction in unemployment, which would not only directly raise output but would also make employees more willing to accept efficiency-enhancing innovations.

Direct relativity bargaining might be criticised as inefficient also on the grounds that it would impose large administrative costs on government, employers and employees. Again, it is not possible a priori to resolve this issue, but my instinct is that the administrative costs of direct relativity bargaining (in which one should include the costs of strikes and similar disruptions) would probably not be much greater than the corresponding costs of the present system.

(iii) *Complexity*

Those experienced in the negotiation and administration of pay may object that direct relativity bargaining would be unworkable because of the complexity and variety of structures and systems of pay, which would make it impossible to find a common denominator in which relativities could be expressed, or to bargain over actual earnings as distinct from basic rates, or to monitor or enforce compliance with directly bargained pay settlements.

It is indeed true that pay systems vary widely between jobs and sectors, and that some of them are very complicated. Some people are paid by the hour, others by the week or month; some are paid by results; some are on incremental scales; many receive premia and bonuses of various kinds; and some are remunerated to a significant extent in fringe benefits rather than cash. In some cases rates of pay attach to jobs, in others to individuals; some jobs have intricate internal gradations; and a given job title may mean very different things in different organisations.

It is also true that this complexity and variety, unless it were compulsorily eliminated, would almost certainly make a centralised system of pay bargaining or control unworkable. But it would not, I believe, be incompatible with direct relativity bargaining of the type I am proposing, namely a *decentralised* system which builds from the bottom up, and which would apply not to basic rates but to every component of pay. It would of course be very convenient if all jobs were paid on, say, a straight hourly basis; but the monthly salary in one job can perfectly well be expressed as a ratio of the basic hourly wage in another job; the target hourly piece-earnings in one job can be expressed as a ratio of the time rate in another job (although in setting such a relative target those concerned would have to assess and take account of the likely amount of drift); and most premia can be expressed as ratios of basic rates. Moreover, there is no reason why a single rate of pay should attach to a job; there could (as in many job evaluation schemes) be a range, within which the pay of individual employees was fixed according to seniority or merit or scarcity.

Needless to say, it would be impossible for any single person to know about, let alone appreciate the significance of, more than a limited subset of relativities. But the strength of a decentralised system is that it is unnecessary for any single person to understand all its intricacies. At the lowest level of bargaining it would, as now, be necessary for those involved to know the details of the internal pay structure of their (say) establishment. But at the second and higher levels of bargaining, those involved would need only a broad grasp of the pay structures at the level below, sufficient to make reasonably satisfactory comparisons and linkages between, for example, different establishments or different industries.

This is not to deny that bargainers at every level, as well as those attempting to enforce directly bargained pay settlements, would face numerous specific problems arising from the variety and complexity of pay systems. They would have particular difficulty, I imagine, with grade drift, fringe benefits and certain types of incentive system, including profit sharing and productivity bargaining. But these seem to me to be not fundamental obstacles to direct relativity bargaining, but problems of detail, which could and would be resolved by employers and employees at the level or levels concerned.

(iv) *Equity*

It may also be objected that direct relativity bargaining would be an unfair system: that it would to a substantial degree permit employers to set pay without regard to considerations of equity; that it would permit powerful unions to enforce their ideas of equity at the expense of the weak (including those who would like employment in a particular job, but cannot obtain it, or lose it, because the incumbent employees have enforced too high a relative wage); and that it would not in itself improve the lot of the low paid, or reduce discrimination against women or racial minorities.

All this I grant. At the same time, I find it impossible to believe that direct relativity bargaining would in these respects be any worse than the present system – and it must be remembered that the government would still be able to enact anti-discrimination laws, to redistribute income by taxation and public expenditure, to promote mobility and retrain the redundant, and to subsidise the employment of the less productive. Indeed, there are two reasons for supposing that direct relativity bargaining would be *fairer* than the present system of pay determination.

One is that it would permit a reduction in involuntary unemployment, which would principally benefit the least skilled, the least productive and the most discriminated against members of the labour force. The other is that it would make the process of settling relative pay more orderly and open. The weak would have a forum in which to plead their case, and could not, as at present, be completely forgotten by the powerful in their scramble to keep abreast of one another. It would be harder for a monopsonistic employer to exploit his employees, who could at the second (or at a higher) level of bargaining invoke the support of their fellow-workers in other establishments. Conflicting views of fairness would have to be publicly and directly compared; and the economic or moral reasons for particular equalities or inequalities of pay would have to be laid bare. The outcome would inevitably be regarded by many as unfair; but the process, I contend, would be more equitable than at present.

(v) *Enforcement*

Before considering objections to the system of enforcement proposed above, which is based on the principle of penalising employers for deviating from directly bargained pay settlements, it is perhaps worth explaining why I favour a system of this kind rather than a system based on penalising employees. One reason is that the latter would be entirely inappropriate insofar as the pressures on employers to deviate are anomic rather than normative. The other reason is that penalties on employees and trade unions have been tried as a method of enforcing pay policies of various sorts, and have failed (Clegg, 1971, ch. VII; Phelps Brown, 1972, pp. 37–8; Donovan, 1968, app. 6). Short of suppressing trade unions altogether, an approach which I have rejected, it has not proved possible to control their wage bargaining behaviour by means of criminal penalties – and it seems unlikely that civil penalties would be any more effective (Adell, 1970).

One possible objection to my proposed system of enforcement is that it would be unfair to employers. Specifically, it might be argued that an employer whose employees refused to accept the outcome of the direct relativity bargaining process and attempted to coerce him into paying above the prescribed rate would be placed in an impossible position.

But this particular objection is misconceived. For the 'impossibility' of the employer's position – the fact that it would cost him more to give in to this sort of coercion than to hold out against it – would be his strongest defence. No rational group of employees would enter into a battle that they were guaranteed to lose. This is not to say that employees in a direct relativity bargaining system would never have a rational interest in coercing their employers. On the contrary, as explained earlier, the exercise of this sort of normative pressure would be an integral part of the system. But its object would be not to cause deviance from previously negotiated rates but to influence the outcome of the next and subsequent rounds of bargaining.

It could reasonably be argued, however, that an employer would suffer unjustly if his desire to arrive at a particular pattern of relativities were frustrated by other employers or by the chairman, and if, as a result, his employees imposed sanctions on him as a way of influencing the future behaviour of other employers or the chairman. But it seems unlikely that this sort of thing would be so widespread or so serious as to constitute a major objection to direct relativity bargaining, especially since the optimal scale of such demonstrations from the employees' point of view would usually be rather limited.

A related objection concerns the fact that the principal loser from some forms of coercion by some groups of employees would be not their employer but the general public or certain sections of the general public. Since this is true also of the present system, it cannot in itself be regarded as an objection to direct relativity bargaining. But it could be argued that in a direct relativity bargaining system the device of holding the public as hostage would be more extensively used than under the present system, since it would provide some employees with a convenient method of exerting pressure on a chairman in cases in which employers disagreed over relativities.

In principle this is a valid objection. But since governments already frequently intervene in disputes which threaten the public interest, the difference in this regard between direct relativity bargaining and the present system would probably not be large. Moreover, the chairman in a direct relativity bargaining system would be well placed in such circumstances, by selecting an outcome which favoured groups with this sort of power, to minimise the amount of damage inflicted on the public. As a result, the degree to which the public actually suffered from collective coercion under a direct relativity bargaining system might well be less than under the present, more anarchic, system.

A further objection to the proposed scheme for enforcing directly bargained pay settlements is that difficulties could arise in the case of public sector employers, and in particular in cases in which the government, broadly defined, was required to penalise itself for deviance. At a technical level, the solution to this problem lies in some sort of separation of powers, which is why I have proposed that compliance should be enforced by the judiciary rather than by administrative tribunals. Even at a technical level, though, this particular proposal is open to the criticism that in some countries it is difficult (because of the doctrine of sovereign immunity) to bring criminal proceedings against the government. And at a practical level, there would inevitably be some discord between the government's interests as an employer and its interests as overseer of the direct relativity bargaining system. But it seems to me unlikely that this would make the system unworkable.

(vi) *Consent*

Finally, it may be objected that direct relativity bargaining could not work because the very conflicts over relativities on which I have laid so much stress are too bitter and profound to be so easily contained. There would inevitably be employees who felt unjustly treated by the process of direct relativity bargaining, and these employees, it could be argued, would willfully or recklessly destroy the system by means of a few large-scale (or many small-scale) strikes in vital industries, which the government would be powerless to resist. Likewise, employers who ran short of labour or who saw the opportunity to pay

237

less than the directly bargained rate might simply cheat on a scale so grand as to make enforcement impossible.

This is the most fundamental objection of all. If the opposition between different normative pressures, and between normative and anomic pressures, were so deep that none of those involved were willing to compromise in any circumstances, then direct relativity bargaining could not possibly work – and indeed there could be *no* non-totalitarian way of reconciling price stability with full employment. More generally, there would be little hope of direct relativity bargaining working unless a great majority both of employers and of employees wanted it to work, and unless most of those involved accepted that, individually, they could not always have their own way.

For my own part, I do not believe that many people are saints, or that all disputes over relative pay can be settled by reasoned discourse, and for these reasons I am proposing a system which would not rely on altruistic behaviour, which would allow anomic forces a major role, and which would permit the exercise of a good deal of force majeure by powerful groups. But I also believe that the great majority of people are sufficiently tolerant, rational and law-abiding that the problems caused by conflict over relativities could be solved, given an appropriate institutional framework. Thus I believe that direct relativity bargaining would be viable, and that conflict over relativities, while playing a very important and conspicuous part in the working of the system, would not actually bring about its destruction.

7.4 CONCLUSION

The most important feature of the above proposals is the principle of direct relativity bargaining itself. I cannot pretend to have worked out its implications or the institutional arrangements required in anything like the depth or detail that would be necessary before one could contemplate introducing it. And a fuller investigation would undoubtedly reveal the need for modifications to the scheme I have outlined, and might even uncover drawbacks so serious that the idea should be abandoned altogether.

Nor do I wish to pretend that direct relativity bargaining could ever be a perfect system, or even that it would in every respect be an improvement on the present system of pay determination. It does seem to me, though, that on balance it would be greatly superior not only to the present system but also to the other alternatives discussed earlier.

Even so, it is a long shot. Institutional changes of this kind cannot, and should not, be hastily made. Moreover, for its full benefits to be felt, direct relativity bargaining would probably have to be adopted in most advanced capitalist countries, since unemployment caused by governmental fears of inflation in one country makes it harder (because of the extent of international trade, and because there are constraints on altering exchange rates, imposing tariffs and running trade deficits) to attain full employment in other countries, even those whose governments are less frightened of inflation.

Thus even if a fuller investigation of direct relativity bargaining were to conclude in its favour, it might be a long time before it was introduced, even in one country. But one could begin to prepare the ground. The government should, for example, promote the amalgamation of separate pay groups within particular establishments and firms, and the wider use of job evaluation and systematic pay comparisons. Employers and employees in different firms, industries and occupations should be brought together as often as possible to discuss the inter-relationships between their various separate pay policies and problems. And it might be worth coordinating the process of pay determination in the various parts of the public sector, to provide a base from which direct relativity bargaining could be extended into the private sector.

What should be done if all attempts at instituting direct relativity bargaining fail? What is the second best solution? The answer, I suppose, is that one should muddle on as at present, with intermittent bouts of wage restraint, chronic and quite rapid inflation, and miserably high levels of unemployment; and simply hope that the result will not be some sort of totalitarian regime. But it is an exceedingly depressing prospect.

REFERENCES

Adell, B. L. (1970). *The legal status of collective agreements in England, the United States and Canada*, Kingston, Ontario.

APL (1976). Accountancy Personnel Limited, *Survey of salaries in accountancy and law*, Autumn, London.

Arrow, K. J. (1971). 'The firm in general equilibrium theory', in R. Marris and A. Wood, *The corporate economy*, London, pp. 68–110.

Atherton, W. N. (1973). *Theory of union bargaining goals*, Princeton.

AUT (1977). Association of University Teachers, *Report on some international comparisons for university teachers*, London (mimeo.).

BIM (1970). British Institute of Management, *Job evaluation: a practical guide for managers*, London.

Blaug, M. (1976). 'The empirical status of human capital theory: a slightly jaundiced survey', *Journal of Economic Literature*, vol. 14, pp. 827–55.

Blinder, A. S. (1974). *Toward an economic theory of income distribution*, Cambridge, Mass.

BMA (1962). British Medical Association, *Recruitment to the medical profession*, London.

Boyle, Lord (1976). Top Salaries Review Body, *Report no. 8: Ministers of the crown and members of parliament and the peers' expenses allowance*, Part II, London (HMSO, Cmnd 6574).

Braff, A. J. (1969). *Microeconomic analysis*, New York.

Braverman, H. (1974). *Labor and monopoly capital*, London.

Brittan, S. (1975). *Second thoughts on full employment policy*, London.

Brittan, S. and Lilley, P. (1977). *The delusion of incomes policy*, London.

Brown, D. G. (1962). 'Expected ability to pay and inter-industry wage structure in manufacturing', *Industrial and Labour Relations Review*, vol. 16, pp. 45–62.

Brown, W. (1971). 'Piecework wage determination in Coventry', *Scottish Journal of Political Economy*, vol. 18, pp. 1–30.

Brown, W. (1973). *The earnings conflict*, Harmondsworth, Middx.

Brown, W. (1975). *Curing inflation*, London (privately published, 4th edn).

Cain, G. G. (1976). 'The challenge of segmented labor market theories to orthodox theory: a survey', *Journal of Economic Literature*, vol. 14, pp. 1215–57.

Cartter, A. M. (1959). *Theory of wages and employment*, Homewood, Ill.

Clegg, H. A. (1971). *How to run an incomes policy*, London.

Corina, M. (1977). 'Cable and Wireless chief resigns over Government freeze policy', *The Times*, 19 February.

Coutts, K., Tarling, R. and Wilkinson, F. (1976). 'Wage bargaining and the inflation process', Cambridge *Economic Policy Review*, vol. 2, pp. 20–7.

REFERENCES

Cripps, F. (1977). 'The money supply, wages and inflation', *Cambridge Journal of Economics*, vol. 1, pp. 101–12.

Crossley, J. R. (1966). 'Collective bargaining, wage structure and the labour market in the U.K.', in E. M. Hugh-Jones, *Wage structure in theory and practice*, Amsterdam, pp. 156–235.

Daniel, W. W. (1975). *The P.E.P. survey on inflation*, London (PEP Broadsheet 553).

Daniel, W. W. (1976). *Wage determination in industry*, London (PEP Broadsheet 563).

Daniel, W. W. (1976a). *The next stage of incomes policy*, London (PEP Broadsheet 568).

DE (1976). Department of Employment, 'The incidence of industrial stoppages in the U.K.', *Department of Employment Gazette*, vol. 84, pp. 115–26.

DE (1976a). Department of Employment, 'Distribution and concentration of industrial stoppages in Great Britain', *Department of Employment Gazette*, vol. 84, pp. 1219–24.

De Jong, J. R. (1972). 'National wage and job evaluation in the Netherlands', in F. Blackaby, *An incomes policy for Britain*, London, pp. 145–60.

Devlin, T. (1976). 'Teachers scorn £11.4 m "dirty money" then change their minds', *The Times*, 21 April.

Diamond, Lord (1976). Royal Commission on the Distribution of Income and Wealth, *Report no. 3: Higher incomes from employment*, London (HMSO, Cmnd 6383).

Diamond, Lord (1976a). Royal Commission on the Distribution of Income and Wealth, *Background paper no. 2: Analysis of managerial remuneration in the United Kingdom and overseas*, London (HMSO).

Diamond, Lord (1976b). Royal Commission on the Distribution of Income and Wealth, *Selected evidence submitted to the Royal Commission for Report no. 3: Higher incomes from employment*, London (HMSO).

Doeringer, P. B. and Piore, M. J. (1971). *Internal labor markets and manpower analysis*, Lexington, Mass.

Dogas, D. and Hines, A. G. (1975). 'Trade unions and wage inflation in the U.K.: a critique of Purdy and Zis', *Applied Economics*, vol. 7, pp. 195–211.

Donovan, Lord (1968). *Report of the Royal Commission on trade unions and employers associations* (HMSO, Cmnd 3623).

Dunlop, J. (1944). *Wage determination under trade unions*, New York.

Dunlop, J. (1957). *The theory of wage determination*, London.

Economist (1976). 'Federal pay – out of pocket', *The Economist*, 11 December.

Economist (1976a). 'Professions – peripatetic', *The Economist*, 18 December.

Fellner, W. (1949). *Competition among the few*, New York.

Fels, A. (1972). *The British prices and incomes board*, Cambridge.

Fogarty, M. (1961). *The just wage*, London.

Fosh, P. and Jackson, D. (1974). 'Pay policy and inflation: what Britain thinks', *New Society*, 7 February, pp. 311–17.

Freeman, R. B. (1971). *The market for college-trained manpower*, Cambridge, Mass.

Friedman, M. and Kuznets, S. (1945). *Income from independent professional practice*, New York.

REFERENCES

Friedman, M. (1973). Letter to *The Times*, 29 August.

Gerth, H. H. and Mills, C. W. (1948). *From Max Weber: essays in sociology*, London.

Godley, W. A. H. (1977). 'Inflation in the United Kingdom', in L. B. Krause and W. S. Salant, *Worldwide inflation*, Washington, DC, pp. 449–74.

Goldthorpe, J. H. and others (1968). *The affluent worker: industrial attitudes and behaviour*, Cambridge.

Goldthorpe, J. H. and Hope, K. (1974). *The social grading of occupations*, Oxford.

Groser, J. (1976). 'Ban on advertising by solicitors should be lifted, the Monopolies Commission says', *The Times*, 30 July.

Hart, H. L. A. (1961). *The concept of law*, Oxford.

Hay–MSL (1976). 'Offices staff pay survey reveals wide variations in rates for similar jobs in London', *The Times*, 19 January.

Henry, S. G. B., Sawyer, M. C. and Smith, P. (1976). 'Models of inflation in the United Kingdom: an evaluation', *National Institute Economic Review*, August, pp. 60–71.

Hicks, J. R. (1955). 'Economic foundations of wage policy', *Economic Journal*, vol. LXV, pp. 389–404.

Hicks, J. R. (1963). *The theory of wages*, London (2nd edn).

Hicks, J. R. (1975). 'What is wrong with monetarism', *Lloyds Bank Review*, October (no. 118), pp. 1–13.

Hines, A. G. (1964). 'Trade unions and wage inflation in the United Kingdom 1893–1961', *Review of Economic Studies*, vol. 31, pp. 221–51.

Hirsch, F. (1977). *Social limits to growth*, London.

Houghton, Lord (1974). *Report of the committee of inquiry into the pay of non-university teachers*, London (HMSO, Cmnd 5848).

Ingham, G. K. (1970). *Size of industrial organisation and worker behaviour*, Cambridge.

Isaac, J. E. (1972). 'Australian compulsory arbitration and incomes policy', in F. Blackaby, *An incomes policy for Britain*, London, pp. 122–44.

Jackson, J. A. (1968). *Social stratification*, Cambridge.

Jacobs, E. (1975). 'Still no peace on piecework for Leyland', *The Sunday Times*, 30 November.

Jaques, E. (1967). *Equitable payment*, Harmondsworth, Middx (revised edn).

Johnson, H. G. and Mieszkowski, P. (1970). 'The effects of unionisation on the distribution of income', *Quarterly Journal of Economics*, vol. LXXXIV, pp. 539–61.

Jones, A. (1973). *The new inflation*, Harmondsworth, Middx.

Kahn, R. F. (1958). Memorandum of evidence submitted to the Radcliffe committee, reprinted in *Selected essays on employment and growth*, Cambridge, pp. 124–52.

Kaldor, N. (1968). 'Productivity and growth in manufacturing industry: a reply', *Economica*, NS, vol. XXXV, pp. 385–91.

Kaldor, N. (1976). 'Inflation and recession in the world economy', *Economic Journal*, vol. 86, pp. 703–14.

Keynes, J. M. (1936). *The general theory of employment, interest and money*, London.

REFERENCES

Kleiman, E. (1971). 'Wages and plant size: a spillover effect?', *Industrial and Labour Relations Review*, vol. 24, pp. 243–8.

Knowles, K. G. J. C. and Robertson, D. J. (1951). 'Differences between the wages of skilled and unskilled workers, 1880–1950', *Bulletin of the Oxford University Institute of Statistics*, vol. 13, pp. 109–27.

Laidler, D. and Parkin, M. (1975). 'Inflation: a survey', *Economic Journal*, vol. 85, pp. 741–809.

Lane, D. (1971). *The end of inequality? Stratification under state socialism*, London.

Leggatt, T. W. (1970). 'Teaching as a profession', in J. A. Jackson, *Professions and professionalisation*, Cambridge, pp. 155–77.

Lester, R. (1967). 'Pay differentials by size of establishment', *Industrial Relations*, vol. 71, pp. 57–67.

Levinson, H. M. (1960). 'Pattern bargaining: a case study of the automobile workers', *Quarterly Journal of Economics*, vol. 74, pp. 296–317.

Lewellen, W. G. (1968). *Executive compensation in large industrial corporations*, New York.

Lewis, H. G. (1963). *Unionism and relative wages in the U.S.*, Chicago.

Lockwood, D. (1958). *The black coated worker*, London.

LPU (1977). 'Many clergymen "face financial struggle"', *The Times*, 10 February.

Lydall, H. (1959). 'The distribution of employment incomes', *Econometrica*, vol. 27, pp. 110–15.

Lydall, H. (1968). *The structure of earnings*, Oxford.

Mackay, D. I. and others (1971). *Labour markets under different employment conditions*, London.

Mann, M. (1970). 'The social cohesion of liberal democracy', *American Sociological Review*, vol. 35, pp. 423–39.

Mansfield, E. (1970). *Microeconomics: theory and applications*, New York.

Marchal, J. and Lecaillon, J. (1958). *La repartition du revenu national*, Part 1, vol. 1, Paris.

Marris, R. (1964). *The economic theory of managerial capitalism*, London.

Marshall, A. (1949). *Principles of economics*, London (8th edn, reset).

Mayer, T. (1960). 'The distribution of ability and earnings', *Review of Economics and Statistics*, vol. 42, pp. 189–95.

Meij, J. L. (1963). *Internal wage structure*, Amsterdam.

Mill, J. S. (1886). *Principles of political economy*, London (People's edn).

Miller, H. P. (1966). *Income distribution in the United States*, Washington, DC.

Mincer, J. (1970). 'The distribution of labor incomes: a survey with special reference to the human capital approach', *Journal of Economic Literature*, vol. 8, pp. 1–26.

Mintz, M. and Kiernan, L. A. (1977). 'Ads of lawyers upheld', *The Washington Post*, 28 June.

Monopolies Commission (1970). *A report on the general effect on the public interest of certain restrictive practices so far as they prevail in relation to the supply of professional services*, London (HMSO, Cmnd 4463).

NBPI (1968). National Board for Prices and Incomes, *Report no. 54: Remuneration of solicitors*, London (HMSO, Cmnd 3529).

REFERENCES

NBPI (1968a). National Board for Prices and Incomes, *Report no. 65: Payment by results systems*, London (HMSO, Cmnd 3627).

NBPI (1968b). National Board for Prices and Incomes, *Report no. 98: Standing reference on the pay of university teachers in Great Britain – first report*, London (HMSO, Cmnd 3866).

NBPI (1969). National Board for Prices and Incomes, *Report no. 134: Standing reference on the remuneration of solicitors – first report*, London (HMSO, Cmnd 4217).

NBPI (1970). National Board for Prices and Incomes, *Report no. 161: Hours of work, overtime and shiftworking*, London (HMSO, Cmnd 4554).

NEDO (1971). National Economic Development Office, *The composition and determination of pay in the U.K. 1970*, London (wall chart).

NES (1970). Department of Employment, *New Earnings Survey 1970*, London (HMSO, published 1971).

Newbould, G. D. (1976). 'Why the middle-class dream turned sour', *The Guardian*, 6 January.

OECD (1961). Organisation for Economic Cooperation and Development, *The problem of rising prices*, Paris.

OECD (1965). Organisation for Economic Cooperation and Development, *Wages and labour mobility*, Paris.

Olson, M. (1965). *The logic of collective action*, Cambridge, Mass.

Ozanne, R. (1962). 'A century of occupational differentials in manufacturing', *Review of Economics and Statistics*, vol. 44, pp. 292–9.

Papola, T. S. and Bharadwaj, V. P. (1970). 'Dynamics of industrial wage structure: an inter-country analysis', *Economic Journal*, vol. LXXX, pp. 72–90.

Parkin, M. (1977). 'Comments', in L. B. Krause and W. S. Salant, *Worldwide inflation*, Washington, DC, pp. 474–86.

Pay Board (1973). *Anomalies arising out of the pay standstill of November 1972*, London (HMSO, Cmnd 5429).

Pay Board (1974). *Problems of pay relativities*, London (HMSO, Cmnd 5535).

Pay Board (1974a). *Relative pay of mineworkers*, London (HMSO, Cmnd 5567).

Pay Board (1974b). *London weighting*, London (HMSO, Cmnd 5660).

Pemberton, J. (1975). *Inflation and the theory of the labour market*, unpublished PhD thesis, Cambridge University.

Pemberton, J. (1976). 'The fight against inflation: what comes next?', *The Banker*, April, pp. 351–6.

Perry, G. L. (1975). 'Determinants of wage inflation around the world', *Brookings Papers on Economic Activity 2*, pp. 403–35.

Phelps Brown, E. H. (1968). *Report of an inquiry into certain matters concerning labour in building and civil engineering*, London (HMSO, Cmnd 3714).

Phelps Brown, E. H. (1972). 'A workable incomes policy for Britain', in F. Blackaby, *An incomes policy for Britain*, London, pp. 31–46.

Phelps Brown, E. H. (1977). *The inequality of pay*, Oxford.

Pilkington, H. (1960). *Report of the Royal Commission on doctors' and dentists' remuneration 1957–1960*, London (HMSO, Cmnd 939).

Pommatau, J. (1976). *Evolution of teachers' salaries with regard to the evolution of prices*, Paris (Federation Internationale des Associations d'Instituteurs: mimeo.).

244

REFERENCES

Reddaway, W. B. (1959). 'Wage flexibility and the distribution of labour', *Lloyds Bank Review*, no. 54, pp. 32–48.

Reder, M. W. (1968). 'The size distribution of earnings', in J. Marchal and B. Ducros, *The distribution of national income*, London, pp. 583–610.

Reynolds, L. G. (1974). *Labor economics and labor relations*, Englewood Cliffs, NJ (6th edn).

Robbins, Lord (1963). *Higher education*, London (HMSO, Cmnd 2154).

Robertson, D. J. (1960). *Factory wage structures and national agreements*, Cambridge.

Robinson, D. (1967). 'Myths of the local labour market', *Personnel*, vol. 1, pp. 36–9.

Robinson, D. (1970). *Local labour markets and wage structures*, London.

Ross, A. M. (1948). *Trade union wage policy*, Berkeley.

Routh, G. (1965). *Occupation and pay in Great Britain 1906–1960*, Cambridge.

Runciman, W. G. (1966). *Relative deprivation and social justice*, London.

Ruud, M. H. (1974). 'That burgeoning law school enrollment is Portia', *American Bar Association Journal*, vol. 60, pp. 182–4.

Scitovsky, T. (1966). 'The trend of professional earnings', *American Economic Review*, vol. 66, pp. 25–42.

Seltzer, G. (1951). 'Pattern bargaining and the United Steelworkers', *Journal of Political Economy*, vol. 59, pp. 319–31.

Shakespeare, R. W. (1977). 'A spanner in the works', *The Times*, 1 March.

Silvestre, J. J. (1971). 'La dynamique des salaires nominaux en France', *Revue Economique*, vol. 22, pp. 430–49.

Simon, H. (1957). 'The compensation of executives', *Sociometry*, vol. 20, pp. 32–5.

Social Trends (1976). Central Statistical Office, *Social Trends*, London (HMSO, annual).

Smith, A. (1904). Edited by E. Cannan. *The wealth of nations*, London.

Sussman, B. (1976). 'How leader groups perceive equality in our lives', in *Elites in America*, a series of five articles reprinted from *The Washington Post*, September 26–30.

Taylor, Lord (1975). 'How pay can be fairly controlled without a statutory policy', *The Times*, 14 April.

Thatcher, A. R. (1976). 'Statistics of unemployment in the United Kingdom', in G. D. N. Worswick, *The concept and measurement of involuntary unemployment*, London, pp. 83–94.

Thurow, L. C. (1976). *Generating inequality*, London.

Tinbergen, J. (1956). 'On the theory of income distribution', *Weltwirtschaftliches Archiv*, vol. 77, pp. 155–75.

Tobin, J. (1972). 'Inflation and unemployment', *American Economic Review*, vol. LXII, pp. 1–18.

Todd, Lord (1968). *Report of the Royal Commission on medical education*, London (HMSO, Cmnd 3569).

Trevithick, J. A. and Mulvey, C. (1975). *The economics of inflation*, London.

Trevithick, J. A. (1976). 'Inflation, the natural unemployment rate and the theory of economic policy', *Scottish Journal of Political Economy*, vol. XXIII, pp. 37–53.

Trevithick, J. A. (1976a). 'Money wage inflexibility and the Keynesian labour supply function', *Economic Journal*, vol. 86, pp. 327–32.

Turner, H. A. (1957). 'Inflation and wage differentials in Great Britain', in J. Dunlop, *The theory of wage determination*, London, pp. 123–35.

Turner, H. A., Clack, G. and Roberts, G. (1967). *Labour relations in the motor industry*, London.

Turner, H. A. and Jackson, D. A. S. (1969). 'On the stability of wage differences and productivity-based wage policies', *British Journal of Industrial Relations*, vol. VII, pp. 1–17.

UCCA (1974–5). Universities Central Council for Admissions, *Thirteenth report*, London.

UCCA (1974–5a). Universities Central Council for Admissions, *Thirteenth report: statistical supplement*, London.

UN (1967). United Nations, *Incomes in post-war Europe*, Geneva.

US (1960). *United States Census*, vol. PC (2) 7A, Washington, DC.

Weiss, L. (1966). 'Concentration and labor earnings', *American Economic Review*, vol. 56, pp. 96–117.

Whitehead, D. H. (1973). *Stagflation and wages policy in Australia*, Camberwell, Victoria.

Wigham, E. (1976). 'Moves towards improving the lot of the low paid worker', *The Times*, 7 September.

Wigham, E. (1977). 'No let-up in the low wage blitz', *The Times*, 17 May.

Wilkinson, F. (1973). 'Earnings and size of plant in the iron and steel industry', Cambridge University Department of Applied Economics, unpublished.

Wilkinson, F. and Turner, H. A. (1972). 'The wage–tax spiral and labour militancy', in D. Jackson, H. A. Turner and F. Wilkinson, *Do trade unions cause inflation?*, Cambridge, pp. 63–110.

Williams, G., Blackstone, T. and Metcalf, D. (1974). *The academic labour market*, London.

Wolfson, M. C. (1977). *The causes of inequality in the distribution of wealth, a simulation analysis*, unpublished PhD thesis, Cambridge University.

Wood, A. (1972). *An analysis of income distribution*, unpublished PhD thesis, Cambridge University.

Wood, A. (1975). *A theory of profits*, Cambridge.

Woodroofe, E. (1975). Review Body on Doctors' and Dentists' Remuneration, *Fifth report*, London (HMSO, Cmnd 6032).

Wootton, B. (1955, 1962). *The social foundations of wage policy*, London.

Wootton, B. (1974). *Incomes policy: an inquest and a proposal*, London.

Worswick, G. D. N. (1976). *The concept and measurement of involuntary unemployment*, London.

INDEX

Adell, B. L., 231, 236
alliances among employees, 43, 228
  in a single job, 44
  in several jobs, 47–52
  within a pay group, 62, 76, 89–90, 91, 93–4
  see also collective action, unions, *and*
    normative pressures, collective
anomalies, 220
anomic, defined, 7, 53
anomic and normative pressures, theory
    of interaction between, 52–60, 64–72,
    80–2, 94–103, 129–65; *see also* anomic
    pressures *and* normative pressures
anomic interdependence, 140–50, 152
anomic pressure function, 65–6, 69, 75,
    81–2, 84
anomic pressures, 52–60, 65–6, 69–70, 81,
    94–103
  on clerical pay, 187, 189
  on direct relativity bargains, 225, 226,
    227, 232–3, 238
  on employees, 58–60, 74–5
  on inter-establishment relativities,
    168–74
  on inter-industry relativities, 175–7
  on intra-establishment pay structures,
    56–7, 183–4
  on managerial pay, 191, 192–3, 194–5
  on professional pay, 196, 197, 198, 201,
    202
  on skill differentials, 181, 182–3
  on wage inflation, 129–65, 204–12, 216,
    217
anomically optimal wage, defined, 65, 81,
    100
anticipation, *see* expectations
APL, 198, 202
Arrow, K. J., 14
Atherton, W. N., 13, 18
AUT, 200n
authority and pay, 30, 31, 185–6, 191, 192,
    194

bargaining power, 9, 11, 171; *see also* collec-
    tive action *and* normative pressures
bargaining units, 76, 81, 154–5; *see also*
    direct relativity bargaining *and* nor-
    mative pressure function

BIM, 183n
Blaug, M., 4, 60
Blinder, A. S., 1
BMA, 199
Boyle, Lord, 31n
Braff, A. J., 13
Braverman, H., 181
Brittan, S., 18, 207
Brown, D. G., 176
Brown, W., 184n
Brown, W. (Lord), 223n

Cain, G. G., 4, 14n, 18
Cartter, A. M., 13
class and status, 29
Clegg, H. A., 18, 214, 223n, 236
clerical workers, 176, 186–9, 230
coalitions, *see* alliances
coat-tail settlements, 121–6, 156, 159–60,
    164
  and anomic pressures, 130, 135, 136, 146
  and incomplete comparisons, 127, 128
  limping, 148
collective action, costs of
  to employees, 44–6, 49, 68, 159
  to employers, 46–7, 48–9, 50–1, 68, 144,
    159
  to society, 218, 233, 236–7
communist countries, 181, 186, 189, 201,
    221
competition, 2–3, 15, 60, 65, 222
  and relativities, 3–5, 17, 168, 188, 195, 201
  and wage inflation, 5–6, 205–12
  see also anomic pressures, shortages *and*
    surpluses
conflict, *see* direct relativity bargaining,
    pay norms (conflicting) *and* anomic
    and normative pressures
consensus, *see* pay norms, non-conflicting
Corina, M., 40
Coutts, K., 19
Cripps, F., 208
critical subset of pay settlements, 122–6,
    127, 128
  and anomic pressures, 130, 135, 136, 146
  in macroeconomic context, 156, 160,
    164, 214n
Crossley, J. R., 168, 170, 175n

247